Rock Garden Design
and Construction

Rock Garden Design and Construction

by the
North American Rock Garden Society

Edited by Jane McGary

Timber Press
Portland · Cambridge

Frontispiece: Cliff at the Montreal Botanical Garden. Photograph by René Giguère

Published in 2003 by
Timber Press, Inc.
The Haseltine Building
133 S.W. Second Avenue, Suite 450
Portland, Oregon 97204, U.S.A.

Timber Press
2 Station Road
Swavesey
Cambridge CB4 5QJ, U.K.

Printed in China

Library of Congress Cataloging-in-Publication Data

Rock garden design and construction / by North American Rock Garden Society ; edited by Jane McGary.
        p.   cm.
    Includes bibliographical references (p.   ).
    ISBN 0-88192-583-7
    1. Rock gardens. I. North American Rock Garden Society.
II. McGary, Mary Jane.

SB459 .R63 2003
635.9'672—dc21
                                                    2002073293

Contents

Part 3   Structures and Containers

Part 4   Regional Styles and Techniques

Part 5   Visiting Public Rock Gardens

Acknowledgments

In addition to the chapter authors, a collective volume of this extensive scope is necessarily the work of many people. Thanks are due first and foremost to the North American Rock Garden Society for funding the preparation of this book and subsidizing its color illustrations. Bobby Ward and Joyce Fingerut were deeply involved throughout the project, defining topics to be covered, recruiting authors, and providing consultation. Tom Stuart is owed particular gratitude for stepping in very late in the editing process as the author of an important chapter.

Thanks are due to the following persons, who also contributed material to this volume: Frederick Case, Judy Glattstein, Nancy Goodwin, Jim Jones, Judith Jones, James MacPhail, Jim McClements, Ernie O'Byrne, and Robert Woodward. We thank those who provided photographs for chapters by other authors: Roslyn Bliss, Todd Boland, Florene Carney, Joyce Fingerut, Phyllis Gustafson, David Hale, Pamela Harper, Sean Hogan, Don Howse, Gwen Kelaidis, Panayoti Kelaidis, Nicholas Klise, Larry Lefever, Nancy Levinson, Baldassare Mineo, Rex Murfitt, Judy Newton, Bonnie Brunkow Olson, Ramona Osburn, David Palmer, Bobby Ward, June C. West, Rhonda Williams, Robert Woodward, and Harvey Wrightman. Neal Maillet of Timber Press, an avid rock gardener himself, provided helpful advice throughout the preparation of this volume.

Foreword: An Invitation to Rock Gardening

PANAYOTI KELAIDIS

One doesn't pass time in a rock garden—in a rock garden, time stops altogether. Simultaneously, the gardener is harvesting the seed from *Draba rigida* on a high ridge in the Caucasus, deadheading a penstemon in Wyoming, sniffing the primulas in Yunnan, and admiring the tulips while buffeted by warm gusts of steppe wind.

Although a steep bank planted with phlox, aubrieta, and alyssum may be called a rock garden, dedicated rock gardeners would call it a rockery. Installing three boulders and a juniper doesn't make a rock garden. The bank becomes a true rock garden when its soil is modified to host a range of plants that could not otherwise be grown there. The rocks themselves may be very few, just enough to provide a strong contrast to the plants and a cool run for their delicate roots. Or they may be the dominant element of the landscape, sculpted into naturalistic strata or talus falls and jeweled with a few small but brilliantly flowered plants or rugged dwarf conifers.

Installing three boulders and a juniper doesn't make a rock gardener, either. Rock gardening, like other profound enthusiasms, often transforms its devotees in strange and wonderful ways. It may be the science of studying rare plants from some of the world's most exotic places that stimulates their minds or the skill demanded to grow alpine plants, with their infinite variety of vegetative form and prismatic flowers. You know you are a rock gardener when someone close to you asks if you *really* need another hundred plants this spring. What a silly question—of *course* you do! You discover you are a native speaker of botanical Latin (rock gardeners are rarely as intimidated by scientific names as they are by precipitous screes). Do you require twenty tons of rock and sand? Dump it right over here, my good man. Do you fly across the continent for a weekend of viewing thousands of slides of obscure plants? My cup of tea exactly!

Soon the convert is planning a vacation around the perfect time to photograph a rare campanula in the Dolomites or the harvest season for good wines and better bulb seeds. Rock gardeners can rattle off the names of mountain ranges and obscure climatic and cultural data for half the countries on the globe. At a rock garden show, the real masters can recognize who grew a plant by the pot or by what sort of mulch is used. (They're also the ones chuckling at the botched labels at the local botanical garden.) Who else could you ask for the precise distance from the nearest airport to the great rare-plant nurseries of Oregon or Scotland? In short, rock gardening is a kind of connoisseurship of lofty plants, places, and people. It is life lived on a very high plane—in my case, literally, in the high plains of Colorado.

Rock gardening is difficult to define precisely because it can be so many different things to different people. Many rock gardeners specialize in woodland plants, whereas others prefer growing bulbs in pots. A few are purists whose gardens host only wildflowers native to their region or only true high-alpine plants. Some don't have conventional, recognizable gardens at all. One of my favorite rock gardens in California might have been imagined by Jorge Luis Borges: the gardener has a fabulous collection of all sorts of wildflowers housed in a few refrigerators in her basement, wrapped neatly in damp paper inside plastic bags. She loves nothing more than to imagine an assemblage of plants—some spring ephemerals, some summer alpines, an autumn-flowering bulb—that she carefully pots up, places under lights, and forces into perfect, simultaneous bloom in November or March, just for the heck of it. She has notebooks filled with algebraic formulas, and those who visit her are astonished and delighted. This is truly a virtual rock garden—there it awaits, in a state of suspended vegetation, like a glossy seed catalog received in January. But the plants here are all real.

Plants are the business of rock gardeners. We study them all winter with a collection of books that is never quite large enough (there are always new plants we can't find in *any* book or even on the Internet). We sow their seeds in autumn and spring, in pots placed outside to chill or on moist paper towels in the refrigerator. Rock garden plants are largely evergreen, and one or another blooms from earliest spring to the onset of winter. If you build cold frames or an alpine house, you can have bloom through the winter as well. Most rock gardeners also photograph plants. To paraphrase Geoffrey Charlesworth, "It doesn't really matter if you have grown a plant unless you have a picture to prove you did." Our slide collections are winter gardens to groom and maintain as well.

Historically, rock gardening has been largely a pursuit of dwellers in northern climes who love to shake off the gray chill of winter with the color of early bloomers, which they subject to a doting passion usually reserved for firstborn children or high-school crushes. Some gardeners collect snowdrops and hellebores with the sort of awesome reverence once reserved for incunabula in medieval monasteries. These enthusiasts are distressed when the visitor, shivering in a dank woodland, can't distinguish the subtle differences among dozens of little white and green bell-shaped flowers or fails to be bowled over by a dingy purple hellebore the grower insists is really dazzling pink, blue, violet, or even yellow. (I alert the reader to another danger that lies athwart the rock garden path: you may fall into a genus addiction so subtly that you find yourself with three hundred pots of saxifrages before you realize you have gone slightly cuckoo.)

But in April and May, everyone on earth is a rock gardener. Garden centers are flooded with customers who want to transform their front lawns into rocky meadows. Landscape architects and designers are kept busy explaining to homeowners why they must not disturb the tedium of their neighborhood by building berms and bringing in tons of pitted limestone. Spouses are distressed to discover the little waterfall they agreed to means that heavy equipment must be rented. Children are surprised that their family is driving out west again this summer. Nerves may fray and tempers flare; but once in a while, we find a garden tucked at the back of a cul-de-sac where the landforms have been shaped so effortlessly and the rocks tucked perfectly in pleasing undulations, with trees and conifers in just the right spots and concertos of pink aethionema, primulas, phlox, and androsaces combining with a lavender froth of veronicas and forget-me-nots. Rock gardeners occupy such heavenly spaces through the force of their wills and the sweat of their brows, when and where they please.

And when the flowers are dormant, there are always books and photos, club meetings, and fellow enthusiasts all over the world to call, visit, or e-mail for companionship. And there are dazzling alpines blooming on the mountains of one hemisphere or the other on any day of the year. What are you waiting for?

Introduction

JANE McGARY with the NARGS PUBLICATIONS COMMITTEE

Most people who are aware of gardens at all have some idea what the term *rock garden* means. To the widest segment of the public, it denotes a raised bed of some sort, studded and probably bordered with stones of various sizes, and planted with compact shrubs and perennials. What we might call the "folk" rock garden is a long-standing feature of North American front yards: usually round, slightly raised, and neatly surrounded with rocks that may have been collected during family vacations. If not devoted to spring bulbs and bedding annuals, it may contain a dwarf conifer or a Japanese maple and such plants as basket-of-gold (*Alyssum*), snow-in-summer (*Cerastium tomentosum*), and pinks (*Dianthus*). It may also feature a miniature wooden bridge or some other ornament.

Making a raised bed bordered by rocks is not a demanding design and construction task. Why, then, has the North American Rock Garden Society (NARGS) sponsored the compilation of this sizable volume on how to build rock gardens? The answer is that people who identify themselves as rock gardeners define the term *rock garden* much more elaborately. The rock garden is not just a design feature; it is also a specialized habitat created to enable the gardener to grow a wide range of plants that demand particular soil and drainage conditions and other factors not available in the ordinary border. Rock gardeners, as Panayoti Kelaidis writes in the foreword, are plant collectors, always trying new and challenging species. To house them, rock gardeners have contrived an amazing array of methods to modify the planted environment. Many of these methods are described in detail in this book.

In this specialist's definition, what makes a rock garden? It usually includes rocks or stonework, but these may not be prominent in the design. In this book you will find descriptions and photographs of gravel berms and woodland gardens, and these fall within the purview of rock gardening because they represent the kind of environmental modification discussed above. Most rock gardens feature changes in level, either on a natural slope or on a raised bed, but completely flat rock gardens have been created where the soil is perfectly drained and the climate not too damp.

Most rock gardeners prefer naturalistic designs and plantings—features that imitate wildland scenes—and true species rather than hybrid plants. Such preferences descend directly from the early days of rock gardening in nineteenth-century England, when the owners of vast gardens erected Alps in miniature or converted entire quarries to their purpose. In North America, this preference has been given impetus especially in the West, by the idea that a region's gardens should reflect its native landscape, featuring plants that can be grown without any or much supplemental water. Nevertheless, many rock gardens contain at least some features that are architectural rather than naturalistic, such as planted stone walls and concrete troughs. In a confined urban setting, naturalism may be out of place. Lawrence Thomas's chapter shows that rock gardening can even be done on a balcony high above the streets of Manhattan.

Many would contend that it is the choice of plants, rather than the garden design, that defines a rock garden. Especially in Great Britain, the term *alpine gardening* is popular; this implies that all or most of the plant material should be native to mountain regions—in the strictest interpretation, from above timberline. Few growers attain this degree of purity, however. A more realistic view would be that rock garden plants share these qualities: small size at maturity (some gardeners insist that they be under 12 inches [30 cm] in height); compact form, often a mat or cushion; flowers large and numerous in proportion to the overall size of the plant; and foliage that is attractive in itself when the plant is not in flower. Rock garden plants comprise both evergreen and herbaceous perennials and shrubs as well as bulbous plants; a few annuals or biennials may be admitted, such as alpine poppies. In addition to flowering plants, rock gardens may include dwarf conifers, small ferns, and small, nonspreading ornamental grasses. Even mosses and lichens may be cultivated.

In summary, then, this book is intended to guide the reader in creating various habitats for an exceptionally wide range of plants from around the world. The kinds of gardens discussed can be made in small spaces; and if the plants chosen are small as well, you can amass an extremely varied collection on even the tiniest residential lot. We invite you to styles and techniques that can expand the pleasure and knowledge you derive from gardening.

Organization of the Book

The many and varied chapters, written by gardeners throughout North America, are organized in five sections. Part 1, "Design Principles and Materials," contains basic information you will need as you read the following sections. Baldassare Mineo, proprietor of one of North America's premier rock garden nurseries, is an artist as well and offers principles and ideas related to choosing the style of rock garden you will build. Nicholas Klise, a landscape architect, introduces the hardscaping elements of the rock garden, such as paths, steps, and walls. Louise Parsons describes the specialized substrates in which plants will flourish. Eamonn Hughes provides a remarkably clear discussion of how to build a stream, waterfall, and pool within the rock garden.

With these tools in hand, we move on to part 2, "Types of Rock Gardens," the heart of this volume. Most of the chapters here discuss classic styles of rock garden construction, including Gwen Kelaidis on berms, Ray Radebaugh on moraine and scree, Harvey Wrightman and Phyllis Gustafson on crevice gardens, Sheila Paulson on tufa features, Jane McGary on dry stone walls and raised beds, Michael Slater on dry sand beds, and Rob and Sharon Illingworth on natural outcrops. Finally, Robert Fincham and John Spain, two avid collectors—of conifers and of cacti, respectively—write about adapting a rock garden to these groups of plants.

Moving beyond the garden landscape, part 3, "Structures and Containers," includes chapters on a number of techniques rock gardeners employ to grow plants they cannot induce to flourish in the open garden, however it is constructed. Here you will learn, from Joyce Fingerut and Rex Murfitt, to make and plant hypertufa troughs; from Lee Raden, to manage an alpine house (a specialized greenhouse); from Jane McGary, to grow bulbs and alpines in cold frames; and from Rick Lupp, to propagate plants in simple structures. Here, too, we encounter Lawrence Thomas's city garden grown entirely in containers.

North America is a vast and varied place to garden, and advice about gardening in one part of the continent is unlikely to apply to the whole. This volume is the first to recognize this diversity in the context of rock and alpine gardening, which heretofore have been discussed primarily from the viewpoints of England, the Northeast, and California. In part 4, "Regional Styles and Techniques," Loren Russell, Jaime Rodriguez, Sandra Ladendorf, Gwen Kelaidis, Tom Stuart, and Michael Chelednik present rock garden styles that respond to their particular climatic constraints, natural landscapes, and locally available materials.

After reading parts 1 through 4, you will have many ideas for your rock garden. To find even more, visit some of the public gardens described in part 5. From Missouri to Alaska and from the Rocky Mountains to Newfoundland, botanical garden curators have constructed rock gardens of appropriate local materials and are experimenting to discover which are the best plants. An extensive selection of books for further reading appears at the end of this volume. We hope you will be inspired to explore them and also to explore the flora of the world—a pursuit that rock gardeners enjoy both in the wild and in their own back yards.

PART 1
Design Principles and Materials

In this section, four experienced rock gardeners introduce important ideas to keep in mind as you design your own garden. Many principles and terms are introduced; for quick reference, see the glossary at the end of the book.

Baldassare Mineo, the proprietor of the famed Siskiyou Rare Plant Nursery in southern Oregon, has surrounded his nursery and adjacent home with display gardens. His chapter on the aesthetics of rock garden design takes readers on a tour of the nursery and explains the thinking behind its remarkably varied and appealing features. Nicholas Klise, a landscape architect, offers advice on laying out the steps and paths of the living entity that is the garden. Because rock plants are best appreciated at close range, successful rock gardens include many paths and viewpoints from which the gardener can work and the visitor see the results. Notice, especially, Klise's comments about surfacing materials; too often, the use of incompatible or inappropriate materials spoils the overall beauty of a rock garden. In a geologically oriented chapter, Louise Parsons gives a detailed introduction to special soil mixes used in rock gardens and the principles behind these concoctions. Finally, Eamonn Hughes, one of the United States' foremost designers and builders of artificial ponds, streams, and cascades, explains concisely how the home gardener can build a naturalistic and leak-proof stream, waterfall, and pond combination. The sound of rushing water is a marvelous complement to alpine plants and stonework.

Rock Garden Design, Style, and Aesthetics

BALDASSARE MINEO

Taste in rock garden design, as in any other branch of art, is subjective, with plenty of latitude for variety and differences of opinion. There may be certain basic rules that many rock gardeners follow (more on rules later), but in essence, it is up to the individual to decide what is "good taste" or "bad taste" when it comes to the design and construction of a rock garden. As a longtime nurseryman specializing in rock garden plants and a lover of artistic design, I urge all gardeners to give attention to creating a well-designed home for their plants.

Fortunately, all of us have the same grand teacher, Mother Nature, who provides rock gardeners with a world full of pleasing examples to study and admire. The best rock gardeners are those that observe general principles of geology, including the forms of rock strata, to create convincingly naturalistic arrangements. It is not necessary to copy nature; instead, learn the principles from it. Reginald Farrer, in *The English Rock Garden* (1925: xxxii), wisely advised how to learn from nature: "To talk of imitating nature, as so many vainly do, is to encourage a rank and empty delusion. To make a thing look 'natural' is by no means to imitate nature. Nature often looks more artificial than the worst form of artificial art; nature in the mountains is often chaotic, bald, dreary, and hideous in the highest degree. By making a rock-garden look natural, then, we mean that it must have a firm and effortless harmony of hill or vale, cliff or slope."

I think rock gardeners are especially inspired by nature because, in the wild, plants grow among rocks and stones almost everywhere, from the mountains to the seashore, from tropical to arctic regions, from deserts to jungles. All over the world, an infinite variety of rocks, stones, and gravel exists in natural harmony with different kinds of plants. It is no wonder that gardeners are drawn to this natural combination and find it irresistibly appealing.

PLATE 1. Autumn color in the display garden of Siskiyou Rare Plant Nursery. Photograph by Baldassare Mineo

What is a rock garden plant? The simplest and broadest definition is any plant that looks good growing among rocks. Alpine plants are a special subgroup: an alpine, strictly speaking, is native to elevations above timberline, the upper limit of true tree growth. The origin of the word *alpine* is connected with the Alps, the great mountain range extending from France through Switzerland and Italy into the Balkan peninsula. But every continent has alpine regions, even some tropical areas near the equator. Plants from above timberline in these mountainous areas are also true alpines. Gardeners casually use the term *alpine* interchangeably with *rock garden plant*, no doubt because plants from alpine regions, with their typical low cushion habit and miniature proportions, are the classic plants of the English rock garden. These plants have particular needs, such as good drainage, specialized soil types, proper light exposure, good air circulation, protection from extreme weather, and root association with rock and gravel. Thus, the goal of the rock gardener is twofold: to create an aesthetically pleasing garden and simultaneously to grow healthy plants by providing the most favorable conditions for them.

The first step in garden design is to develop the concept. A mountain trail that passes beautiful rock outcrops dotted with interesting miniature plants is the vision many rock gardeners bring home when it is time to design and build their own gardens. Choosing the style and designing a garden is a very personal, individual endeavor. It starts with a vision, but how it evolves physically depends on many factors. Sometimes these factors shape the result into something rather different from the original vision—visions aren't always practical, but they are a wonderful way to begin the design process. When it is your time to design a rock garden, let your imagination soar. Envision what you would like to see. Listen to your creative mind.

We must be practical, however, and we usually must design within the scope of our particular setting. I have several rock garden areas in my 2-acre (0.8-ha) garden. Visitors entering the garden gate of my home step immediately into the display gardens for Siskiyou Rare Plant Nursery, my business next door. The first is the pumice garden, a fairly typical front-yard space where I removed the lawn and transformed it into a rock garden. Here I used lightweight volcanic pumice from the nearby mountains to edge raised beds of scree soil (see "Soils" and "Moraine and Scree Gardens"). The island beds, surrounded by meandering paths, are of varied heights. Some rise only about 2 inches (5 cm) above the original grade; in others, the pumice edging is built up to a height of 2 feet (0.6 m), which allows for the creation of deep scree beds of varying levels, sloping surfaces, and even small cliffs (if you use your imagination).

Once the rock and soil were in place and planting began, I had a multitude of areas to suit a wide assortment of plants. I achieved what I had envisioned for this garden: many different visual settings, varied aspects providing light exposure ranging from full sun to shade, and soil conditions ranging from deep to shallow scree. In addition, there are areas of open scree and others of dense rockwork where the crevices offer special planting pockets. Apart from these practical accomplishments, however, I had created something aesthetically pleasing. The paths invite visitors to wander through this little garden, and the plants

PLATE 2. The crevice-style feature in the Siskiyou Rare Plant Nursery display garden in Medford, Oregon, built by Josef Halda, rises high above the gently sloping site, supported by massive boulders. Large plants can be accommodated in a rock garden of this size. Photograph by Baldassare Mineo

contentedly growing in appropriate conditions draw visitors closer for a look (see "Paths and Hardscaping").

I faced certain limitations when I built the pumice garden—especially the flat, uninteresting grade. The shape of the garden had many constraints, too: two driveways, a concrete walk to the front door, and the house itself bounded the area. In other words, I was working within a frame, and I had no interesting natural land features such as rock outcrops or changes in level. More often than not, in suburban locales rock gardeners start with similar sites. Most of us want a naturalistic style, not the more formal design such a setting suggests, but we have to face facts. In an urban or suburban setting, where property lines and structures create both space limitations and visual impact, gardens necessarily blend natural rock formations with somewhat formal surroundings. The naturalistic rock garden is inevitably a contrasting element within a landscape of pavement and buildings; the challenge to aesthetics is to make that contrast a charming one.

PLATE 3. Rock features and even troughs blend with water in the Illinois garden of Waid Vanderpoel. Photograph by Baldassare Mineo

A tastefully designed rock garden, regardless of its surroundings, becomes a unique oasis because of the size and character of the plants. Most rock gardens, even large ones, have a welcoming, intimate quality. Once inside a rock garden, something magical happens. Because the rocks are relatively small, the garden offers a series of vignettes of rocks and plants. The visitor focuses on the many harmonious groups and is transported into this miniature world, visually filtering out the surrounding elements.

How do we create a pleasing, naturalistic rock garden without directly copying nature? First, the rockwork and the various materials (boulders, rocks, and gravel) and plants must be combined aesthetically. Shop around and take some time to plan what materials to combine in your garden. Choose rocks to suit your site. If your garden is within an urban setting, select boulders and rocks that are in scale with nearby elements such as buildings, fences, walls, driveways, and sidewalks. Conduct a study of the kinds of rock available in your area. You may be able to collect rocks from public lands at no charge (although a permit may be required), or you may need to purchase them. It is usually wise to use rock that comes from a source as close as possible to your home—it will always feel more natural to you and to visitors—and try to use just one type of rock. Next, carefully select a gravel mulch that blends well with the larger rocks; the goal is to have the gravel appear as if it consists of small pieces broken off the larger rocks. In siting your new plants, keep in mind each one's potential size. Don't allow large plants to cover up the rock arrangements, or be prepared to control plant growth with regular pruning.

A garden implies some degree of artistry in arrangement; however, most rock gardens simply evolve and grow as the gardener acquires an ever larger plant collection. The gardener's depth of concern with aesthetics determines how much effort he or she makes to arrange the expanding number of beds and paths into an artistically pleasing whole. Don't let uncontrolled expansion of the rock garden lead to an awkward lack of design. Beware lest the growing plant collection cause your garden to expand like a sprawling city with too little thought for overall planning and traffic circulation.

In another part of my garden is a more naturalistic, large-scale feature: the crevice garden, built by the Czech expert Josef Halda, a botanist, mountain climber, and stonemason. It is situated within a large space surrounded by trees and shrubs, an excellent screening background for this massive feature. The viewer's eye goes from the intense rockwork and plantings of the crevice garden to the green background and on to the sky. This provides a wonderful setting to enter and enjoy a rock garden. The visitor feels entirely immersed in the garden experience because there is little distraction from buildings or other structures. Although it may not always be possible, try to create a setting for your garden that allows for many views without distractions.

The preceding discussion has assumed that you want a naturalistic rock garden, but rock gardens can also be formal in design. In another part of my garden, I built and planted raised scree beds edged in split-face (textured) concrete block, one course high. When placed end to

PLATE 4. A planted retaining wall provides a home for rock plants in a setting of lawns and larger plantings in the garden of Amy Stewart, Toronto, Ontario. Photograph by Baldassare Mineo

end, with the tops covered with soil and overhanging plants, the blocks resemble quarried granite. The lines of this garden are straight and set at right angles. Such a formal rock garden is especially appropriate near a building or other architectural element, where the garden becomes an extension of the structures. My formal scree garden has no rocks within the beds. The block edging is the only stone in view, and the plants on display are the primary focus. They are placed informally in a patchwork of interesting textures and floral combinations. Other formal rock gardens use rocks and stones among the plants, but arranging the rocks and plants naturalistically makes the stark lines more informal.

A rock garden can be a combination of formal and informal (or naturalistic) design. Frank Cabot, in his garden in Cold Spring on Hudson, New York, designed chest-high raised beds of beautiful, rough, natural stone stacked artistically (see "Planted Walls and Formal Raised Beds"). The four tall walls of each raised bed form stark rectangles. The surfaces of the planting space are enhanced with naturalistic rock

PLATE 5. Skilled masonry forms the raised beds and their background at Stonecrop Garden and Nursery in New York. Photograph by Pamela Harper

formations. Both walls and upper surfaces are effectively planted with choice specimens. Excellent variety in sun and shade exposure is achieved with this design. The scheme is a grand example of a formal design combined with naturalistic rock and plant arrangement.

Almost all rock gardeners are artistic. From the gardener who removes the sod from the middle of a flat lawn and begins to create his or her first masterpiece to the skilled alpine grower who successfully nurtures the most demanding species in crevice or trough, all devote remarkable intelligence and effort to their living—and thus ever changing—works of art.

FURTHER READING

Joachim Carl, *Miniature Gardens*; Reginald Farrer, *The English Rock Garden*; H. Lincoln Foster, *Rock Gardening*; Baldassare Mineo, *Rock Garden Plants: A Color Encyclopedia*; Graham Stuart Thomas, *The Rock Garden and Its Plants*

Paths and Hardscaping

NICHOLAS KLISE

Almost any type of garden-making seems more transitory than the rock garden. A perennial border can be—and probably should be—dug up and rearranged every few years; woody plants can be cut down and regrown. The rock garden you are contemplating, however, may persist as a landscape feature long after your house has been abandoned or replaced. Making structural changes in a completed rock garden is such a monumental job that few attempt it. No one likes to rip up paving, remove rocks, and change grades. Therefore, you will want to plan the layout very thoughtfully.

Regardless of the style, size, and horticultural intent of the rock garden, many things have to be thought through before construction begins. Among the most important considerations is access: the paths visitors will walk to see the plants. Because a rock garden is typically furnished with small, subtle plants that invite close

PLATE 6. Brick pavement transitions to flagstone set with rock plants in the garden of Amy Stewart, Toronto, Ontario. Photograph by Nicholas Klise

inspection, paths should shorten the focal length between the plants and their admirers.

Paths are a part of the actual construction, not adjuncts or after-thoughts; they are an integral part of the composition. Indeed, paths are so necessary to the cohesive integrity of the garden that they should be the genesis of any garden plan. Major paths are the conventional walk-ways used by visitors, but gardeners also have private pathways to the plants. They know where to step into planted beds, where to jump from rock to rock, and where to crawl on hands and knees. This network of concealed, secondary access routes is not discussed here because its ad hoc character defies analysis and it is not actually constructed.

It is disconcerting to find oneself in a wilderness without a trail or in a landscape without direction. Good paths don't just happen; they are not just the leftover space between plants. Aside from their obvious utility, paths serve as the garden-maker's orchestration of the events that compose the garden. They are the visitor's road map.

The paths in a naturalistic style rock garden should generally be low in grade. They look best when they are actually excavated below the surrounding terrain. This is true in both a sunny alpine garden and in a shady woodland site; the obvious exception is a boardwalk through a wetland. The reason for this low grade is to make the path appear to be worn into the landscape by use, imitating the effect of primitive travel-ers through a natural landscape. Even though you probably don't expect hordes migrating through the garden, this is an easy way to indi-cate that it is *here* that people walked before you, taking the logical route of least resistance. Such paths should look effortless, just like the artful rendering of the entire rock garden.

Paths are above all linear, leading eyes and feet onward. We have implicit trust that this well-worn path leads somewhere, so a path should never end abruptly, without warning. It should bring the walker back to the beginning, or it should connect with other paths. If the rock garden is an island element, it should be surrounded with a beltway path that isolates the garden from an encroaching lawn or other

PLATE 7. A flagstone path through the rock garden of Pat Tucker, Ontario, Canada. Photograph by Nicholas Klise

invasive plants. If a path does terminate, it should do so with ceremony, at a vista, a piece of architecture, or an aged tree. Whatever the terminal feature, make sure that it is worth the round trip. This concept of a path that leads somewhere is perfectly exemplified by the path to the tea-house in a traditional Japanese garden, where the walk to the structure, the wait at it, the entry into it, the ceremony within, and the walk back all meld into one spiritual experience.

An important dimension to consider is width. A path for one person should be about 2 feet (0.6 m) wide (figure 1). A path for two people walking side by side needs to be about 5 feet (1.5 m) wide. A wheelbarrow can traverse a one-person path, a garden cart or lawn tractor needs much more clearance, and a truck or car requires at least 8 feet (2.4 m). Be generous in planning for width—paths can rarely be too wide—but resist the temptation to think in absolute minimums. In fact, the width does not have to be consistent throughout the path's length—in other words, the edges do not need to be parallel. It is more interesting visually to have the path narrow and widen, each edge taking an independent curving line. Especially at turns, such as a switchback on a slope, a wider spot signals the change in course. A widening can also indicate a rest stop, especially if there is a place to sit.

Another dimension that may not be obvious to the novice garden-maker is height. A certain amount of air space is needed for a person to walk unhindered along a path (figure 1). There is no worse fault in garden etiquette than inviting a visitor down a path to be smacked on the head by a tree branch. Even if you enjoy plants brushing your legs and have become used to ducking at the right moment, it is unlikely that others will enjoy experiencing your garden in such a tactile way. Thus, paths must have minimal width not just on the ground but also up to a height of 7 feet (2.1 m). If you garden in a wet climate where plants bow under the weight of rainwater, take this into account. If you grow dangerously spine-tipped desert plants, be especially cognizant of safe distances between visitors and plants. Remember, paths that appear excessively wide when the garden is new will look more in proportion when the plants mature.

FIGURE 1. A single-file path should be a minimum of 2 feet (0.6 m) wide, with ample clearance to a height of 7 feet (2.1 m). Drawing by Sukey McDonough

2'- 0"

There are many materials for surfacing paths. Choosing one is a matter of sifting through a long list by first narrowing it to what is locally available. Often the most expedient course is to seize a serendipitous windfall of material. If your brother-in-law has six tons of brick to give you, don't hesitate. I happen to have a creek through my property that provides an unlimited supply of rock, gravel, and sand; of course, that is what I use. However, don't use an inappropriate material simply because it is available. The surface of the path should be smooth and serviceable, but it should also be appropriate to the horticultural and aesthetic intent of its garden area. Don't use the same surfacing throughout a garden with varied environments. There is nothing aesthetically wrong with combining different materials and various construction techniques in even a relatively small rock garden.

After you have identified one or several readily available materials, confirm their suitability by imagining how they will look in the rock garden. Paths in a rock garden have to incorporate two seemingly contradictory attributes. They must be conspicuous and obvious in *peripheral* vision, yet they must be harmonious and unobtrusive in *direct* vision. When you look directly at it, the path should seem unremarkable, logical, appropriate, simple, effortless—not noteworthy in and of itself. But when you are not looking at it, its subliminal presence should be enough to direct your movement. An edging is generally not needed if an appropriate path material is used, because the material itself in juxtaposition with the surface of the planted areas lends enough definition.

In a rock garden where rock chips are used as a mulch, the most suitable surface for the paths may be the same rock crushed to a smaller diameter and pounded into a larger aggregate that serves as a foundation; this is then surfaced with fines (sand and dust) of the same rock pounded down into the larger aggregates, creating a smooth paving. Although this path is made of the same rock as the garden, the building technique makes it both conspicuous and functional. Rounded pea (or river) gravel, which does not compact, is often used as a rock garden mulch, but it is useless as a path surface for that very reason. Also, on an incline the ball-bearing quality of pea gravel makes it dangerous.

Different stone may be used, however, and even concrete is not out of the question. With stone or concrete, the overriding consideration is color: you want the paving to blend with the color of the rock used in the planted areas. Color is difficult to talk about because its perception varies among viewers and depends on the quality of ambient light. Colors that look harmonious in New England may look terrible in Arizona; consequently, each garden-maker needs to decide on color based on the local environment. But there are some general guidelines: if the rock used in the garden is in the yellow-to-brown range, use paving that is somewhat brown; if the rock is in the white-to-gray range, use paving that is sympathetically gray. It is wise to use paving slightly darker than the dominant color of the garden rocks.

Concrete can be any color or texture—not just the light gray of most sidewalks. A very attractive path can be fashioned from professionally formed, stamped, and colored concrete that duplicates the look of cobble-

PLATE 8. Free-form poured-concrete stepping stones. Photograph by Nicholas Klise

stones, Belgian block, brick, or some other stonelike material. When such paving is executed perfectly, its artificial character becomes camouflaged by a few years of aging; in time, it can become the most treasured attribute of the garden. This option is worth exploring if you are constructing a rock garden in a new landscape, but I would be very cautious about inviting concrete trucks and workers into an existing garden. The limiting factors for the garden-maker are whether an appropriately natural-looking pattern can be produced and whether local contractors are skilled enough. The do-it-yourself concrete forms sold to create ersatz paving can never produce a result equal to professional work, even after days of backbreaking work hauling and mixing the concrete. Existing concrete— either broken pieces of recycled paving or cheap patio blocks—can easily be colored a burnt ocher hue with liquid chelated iron, sold in garden centers as a nutritive supplement for plants (with a warning on the label not to spill it on the concrete sidewalk for fear of staining).

Many people who live in the great forested environments of the eastern United States and Pacific Northwest build rock gardens under trees, usually referring to them as "woodland" or "shade" gardens. Here, different path surfaces are appropriate. Although organic mulch material (for example, bark, cocoa hulls, or nutshells) is the usual choice, it may not be the best one. The problem with using mulch as a path surface is that it does not contrast enough with planted areas mulched with identical or similar organic material. Moreover, the path needs annual topping up and thus develops a crown higher than the planted areas— again, paths should be lower. One way to mitigate the build-up problem is to use weed-block landscape fabric under the organic mulch. Select a strong, high-quality woven product manufactured for the nursery trade rather than the perforated polyethylene sheet material available in most home and garden stores. Placed under the organic material, this fabric not only prevents germination of weed seeds and perennial regrowth but also slows the decomposition of the path material by isolating it from contact with the soil. Another problem in a woodland garden is the abundance of fallen leaves that obscure the paths. You can remove the old mulch annually and apply a new layer of a slightly different color, or simply skip the mulch because it and the leaves have to be removed periodically to define the path.

Moss, a glamorous and luxurious path surface, is easy to cultivate on the clay subsoil on my property, so I have confined the mulch to the planted areas and transplanted moss to the paths. Moss paths can be weeded with glyphosate herbicide (such as Roundup®) because it kills only vascular plants; however, you must use only straight glyphosate without an added surfactant (a wetting agent, such as dishwashing detergent), which does kill moss. Despite the common misconception, most mosses require a good deal of light and die if deprived of it by a covering of fallen leaves. In small areas you may be able to keep up with leaf fall by using a broom or rubber-toothed rake, but on larger paths you will find a leaf blower or vacuum more efficient. A regular metal or bamboo rake pulls up the moss.

Another paving that always looks handsome in shade is asphalt, especially when dark brown crushed rock is used as the aggregate.

PLATE 9. Mossy paths in the woodland garden of Morris West and Nicholas Klise in Pennsylvania. Photograph by Nicholas Klise

Asphalt doesn't work well in sun because it is the wrong color and gets hot, so garden-makers have developed a strong but irrational prejudice against it. I would be apprehensive about installing asphalt in an existing garden simply because of the access and equipment needed, but for new construction it should certainly be considered. Asphalt is readily available, simple, unassuming, and the right color for a shady path.

Turf, or lawn grass, is probably the least reasonable surface for a path. Besides the endless maintenance it requires, constant traffic is the very thing that hurts it most. If the rock garden is being constructed as an island in a lawn and will be as close as 8 feet (2.4 m) to shore— another planted area, a structure, or a paved area—it is wise to eliminate the intervening grass and replace it with the same material used in the beltway path. Not only does this strategy free the time needed to maintain the insignificant strip of grass, it also helps to integrate the rock garden visually with the surrounding landscape elements.

PLATE 10. A wooden walkway spans a low spot in the Memorial University Botanical Garden, St. John's, Newfoundland, and keeps visitors from walking through sensitive plantings. This type of pathway can be used without the railings in a private garden. Photograph by Todd Boland

In gardens that are not completely flat, the rock garden is likely to be situated on a slope, and this brings us to the next set of problems in path design. In a larger rock garden, there are probably some ups and downs. Any change in elevation should be accomplished with a ramp rather than steps, if at all possible. It is easier to negotiate a ramp, on foot or with wheels. Nonetheless, ramps take up a lot of room, and you may not have the space for a gentle hill climb or a switchback. I do not recommend a slope of more than 20° from the horizontal. If there is room and you need to gain more elevation than can be achieved with a single ramp, combine shorter ramps with several small sets of steps: always try to build your elevation gain into the path and use as few steps as possible. Stairs are complicated and costly to build, and they are also prime sites for accidents.

It may be impossible to avoid using steps, however, so here are some general pointers. Exterior stairs should be designed differently than interior stairs, and the difference is one of scale. Things outdoors need to be bigger in every respect to look logical and to verify their presence. Garden steps should always be at least as wide as the adjacent path and can be wider. People should move along exterior (and especially garden) stairs much more slowly than interior ones: the height of the risers is shorter and the width of the tread deeper (figure 2). Gaining elevation on this type of slow stairway takes more steps than, say, a ladder, which would be very fast. The proportion of a 6-inch (15-cm) riser to a

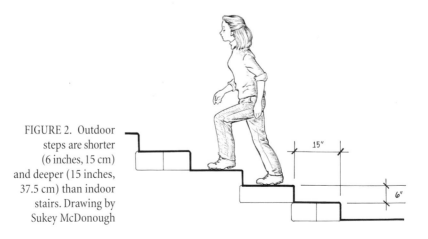

FIGURE 2. Outdoor steps are shorter (6 inches, 15 cm) and deeper (15 inches, 37.5 cm) than indoor stairs. Drawing by Sukey McDonough

15-inch (40-cm) tread provides a comfortable cadence on exterior stairs. Anything slower seems frustrating, and anything faster seems obstructive. An immutable rule is that, whatever the proportion of tread to riser, once begun, the rhythm must continue exactly the same to the end of the flight. Nothing is more likely to result in tumbles, bloodshed, and lawsuits than a flight of steps with irregular proportions. Don't build your own garden steps without fully understanding their design and carefully planning their construction.

Garden stairs can be constructed of various materials, but they are usually built with materials different from those used in the path leading to them. The same principles apply: select material that is appropriate, available, serviceable, unremarkable, and, even though different from the path, not at odds with the general aesthetic intent of the garden. The riser can be different from the tread; for example, the riser can be fashioned from pressure-treated wood or concrete, and the tread surfaced with the path material—a pleasing way to integrate the stairs into the path. Aged granite curbstones make the most beautiful garden

PLATE 11. Setting concrete lintels for a flight of steps in the garden of Morris West and Nicholas Klise, Pennsylvania. Photograph by Nicholas Klise

PLATE 12. The completed lintel stairway. Photograph by Nicholas Klise

steps, but they are not universally available, and even if they were, only a few could afford to use them. A simple and affordable substitute is premanufactured concrete lintels, available in most areas from companies that make them for architectural applications. Although lintels come in standard sizes and a standard gray, the manufacturers usually can make custom sizes, colors, or surfaces (mine are surfaced with bluestone flagging).

Garden steps can be discreetly planted with tiny perennials or mosses as long as the result does not impede walking. The same is true of any paving. The plants must be very low and their growth controlled so as to not obstruct or even visually interrupt the onward thrust. Any plant in a path suffers occasional abuse, so choice plants should be displayed with the dignity they deserve, safe from the footfalls of garden visitors.

The hardscaping of a rock garden—the garden architecture— differs from the horticultural aspect of garden-making in that its beauty and utility do not evolve out of trial and error. The rocks, paths, and steps have to be designed, positioned, and installed with careful forethought. On this foundation, a rewarding garden will grow a lifetime of pleasure.

Soils

LOUISE PARSONS

Writers on rock gardening typically devote much space to precise formulas for soils. Because many rock gardening books have been written in England, these formulas usually call for ingredients that North American gardeners cannot obtain, such as sterilized leafmold and John Innes No. 2 compost. Experienced growers know, however, that most plants can be induced to succeed in a variety of soil mixtures. This chapter does not offer magic formulas and secret ingredients; instead, it provides a general understanding of what soils can adjust the odds in your favor.

Soil mixtures can be as simple or as complex as you wish. Rock fragments are usually the main constituent of rock garden soils; however, under all but extreme conditions of heat and humidity or excess moisture, it is possible to maintain a successful rock garden simply by using what is commonly called "good garden soil," or ordinary dirt. Sometimes this strategy is even an advantage: for example, Robert Nold in high, dry Colorado grows a vast array of choice rock garden plants by using the water-holding capacity of ordinary dirt.

For greater rewards, however, you will probably need to tailor your soil choices to your planting preferences and climate. Concoct soil mixtures to increase the range of plant choices, rather than to battle the elements. If your climate features too much moisture for plants from high, dry places, you can make the soil leaner by adding rock materials such as sand and grit. In fact, you can even garden in beds of pure sand or coarse grit (see "Moraine and Scree Gardens" and "Dry Sand Beds"). Scree mixtures widely used for growing alpines in pots have an average moisture retention of only 10–15 percent; this seemingly low moisture is held constant with regular but spare watering, but it is difficult in such mixtures to achieve acceptable dryness without crossing the line into deadly desiccation. If rainfall is seasonally cyclic in your area, compromise is necessary, but you can still use soil mixtures to advantage, especially if you take into account the dormancy cycles of the plants. Increase the retentiveness of the soil to keep plants alive in dry seasons, and use slopes and crevices for drainage during the wet part of the year.

You can also respond to the temperature requirements of plants with soil and site choices. To grow bulbs that require a warm, dry summer dormancy, you can provide an especially stony spot with well-aerated soil and a southwestern exposure. Alpines that need a cool root run benefit from moisture-retentive humus in the soil and placement on the northern side of a rock.

A rock garden can be grown in relatively heavy soil. Even if your soil is clay, don't despair. Clay has many virtues. It is a vital delivery system for mineral nutrition. The structural properties of clay—for example, cohesion, the stickiness or heaviness that gardeners curse—make it an excellent stabilizing mortar and foundation for rock garden construction. You can fill in pockets and crevices with stony scree mix. Many plants do best with access to both types of soil, profiting from the drainage of scree and grit mulch on top while putting down roots into heavier soil below. Clay-rich buried soils are characteristic of many alpine environments: in rocky places finer, heavier soils form from the bottom up (for an excellent diagram of this phenomenon, see Koerner 1999, 63).

Christian Koerner points out in *Alpine Plant Life* (1999) that the local diversity of alpine soil types is high when compared with that in lowland regions, including lush alpine meadows, natural sand beds, screes, and bogs. Even in a small garden, you can vary the major soil ingredients by proportion alone to imitate this diversity. Creating soil variety need not require importing many exotic ingredients; it can be achieved by varying the proportions of those readily at hand.

From Nature to Rock Gardens

Alpine and rock gardeners enthusiastically take cues from nature. We attempt to imitate rocky places with varying altitudes, latitudes, and soil types. Let's now look more closely at alpine and rocky environments for cues to understanding soil.

HOW SOILS FORM. In geomorphic (that is, landform) terms, rock plants typically grow in young, high-energy environments. The processes that break down minerals into soil and scree are rapid. *Scree* is broadly defined as loose rock material found in the mountains. The term *detritus* is used to denote loose rock fragments in general. Water, wind, temperature, soil-dwelling organisms, parent rocks, and gravity influence soil formation and characteristics. In nature and in the garden, the interplay of all of the elements is ongoing and dynamic. In the alpine environment, diverse soils may form in small pockets and provide special niches for plants. Rocks are wedged, chipped, and shed by the repeated action of frost and sharp night-to-day temperature changes. Glaciers pluck and transport rocks great distances in a geologically short time. Glacial by-products range in size from huge blocks and boulders to a dust-fine, mineral-rich material called *glacial rock flour*.

The colorful term *rock jumble* is used to describe the typical mass of unsorted rock material associated with active glaciation. It may seem like heresy to say this in a manual on rock garden construction, but aesthetic and practical considerations aside, you could use a dump-truck load of unsorted rocks, gravel, sand, and soil—even some mud—to create a rock garden faithful to natural geologic environments in the mountains. This seemingly chaotic mix of unsorted rock and soil material is called *till*. Even without glaciers, mountainous regions are often characterized by some chaos. As I look out my window at the beautiful Oregon Coast Range, I view a landscape whose present-day features are largely the product of landslides. Contrast this with a mature lowland river plain, where rock and soil materials are well sorted and nicely graded with respect to particle density and size.

Detritus shed from rocky places forms an environment for rock plants, regardless of elevation. In true alpine regions, frost-wedging creates scree composed of angular rock fragments. In the garden, however, the term *scree* generally denotes any soil with a high proportion of rocky material. A rich scree has more soil, compost, or loam, whereas a lean scree has more rock or sand. You may also encounter the term *talus* for rock debris (usually of larger sizes).

WATER AND SOILS. Water in alpine regions contains abundant minerals, both dissolved and suspended in solution. In these geologically young environments, slopes tend to be steep. Unconsolidated material moves easily at rates varying from active creep to sudden landslide. Water and ice lubricate much of this activity. Certain true alpine plants have evolved to thrive in areas of continuous soil movement, a condition difficult to duplicate in the rock garden. These species tend to be short-lived, both in gardens and in nature. Considering the effort required to construct a rock garden, you want it to stay in place rather than creep and slide downhill, as it might in nature.

In all soil-related processes, from the mechanical breakdown of rock to the micro-delivery of nutrients to plants, water (or the lack of it) plays a critical role. In addition to being a delivery mechanism for mineral nutrition, water leaches out compounds harmful to plants, such as alkalis and salts. One of the unique characteristics of alpine soils is the extent to which they are consistently percolated with fresh, remarkably pure, yet mineral-rich water. Moisture affects the structural characteristics of soil profoundly; indeed water content affects soil texture as much as the actual composition does. During garden construction, you can use water to help settle soil gently into crevices and planting pockets, just as nature does. Designing slopes and using free-draining, or open, soils prevents stagnation, which harms plants by depleting the supply of oxygen to the roots and hosting pathogens.

SOIL TEMPERATURE AND ORGANIC CONTENT. Temperature, too, plays a critical role in shaping soil characteristics and in regulating the supply of organic matter that, contrary to popular belief, is needed by many alpine plants. Cool temperatures limit the growth of soil-borne pathogens. In cool soils, the decay of organic matter is relatively slow. Although there is less organic matter in alpine regions than is typical at lower elevations, this slow decay rate allows organic matter to persist, so localized alpine soils may be surprisingly rich. A small leaf or twig that would decay in less than a year in my temperate lowland garden might take two or three years to do so above timberline. Decayed moss and lichens in rock crevices are often overlooked as typical alpine organic components. If you visit mountain regions to observe plants in the wild, look closely at their bases. You may see that a lovely alpine primula is growing in a rock crevice generously lined with pads of old moss. Including as little as 5–10 percent organic matter in the soil can increase your plant choices. This material provides minute but crucial slow-release nutritional and moisture benefits to crevice plants.

FROST ACTION. The formation of ice crystals in soil is often cursed by gardeners, yet it is vital in soil formation and enhancement in the alpine realm. Although it is distressing to find plant treasures heaved out by frost, this constitutes a natural cultivation and continual aeration in alpine soils. Some plants are lost this way, but the overall benefits are many. If an adequate proportion of gritty material is present, ice crystal formation in volcanic material produces a wonderfully fluffy medium called *popcorn soil*, the favorite home of such choice plants as *Dicentra uniflora*. Frost-heaving damage to plants is most pronounced in areas of greatest daily temperature fluctuation. Shading the affected area from winter sun can mitigate this problem. A loose rule of thumb to cope with seasonal variations such as frost and rainfall cycles is to plant deeper-rooted plants or tougher shrubs in the most exposed areas of the garden.

WIND-DEPOSITED SOILS. At high latitudes and altitudes, winds are strong and may transport material to create a rich soil called *aeolian* (that is, wind-blown) soil. Once deposited, this soil is termed *loess*; it is composed of dust from minute rock fragments and organic materials. The wind sorts this material by size and transports it vast distances. Loess is fine-grained and more uniform in texture than scree, but it may contain identical ingredients. Sandy river loam, widely available to gardeners, is a good approximation of loess.

PARTICLE SHAPES. Now let's look in detail at a basic difference among rock particles of any size, from flour to boulders. A lowland marine or river environment tends to produce rounded particles in the process of weathering and transport. By contrast, the rock particles from a higher-energy environment such as the glacial realm are often angular and sharp; even when they become somewhat rounded, the particles' shapes tend to be irregular. In a lowland outwash plain or riverbed, however, even the boulders are rounded. In theory, perfectly spherical particles would arrange themselves in such a way as to produce maximum pore space; in nature, however, the existing rounded rock particles have opposing flat surfaces that give them a directional character and cause them to layer, or shingle. Considering inevitable compaction and con-solidation, the interconnectedness of pore space in angular, irregularly shaped sharp material gives it better drainage properties.

Pore, or void, space is important to most alpine and rock garden plants not only for drainage but also for transfer of oxygen. Porosity maintains the soil's vital system of microorganisms and life-giving soil air. In a reciprocal relationship that maintains porosity, plant roots facilitate the passage of soil gases and the transfer of nutrients. The soil of any healthy garden is a complex and dynamic ecosystem. (For a description of a simple way to determine the porosity of a garden soil, see the chapter "Moraine and Scree Gardens.")

SOIL COHESION. How well a soil hangs together, cohesion, is another important characteristic. Sometimes cohesion is mistakenly referred to as "structure"; properly, the term *structure* refers to the collective phys-ical properties of soil as they relate to the arrangement of particles in the soil, including cohesion. Pore space in soil has a strong influence on its structure, especially its drainage and aeration. Cohesion is desirable, up to a point. You want enough of it for the soil to hold together, but excessive cohesion interferes with porosity and permeability—and thus with drainage. An open soil has the abundant pore space needed by most rock garden plants.

THE WORLD BELOW THE SURFACE. Video technology lets us observe the dynamics of soil and plant root interaction. At the Environmental Protection Agency Laboratory in Corvallis, Oregon, scientists study root activities with the aid of a microscopic video camera on a probe, an instrument dubbed a *microrhizotome*. In this seemingly dull world beneath our plants lies a complex and subtle interplay of living organisms with minerals, water, gases, and the products of decay. This microscopic world hums with activity vital to plant growth. Microorganisms and insects glean and cultivate soil. The balance of microlife and micronutrients maintains the health of the system.

The more you can go with the flow of nature, the better. Even if you start out with a bed of pure, graded silica sand, over time a complex miniature ecosystem will surely develop, with its own biotic community. You may see something happening that you don't like, such as the formation of an algal mat or crust. The presence of even a small amount of native soil, rock, microorganisms, and burrowing soil organisms such as benign worms and insects can help to prevent this. No natural force is inherently bad for rock garden soil; it is bringing them into a desirable balance that is the key to success. For example, soil compaction is not altogether detrimental—it provides good root contact and moisture retention—but *excess* compaction is a serious problem. Bioturbation, the stirring up or burrowing of soil by organisms of all sizes from the microscopic to the mammalian, is not inherently harmful, although it is distressing to find treasures uprooted by voles or moles. Seldom can we arrest the forces of nature, but we are in a good position to balance them. There are always trade-offs: we need some organic matter for nutrient delivery and the transfer of vital soil gases, yet too much can result in excess water-holding capacity.

Types of Rock

To help you explore possible local resources, I provide an overview of the most common rock types available in North America. For more specific information, consult your state geological survey; those organizations usually have inexpensive publications on rocks of the region and may be able to suggest sources.

VOLCANIC ROCK PARTICLES. Gardeners in far western North America have easy access to volcanic rock. Pumice, scoria, and perlite are the three main types of volcanic scree materials encountered in nature and in the rock garden. They are widely available throughout North America but may be expensive in nonvolcanic regions. Both pumice and scoria are rocks ejected from a volcano during a violent eruption. The magma from which volcanoes erupt contains dissolved gases under pressure. As it rises and the eruption begins, pressure is abruptly released, and the dissolved gas rapidly forms copious bubbles. When the lava is blown out, the particles cool very rapidly and holes and pores are formed. Not all eruptions produce the bubbly stuff—the viscosity of the parent magma also affects the violence of the eruption. Magmas rich in glass and gas produce the most foam. Runny material loses gas readily, so the less viscous iron-rich basaltic volcanic rocks are not as bubbly. Both pumice and scoria are what geologists term *vesicular* (that is, full of tiny holes) lavas, but they differ in chemical and mineral composition. A competent volcanologist can distinguish the two in the field on the basis of color and heft alone. If a rock is bubbly, dark, and heavy, it is scoria. Pumice is light colored and has an especially high percentage of frothy glass, which is why it is known as "the rock that floats." Scoria has more iron and magnesium and less glass; it has a greater variety of minerals and thus more trace elements.

Pumice and scoria are excellent rock garden materials, either as mulch or as soil additives. Volcanic rocks are available in the trade in various sizes. If you are considering using volcanic material as a scree component, scoria is a slightly better choice from the standpoint of mineral nutrition. Both rocks alter eventually to clay (especially in the presence of acidic components such as peat), but in the lifetime of a garden, this alteration will not affect the character of the soil adversely. The clay produced from scoria, even in tiny amounts, is excellent fare for many plants. Pumice quickly alters to a very sticky clay, but it won't do this significantly in the lifetime of a garden or trough. Excess fines or dust from pumice, however, can act as an adhesive.

Perlite is a commercial product made from hydrated pumice, either artificial or natural. Because perlite is nearly pure glass, it may contain short but complex microscopic threads, or spicules, that are spun in its production. For this reason, it is very important to protect yourself from inhaling dust from perlite. It is light and will float to the surface of soil. Perlite is expensive, and because it dries out very quickly, it is a poor choice for use in an open garden.

GRANITES. When magmas are slowly cooled at deeper levels beneath the earth's surface instead of erupting, intrusive or crystalline igneous rocks result. Although they have a great deal of geologic variety, in the commercial trade these slowly cooled crystalline rocks are often called "granite." In granites, you can see discrete mineral grains, blebs, or crystals. The most common granites are feldspar, quartz, amphibole, and mica. All have great color variety, and granite grit is one of the most attractive mulches for a rock garden. Granite is widespread in the Rocky Mountains, the Sierra Nevada of California, most Canadian provinces, and outcrops and glacial deposits in the Atlantic and New England states. It is found locally in many other areas. Granite makes excellent rock material for soil-building, but if it is mined and crushed, it may be expensive, because this hard stone requires a great deal of energy to process. Fortunately, granitic gravel deposits are also widespread. Even when partially crushed, these make an attractive mulch and soil additive. If granite is expensive in your area but you want to use it to match rocks, consider using a less expensive grit mixed into the soil, with some granite mixed into the grit mulch. The color variety helps bring visual harmony to otherwise mismatched materials.

METAMORPHIC ROCKS AND ROCK MATERIALS. Metamorphic rocks run the gamut from high-grade gneisses (which closely resemble granite in their massive and grainy or crystalline character) to slates and marbles. Gardeners complain of the biotic barrenness of metamorphic areas, and there is some geologic basis for this. The processes of metamorphism tend to lock up important soil-building minerals chemically; however, these same processes may also make certain minerals more available.

The extreme of locking away elements and minerals from plants is represented by higher-grade metamorphism (more intense in terms of temperature and pressure) in basaltic rocks, which produces serpentine. In spite of their reputation of being toxic to plants, serpentines and their derived soils support many alpine gems. I would not hesitate to use serpentine, with its exquisite jade-green hues, to build a rock garden.

Under an even more intense regime of temperature and pressure, crystalline metamorphics such as schists and gneisses form. These tough rocks have a massive texture and may have attractive swirls of microfolds that echo the intense pressures they have undergone. Because they tend to lack directional cleavage, building with them is a challenge. The detritus from high-grade metamorphics tends to be chippy yet very hard. Although slate is not an especially popular material for rock gardens because of its strongly planar cleavage, the tougher grades make wonderful crevice gardens. Slate chippings or grit can be used as a soil additive, but try to obtain hard, high-grade material; low-grade slates tend to be soft and crumbly, even when they at first appear to be hard.

If you live in an area with lower-grade metamorphics such as slate, consult the local agricultural authority to find out if soils derived from local metamorphic parent rocks suffer from any noteworthy mineral deficiencies. The occasional application of a weak fertilizer may correct this. Remember, however, that many rock plants prefer nutritionally lean conditions.

LIMESTONES AND DOLOMITES. You are fortunate if sandstone, limestone, dolomite, or marble is available locally in any form. Calcareous chippings are a premier rock garden soil additive. Calcium-rich, or limey, soils are home to many of the finest rock garden plants, including many saxifrages. In this context, *lime* refers to limestone (calcium carbonate) and dolomite (calcium-magnesium carbonate), which are both non-caustic even when hydrated.

In general, transported rock materials do not significantly affect the pH of soil. Rock types do affect the pH of the soils that are derived directly from them, but this process occurs over a much greater time span than the life of even a very old garden. The original rocks from which a soil is derived are called *parent rocks*. A rule of thumb is that it takes a hundred years to accumulate 1 inch (2.5 cm) of topsoil. The minerals found in most rocks are very stable and do not break down enough to become available to herbaceous plants within their lifetimes. This is why using limestone (or recycled concrete) in your rock garden will not in the least limit your ability to grow acid-loving plants such as members of the Ericaceae. Azaleas and rhododendrons do fine in limestone regions of Kentucky, and there are many acid-loving plants growing naturally in the Burren, a limestone region in Ireland that abounds with choice rock plants. Sufficient acidity is supplied by the organic component of the soil.

For either established plants or seedlings, pH changes are best made gradually. If you do want a limey soil in some location for growing plants that truly demand it, and you don't have a soil rich in calcium in a natural form available to plants, you can purchase an extremely fine-textured hydrated lime that is granulated for ease of handling. Hydration is one of the major processes of nature that makes minerals and elements in soil available for plant nutrition. When used sparingly, hydrated (or quick) lime works wonders for lime-loving ferns, saxifrage, and other plants—a kind of tufa in a teaspoon.

Tufa is a soft, lime-rich rock beloved by rock gardeners (see "Working with Tufa"). It is formed when calcium-bearing freshwater springs well up through alkaline lake water that is rich in carbonates and organic debris. The resulting precipitate is soft calcium carbonate that also contains hydrated lime and other minerals. Roots of calcium-loving rock plants can easily penetrate the soft rock. Another soft limestone rock is travertine, formed in hot springs, which has all the virtues of tufa and can host a splendid variety of rock plants.

Quick lime also contains pure calcium. Contrary to popular belief, natural lime-rich rock materials and quick lime are not at all caustic. Caustic lime is calcium oxide produced by special cooking and hydrating of calcium; this is an ingredient in the cement bagged and sold for home use. As discussed in "Making Troughs," this is why you should always wear gloves while working with cement; finished troughs are not caustic, however, because the reaction quickly stabilizes, and cement that has been even briefly cured won't burn plant foliage or roots.

SANDSTONES. Sandstones and the soils derived from them are desirable rock garden materials. Arenites, clean sandstones with a mineral-rich matrix, are found in many attractive colors. Some formations have interesting bedding and rock cleavage that enhance their use in rock garden design. The north-central regions of North America have widespread arenite formations, as does the American Southwest. Sandstones with a matrix of lithified (hardened into rock) mud are called *graywackes*, or dirty sandstones. The best graywackes are those that have undergone low-grade metamorphism—fortunately, most of them have. Some graywackes are fine grained, quite soft, and crumbly; these may alter quickly to heavy clays. Graywackes can be a good source of rock garden soil material.

CONGLOMERATES. Conglomerates, sedimentary rocks composed of pebbles hardened in a matrix of sandstone or mudstone, are especially attractive. Because they have been through extensive cycles of weathering and transport, conglomerates frequently contain very hard rocks such as quartz. The colorful detritus and soils derived from these so-called pudding stones are choice material. Many conglomerates have undergone low-grade metamorphism, which makes them harder and tougher.

Breccias are conglomerates with angular fragments rather than pebbles. They are also terrific rock garden material in both the whole rock and fragmented forms. An especially choice example is the Beekmantown formation in Pennsylvania, a breccia composed of limestones and dolomites.

Soil Components

Obtaining rock and soil ingredients is a major step in the construction phase, and transporting them is the major expense (in money and physical labor) in creating rock garden soil. This section discusses various potential components and how you can manipulate their proportions.

No book can substitute for local advice, preferably from seasoned gardeners. Don't hesitate to imitate as well as experiment. But, what if your area has few rock gardens? Northern Texas and southern Oklahoma, for example, possess a thick blanket of heavy clay soils derived from repeated cycles of weathering and erosion of very ancient granites and sandstones. With hot, humid summers, relentless wind, and flat terrain, it hardly seems like rock garden country; nevertheless, you can make a lovely rock garden here. The limestones and sandstones of the Arbuckle formation and the stony soils derived from them are ambrosia for many rock-loving plants, including such beautiful Texas natives as *Penstemon cobaea* and *Castilleja indivisa*. Texas rock plants include an impressive list of composites and bulbs. Moreover, such a garden would weather summer thunderstorms and seasonal winds far better than the typical perennial bed or cottage garden.

FINDING LOCAL RESOURCES. It is both enjoyable and worthwhile to become acquainted with your local geology. Contact a nearby university or public library to find a government or private geologist, and learn a bit about available rock resources. In many areas, local geologists offer get-acquainted field trips. Agencies such as state or provincial highway or mineral resource departments provide information on obtaining rocks. Soil conservation or environmental services agencies publish reports on soils and geology throughout the United States and Canada. If you find an especially attractive rock formation in your area, you can use a geologic map to find quarries that might be sources for that rock type. Geologic or topographic maps show locations of quarries and borrow pits, shallow areas where rock is excavated and crushed for road projects and winter graveling. You may be able to obtain a detailed local soil survey from your local garden club or chapter library.

Some agencies, such as the Bureau of Land Management and the U.S. Forest Service, issue low-cost permits to haul materials for home or group projects. Remember that commercial mineral rights may be in effect on any naturally occurring rock, even a seemingly common one. Always seek permission before removing any rock or soil materials. Consider issues of trespass: ownership of mineral rights and all lands in North America is a matter of public record. For information, contact your state or provincial geologist or department of mining industries.

If outside your window you see flat prairie, you may not realize that underneath it is a wealth of buried ancient glacial deposits that can provide first-class material for rock garden soil. In the not-too-distant geologic past, glaciers covered a significant portion of North America. In addition, wind and water carried glacial soil nutrients in which alpine plants thrive far beyond the direct reaches of the ice sheets. Although somewhat altered from their true alpine state, these deposits are gold mines for the rock gardener. Most areas also have many buried streams and gravel deposits.

ADAPTING NATIVE SOILS. Local advice from experienced gardeners or county agents can help you learn about the quirks of your native soils. For example, some clays have very specific properties of adhesion, particularly to the common, yet highly variable, mineral feldspar. If you have a clay-feldspar incompatibility, mixing in grit or sand that contains large quantities of feldspar will produce a nasty, concretelike soil. Some soils are gypsum-receptive, whereas others are not: adding gypsum, often recommended by general gardening manuals, does not automatically balance or even influence pH in all soil types. Still other soils contain a clay that adheres to gypsum, producing a concrete or crusty hardpan. You can spend a lot of money on this popular additive, only to make textural problems worse.

In some soils, the drying out of even a thin portion of the topmost layer can cause the soil to limit upward flow of the soil pore water, so that the soil may feel dry on top and still be saturated beneath. This blocked conductivity is an effective barrier against water loss, a saving grace in desert soils but potentially disastrous to irrigated gardens. Plant roots help subsurface water pass this barrier, but rock gardens, especially new ones, may be too sparsely planted for this process to occur.

ROCK GARDEN SOIL INGREDIENTS. The three major components in rock garden soil are rock particles (or detritus), loam, and organic material. Lean soil, or scree, consists predominantly of rock particles. As long as you maintain excellent drainage, you can vary the proportions of materials almost infinitely. A typical rock garden soil may contain 2 parts ¼-inch or smaller (5- to 7-mm) rock fragments, 1 part sandy river loam, and 1 part composted forest humus or other organic matter. The Appendix provides information to help you evaluate soil ingredients.

Typically, rock particles are mixed loosely into the soil of the rock garden and also used as a top-dressing, or mulch. Shop around for aggregate material. The two basic, widely available choices are: (1) natural gravels and sands mined from river or glacial deposits; and (2) aggregates made from crushed quarry rock. Both types have pros and cons. Be aware that the terminology for rock products varies by region; for instance, the term *pea gravel* can mean anything from a material that resembles coarse sand to a uniform gravel the size of peas.

Some gravels are partially crushed, and this may be desirable for compaction and stability. You don't want material that packs too tightly, but you might not want it to be too unstable and slippery, as rounded pebbles are. Because angular fragments can interlock, they have what is called (in the romantic language of geology) a good "angle of repose." This is the natural angle at which unconsolidated rock material can be piled and still maintain slope stability. Take a shovel or scoop and pile up the material into a mound until it starts to slide away and downward; when a miniature landslide has occurred, the material has exceeded its angle of repose. If the material has some interlocking qualities, it will have a steeper angle of repose. A variety of fragment sizes increases the allowable angle of repose. This is a desirable characteristic in rock garden construction, especially if you wish to use slopes to enhance drainage or to place material in crevices and have it stay put. There is even a significant difference in angle of repose between beach sand, with its very rounded particles, and the more angular builder's or quarry sands. These principles work with all sizes of material. Soils themselves also have slope stability.

In spite of the existence of North American standards for sized construction aggregate, the variation in type and quality of material is very wide. Try to obtain grit that has been washed free of mud and contamination. It should not be washed perfectly clean: the presence of some fines is desirable for moisture retention and the availability of mineral nutrients. However, you will be very frustrated if the material you work with has gobs of sticky mud or creates an outwash of thick slurry every time it rains. If you visit a pit and observe the material heaped up, it may appear cleaner than it really is because rain has washed most of the goo off the surface. Both clean and dirty materials are used in construction; dirty aggregate is used to maximize compaction—not a desirable trait in a rock garden.

To accommodate the diverse needs of the construction industry, gravel is available in most areas in an assortment of sizes. For scree and grit mulch, you want rocks with a roughly ¼-inch (6-mm) diameter or less; an ideal range is particles from ¼ inch down to coarse sand size (6.0 to 0.2 mm). Look up "sand and gravel," "rock products," or "construction aggregates" in a telephone directory, and you are certain to find a source. Some of these firms have websites that include photos of the materials they offer. If you live in an area remote from construction development, you may still be able to locate a source for aggregate used in road maintenance. A word of caution for those living in the Deep South: many resources for sand and gravel are offshore, where ancient river fan deposits are mined to provide sand and gravel for construction in areas covered with thick alluvial deposits of clay. These products may have a salt content not acceptable for garden use, so specify your need for salt-free material.

Start with a basic soil mixture of aggregate, sand, loam, and organic matter, and then experiment with select areas in your rock garden where you add smaller quantities of imports, or exotics. For example, you might try a commercially prepared turf-soil amendment, such as particles of fired and hardened clay called "calcined clay" (a proprietary name is Turface®). This material is expensive, but it has the virtue of retaining moisture while allowing very free drainage, a real benefit for fussy alpines. You might want to try recycled materials such as crushed concrete, which can be used beneath a grit mulch if you don't like its appearance.

Most native soils contain good loam, which is a suitable rock garden soil ingredient. If your native soil contains extremely heavy clay, such as adobe or deep-marine blue clay, you may realistically decide to import the loam component. Check with your local agricultural extension or government soil service for an equivalent of sandy loam or loess that is available in your area.

The ideal soil contains organic matter in various stages of decomposition. The best organic component is a high-fiber one that will last longer than the typical leaf compost sold for use in vegetable and perennial beds. One organic material popular for use in rock or woodland garden soil is the mundane rotted sawdust, which, happily, is also one of the longest-lasting, most widely available, and least expensive. Fresh sawdust from cabinetmakers or planing mills may be available, even if you are distant from timber areas. If you can obtain only fresh sawdust, you can initiate the decaying process by dampening it and further moistening it with a weak solution of lawn fertilizer. Decaying wood consumes nitrogen and may temporarily deplete soil, but this is a concern only during the initial period of decay. Another ordinary organic constituent that works well for some (but not all) rock garden plants is decayed bark fines, handled like sawdust. Leafmold, especially that derived from oak leaves, is another long-lasting organic component.

Some rock gardeners avoid using manure, but others swear by it, especially if it is buried well below the surface. Manure may be used, if well rotted, as a portion of the organic component. Rotted barnyard litter, composed of manure and sawdust or straw, is a fine soil additive, and many alpines thrive in its presence. Be sure that it is well aged and free of large, hot lumps. You can run litter through a coarse sieve or purchase it prescreened from a landscape supplier. How long you should age it depends on your climate. In a mild, damp climate, litter will be well aged in a full year; in a colder or drier climate, it may be better after three years. If you have farm animals, you can process the litter by using a simple wood frame of ¼-inch (6-mm) hardware cloth placed over a wheelbarrow or garden cart; simply screen as you shovel. Stable litter from horse manure contains many viable weed seeds. To kill them, you can solarize it briefly: spread the aged manure out to the depth of 1–2 feet (0.3–0.6 m) in full summer sun, cover it for two or three weeks with clear plastic, and allow it to cook.

If you have access to decayed, mixed forest products such as bark and duff (rotted coniferous organic debris) or mull (the deciduous equivalent), these make a fine organic addition. Peat, either fresh or milled, is also good, but some people dislike its tendency to resist rewetting if allowed to dry out. For the best of all possible worlds, mix several types of organic additives. For example, peat and well-aged manure improve each other when mixed. Whatever you choose for organic additives, keep some on hand over the years and stir in a bit as you cultivate, plant, and replant portions of your rock garden. This rejuvenates the soil, replacing what has been lost to decay.

There is one urgent caveat with regard to using organic matter in rock garden soil. In climates with a pronounced wet or humid season, excess organic matter can cause stagnant soil conditions that may quickly kill some rock plants. In such climates, you may wish to test proportions in some large containers with drainage. Water a mixture copiously and observe how long it takes to dry out under whatever conditions of duress you expect. If the mixture drains slowly or stays sopping wet, you need to decrease the amount of organic matter used.

FERTILIZER. Rock plants vary widely in their nutritional needs. In addition to traditional alpines, the selection of rock garden plants increasingly includes many native to rocky nonalpine and pedocal soils (relatively alkaline soils rich in calcium and associated nutritional minerals). If you are using a soil mix that consists largely of unaltered freshly crushed rock material and little or no clay or loam, you are likely to need a program of consistent but weak applications of balanced fertilizer. As a rule of thumb, use fertilizers at low strength, one-quarter to one-half the recommended dosage for border plants. Although fertilizer may appear to improve growth in ways such as increasing leaf size and plant mass, it may also make plants more vulnerable to rot and disease. This effect is most pronounced if you apply excess nitrogen. Rock plants have thrifty ways, and their growth is naturally restrained as an adaptation to a harsh environment. Choose a fertilizer formulated for encouraging bloom rather than leaf growth, with a relatively low proportion of nitrogen to phosphorus and potassium.

Guidelines for Handling Soil in the Rock Garden

The following tips will help you to create a soil environment for good growing, and they'll also spare you a backache or two. There is no need to stir soil mixtures laboriously in a wheelbarrow. Mix soil on a tarp laid on the ground near where you intend to use it. To mix a small batch quickly, spread layers of the ingredients on the tarp with a rake, then pull the corners of the tarp toward the center one by one. Rake the heap out again and repeat the process to mix. Two people can work with a larger tarp, rolling the soil heap from end to end.

To move rocky soil, construction supply houses offer heavy metal scoops, or you can use a large tin can or pail. A trenching tool is a narrow shovel with scooping capacity, well suited to handling rocky soil; also known as a telegraph spoon, this tool is designed to remove heavy material such as gravel from deep holes. A small pry bar, or gem scoop, is a valuable tool; a roofer's tear-off bar is a fine substitute. One of my favorite tools is one I can recommend only for the reasonably strong: a digging bar, a 4- or 5-foot (1.2- or 1.5-m) long, very heavy bar with a chiseled end and a rounded end. It is handy for moving rocks and wedging them in place, but it requires strength to manage without muscle injury. If you can manage its weight, this bar can actually spare your back and knees.

Give careful consideration to using a small tractor or grader, which can be rented and can save hours of time and much wear and tear if you are comfortable operating machinery. It may be worth your while to hire an operator with a front-end loader to move heavy soil and rock materials into position. If you do, be sure to find one with whom you can communicate easily and who has experience handling landscape materials with precision and sensitivity. It is important that soil materials not be overhandled with machinery.

Avoid excess compaction or mixing of the soil. Gravity is relentless and is going to compact the soil over time. Handling soil lightly not only spares your wrists and back, it also helps maintain air space. Avoid overmixing during construction and soil placement. If unevenness really bothers you, you can always do additional mixing as you plant. This unevenness, however, gives the garden a more natural look: remember that lovely chaos described earlier. You can also avoid compaction by making paths for wheelbarrows, carts, or heavier equipment. If the garden is large, you can break it up into smaller gardens. This will go a long way toward saving your back, too. On a smaller scale, create areas—perhaps large flat stones—to step and perch on while you weed, plant, and groom.

The use of geofabric, used in roadbed construction, can help create a better foundation for the rock garden. This material, which is heavier and much longer-lasting than the landscape fabric sold at garden centers, is available in assorted grades and characteristics. It is designed to spread the load and will help prevent the rock garden or raised bed from sinking over time. The use of geofabric also prevents soil reversion, or excess mixing of native soil into the rock garden by earthworms. It is especially valuable under low scree beds in moist temperate climates, where worms or burrowing animals can contaminate the scree with heavy native soil in just a few years. Geofabric, when installed taut, strongly discourages moles and gophers. If geofabric is unavailable, you can use woven plastic nursery groundcloth to similar effect. A general word of caution, however: when any distinct drainage horizon is created, water can quickly collect at the base of the area of more rapidly draining material—it will either run off somewhere or create an undesirable stagnant spot. The more abrupt the horizon and the larger the difference in drainage rate between the soils, the more severe the problem. Runoff must be accommodated, or the water must be able to permeate freely to the soil below.

Once your garden is full of thriving rock plants, their busy roots will cultivate their own soil nicely. With good soil, there will be no need for the laborious cultivation and digging associated with other types of gardening. If at first you seem to have built more garden than you have plants for, don't hesitate to install some easy, temporary plants to maintain soil health. If you choose species that are not too invasive, you can always remove them as your range of tastes and acquisitions increases.

Water: A Natural Addition to the Rock Garden

EAMONN HUGHES

The sight and sounds of water in the landscape captivate our senses in a way that stirs deep within our souls, probably because all life originated in water and needs water to survive. Whatever reasons we devise to explain the effect that water has on the human psyche, the simple fact is that the movement of water in the garden washes away the stresses of daily life. Once you have a garden with a water feature in it, you will never again want a garden without one.

A water feature is a natural addition to the rock garden. If you look to nature for inspiration, you will see many places where water has

PLATE 13. A water feature designed by the author. Photograph by Eamonn Hughes

sculpted the terrain as it courses through alpine slopes and screes. In addition to the dynamic aspect that water adds to the rock garden, it creates a more humid microclimate. This allows you to expand your palette of plants to include species that thrive next to and even in water.

If you decide to use a water feature in your rock garden, proper planning is vital. Time taken at this stage ensures that you will enjoy this element for many years to come. This chapter describes the design and construction of a fairly typical water feature incorporating a length of stream, a pond, and at least one waterfall or cascade. As you plan the placement, type, and size of the feature, you should consider the following questions carefully.

WHERE SHOULD I PLACE THE NEW GARDEN SO THAT I WILL GET MAXIMUM VIEWING AND ENJOYMENT FROM IT? In many regions, people are cooped up indoors during the winter months. If you live in such a region, your waterfalls or other features should be easily seen from the windows of your house's living area. You can add lighting to extend the enjoyment into the night. Water sounds can help to mask traffic and other neighborhood noises, so placing the feature close to an outdoor patio or deck also works well. It is inadvisable, however, to build large waterfalls too near the main sitting areas: too much water volume can be more irritating than soothing.

WHAT IS MY BUDGET? WILL I BE ABLE TO ADD TO THE FEATURE WHEN I HAVE MORE RESOURCES IN THE FUTURE? Your budget determines how much of the heavy work you can hire a contractor to perform and how much you will do yourself. A water garden need not remain a dream because of a present lack of money. You can plan to complete it over several years, and if you incorporate future changes into your initial plan, the final result will appear to be a unified project.

WHAT SAFETY ISSUES SHOULD I BE CONCERNED ABOUT? Water gardens, like swimming pools, are legally classified as attractive nuisances. You may have to get construction permits for the water garden, so check with your local authority to see if there are any restrictions on the size or depth of ponds. Be aware of the intrinsic danger of water to young children, even if you have none of your own. They will be drawn to the moving water, and you need to provide for their safety.

Once you have answered these questions, it is time to do some serious planning. The effect you are after is that of a naturally eroded landscape where the water appears to have carved its way through the rock face. The surrounding rock placement must give the illusion of eroded bedrock.

Certain principles are fundamental to achieving a pleasant, natural-looking rock garden. When we look at rock gardens, we love some of them immediately; many, however, we are polite about to the owner, but there is something that we do not like about them. Often we cannot define what that something is. The most common problem involves rock placement. To understand this, we must look at how rock is formed and how water and weathering affect rock faces in nature.

When most rock was formed, it had strata (layers) that developed either while volcanic rock was cooling or as layers of sediment were laid down. These strata tend to be horizontal except where ground forces have pushed them up. In all my work building rock gardens and water features, I try to maintain a plane that is horizontal across the whole area. This horizontal plane is also the easiest to work with. As you set your rocks into place, step back and check that you are keeping at least one side of the rock in this plane. Use the largest rocks at the base of the garden and gradually reduce their size as you work toward the top.

Lay two hoses through the proposed waterfall or cascade area. Each hose represents one edge of the proposed streambed. These will give you a visual idea of how the water will flow through the new rockery. Experiment with the hoses, laying them to meander along the slope.

You need not keep them parallel all the way; be creative by widening the streambed in some spots. These wider sections can become small beaches that you can plant later with aquatic marginal plants.

At the bottom of the waterfall will be the pond from which the water is recirculated. Make sure that the size of the pond is in balance with that of the entire rock garden. Wrap the pond along the base of the garden slope as far as your budget allows. The regret I hear most often from other pond gardeners is that their first ponds were too small. Once the water garden bug has bitten you, you will want more area for the new plants you acquire. After you have decided on the best location for the waterfall and pond, the hard work begins. The following is an outline of the basic procedures for installing a natural-looking feature with liner and rock.

PREPARING THE POND SITE. Referring to your plan, mark out the outline of the new watercourse with athletic-field chalk, spray paint, cat litter, or flour. Use a builder's level set on a long, straight board to check the elevations around the pond perimeter. It is critical that the margin of the pond be level. You may have to cut and fill the soil to achieve this.

EXCAVATION. Small ponds can be excavated by hand. Dig out one shovel's depth at a time from the entire pond area. It is a good idea to allow for a shelved area, particularly at either end of the new pond, which can be used later as planting beds. Usually shelves are only 12 inches (30 cm) deep and at least 18 inches (45 cm) wide. Continue excavating down to the bottom of the pond. The depth is determined by how you want to stock your pond. If you want only a few goldfish to keep down mosquito larvae, then 15 inches (38 cm) is perfectly adequate, but if your taste runs to Japanese koi and the larger water lilies, you will have to excavate as deeply as 3 feet (0.9 m). It is best to slope the bottom of the pond to form a deeper section at one end. You can place the pump in this deeper area later, and it will make cleaning out the pond much easier. The sides of the pond should be almost vertical to discourage predators such as herons and raccoons from wading into the pond after the fish.

Once the pond is fully dug, you can start excavating upstream for the waterfall or streambed. Be sure to make this watercourse wide and deep enough so that after you lay rock on both sides, you still have plenty of room for the water. When completed, the waterfall excavation should present a stepped staircase effect. For a streambed, excavate longer, gently sloped sections.

CHOOSING, MEASURING, AND LAYING THE LINER. Looking at the specifications of the various types of liners available can be very confusing. For the liner, I recommend either butyl rubber or EPDM (a synthetic form of rubber). I have used these liners for more than twenty-five years and have never had a failure. They are flexible but tough, and best of all, they are stable to ultraviolet light, so they will not deteriorate in the sun.

Next, you must work out how much liner you need. Drape a cloth measuring tape loosely on the sides and bottom of the pond along its greatest length. Allow an extra 12 inches (30 cm) on each end. This will give you the length of the liner needed for the pond. Repeat the process to determine the width, again allowing an extra 12 inches on each side. For the waterfall section, allow an extra 12 inches at the top of the waterfall and then measure down the centerline to the bottom of the pond; this gives you the length of the waterfall section of liner. For the width, measure across the widest part of the stream or waterfall, allowing at least an extra 9 inches (23 cm) on each side. When you lay the liners, you will not have to glue them together if you allow for the amount of overlap stated above.

Whether you need to put a 2-inch (5-cm) layer of sand under the liner depends on the underlying soil. If it is very rocky or if you have cut off many sharp roots during excavation, then sand is required; if the base is clean soil or clay with no rocks, no sand is needed.

PLATE 14. The first stages of laying out a waterfall. Photograph by Eamonn Hughes

Drape the pond liner into the excavated area and center it as well as you can. Wearing smooth, flat-bottomed shoes, you can walk on the liner and press it into the corners. Next, lay down the streambed liner and allow it to overlap into the pond. This is the water containment area. If water never rises above the edges of the liner, it cannot leak. As you set everything inside the liner, do it in such a way that water will not be forced over the liner's edge.

The black liner is unobtrusive and need not be covered in the pond area, but the shallow stream will look better if it is covered with water-rounded gravel of mixed sizes, which helps to hide the liner and makes your finished water garden more naturalistic. Be sure that any stone placed on the liner is not sharp enough to cut it if children or pets wade in the stream. In shallow pools where the water flow slows, the bottom can be sandy, as it would be in the eddies of a natural stream.

MIXING MORTAR. The rocks are to be set using mortar. In many areas, mortar is available in premixed bags, a convenient way of purchasing supplies. The basic mortar is 3 parts sharp sand, 1 part Portland cement, and ¼ part lime. If you are using premix, empty it into a wheelbarrow and slowly add water until you have a very thick, sticky paste. Do not allow the mortar to get runny, or it will leave marks on the rocks.

SETTING ROCKS. The setting of the stone is the most important phase of the project. The placement of the rock determines the finished feel. Remember that you are trying to make it look as if the water has eroded a channel through the soil and bedrock of the rock garden.

First, choose the largest rocks that you can manage to get into place. Use these pieces as anchor rocks on either side of the falls and along the streambed. Place a few flatter slabs around the edges of the pond. Mix

PLATE 15. The rocks are laid once the foundation and liner are installed. Photograph by Eamonn Hughes

the mortar and lay a 2- to 3-inch (5.0- to 7.5-cm) mortar bed on top of the liner, roughly matching the footprint (shape of the base) of the rock you are setting. Lift the stone into place and ease it into the mortar. The mortar consistency needs to be stiff enough to support the rock in place. In setting these main rocks, remember to choose a flat face and set this face on a horizontal plane. (If this talk of planes confuses you, think of it in terms of whether you can sit comfortably on these rocks. You are trying to get flat tops on each piece.) When the rocks have been set, stand back, and you will see the subtle effect of this technique. If any rock is not level on top, adjust it now before the mortar bed hardens. Once all the main rocks are in place, you can infill with rocks of various sizes, giving the illusion that they have sloughed off the old rock face. Be careful not to use too much mortar in setting these smaller rocks: you only want to secure them from behind, and you do not want to see any mortar oozing through the joints.

PUMP SIZE AND INSTALLATION. Before you finish the edge of the pond, you need to place the return hose line for the pump. If you are using a submersible pump, place it in the lowest area of the pond and bring black flexible tubing up over the edge of the pond; bury it in a channel leading to the top of the waterfall and stream. You can lay some loose rocks to hide the hose.

It is best to discuss with your local water garden supplier the size of pump you should use, depending on the volume of water that your pond and stream will accommodate. Often these stores have displays showing the flow produced by various pumps; by looking at these, you can choose a pump that will give you the effect you want. Here you can also get advice on running the power supply to the pump. You can install the electric line for the pump yourself, if you follow the appropriate electrical codes in your area for outdoor installations. It may be better, however, to have an electrician do this. Remember that water and electricity are a dangerous combination, and you must protect yourself and others.

PLATE 16. A finished
waterfall designed by
the author. Photograph
by Eamonn Hughes

You are now ready to fill the pond with water and begin enjoying
your new creation. When you turn on the pump for the first time, you
may see that the water is not flowing quite as you thought it might. Just
turn it off, set another small rock, and try it again when the mortar
hardens. Soon you will achieve the desired effect.

FURTHER READING

James Allison, *Water in the Garden*; Helen Nash and Eamonn Hughes,
Waterfalls, Fountains, Pools and Streams; Perry D. Slocum and Peter
Robinson, *Water Gardening, Water Lilies and Lotuses*

PART 2

Types of Rock Gardens

In North America, the term *rock garden* has been extended to cover numerous specialized garden features for growing unusual plants. These plants, native to a multitude of climates, latitudes, and elevations around the world, flourish only in conditions quite different from those that exist in an ordinary garden setting. Rock gardeners modify the existing topography, soils, sun and wind exposure, and moisture patterns to welcome a wide range of plants. At the same time, they try to create settings in which wild plant species look natural. Unlike dahlias or hybrid tea roses that can be regimented in formal beds, such plants look best in informal gardens, combined with companions of similar scale and with natural rocks and other structural materials.

The chapters in part 2 describe more than a dozen different kinds of specialized habitat gardens. Each was written by a gardener who focused on that garden type in response to local climate and terrain and his or her individual enthusiasm. The first seven essays present different approaches to classic rock gardens in which stone is prominent and the gardener wants to accommodate alpine and other dwarf plants. Finally, two specialist collectors explain how to design and plant rock gardens to house large numbers of conifers or cacti and succulents.

Before you decide to install one of these specialized features in your garden, read the appropriate chapter in part 4, "Regional Styles and Techniques," to find out how they will work for you. Notice the geographical perspective from which each author is writing. For example, the chapter "Dry Sand Beds" was written based on experience in Pennsylvania, where precipitation falls year round; if you live in a dry-summer climate, you may need to provide supplemental moisture to your sand bed. In regions with mild, wet winters, the screes, berms, and xeric gardens described by Coloradans Ray Radebaugh and Gwen Kelaidis would require a different range of plants and, perhaps, some winter cover.

Almost all the features described in this part can be made in a wide range of sizes and shapes. If you have a truckload of tufa, you can make a feature like that described by Sheila Paulson in "Working with Tufa." If you can obtain only one or two small pieces, however, you can use them in a small trough or even cement them into a large clay saucer for a portable garden. The berms Gwen Kelaidis has created in her garden are massive features, but the technique can be used in a garden of any size. The larger the feature, the more varied in size its plants can be. But there are so many tiny plants available to rock gardeners that even the smallest crevice bed, tufa boulder, or planted retaining wall can host dozens of brightly flowering specimens.

Berms: Raising a Rock Garden
above Flat Ground

GWEN KELAIDIS

Some rock gardens are built in response to the existing terrain. A steep slope or rugged rock outcrop is a natural inspiration for growing small shrubs and perennials—but many residential properties are flat or nearly so. The gardener with a flat piece of land has several options. One is to cut and fill, changing the contours with excavation to create depressions and elevations. Another is to work with the flat ground without excavating, in which case it is necessary to use the elevations of berms or other raised features to provide contour.

A berm is a substantial ridge of soil. Built up around the perimeter of a residential lot, berms improve privacy and add interest. They can emphasize the height of screening trees or shrubs planted on them, or they can bring perennial plantings closer to view. A garden creator can use a berm to separate areas of the garden, block the view of a mean-dering path, and create allure and adventure in the garden. What new delights lie beyond the ridge? How does the prospect change as we walk through the garden? One more advantage will warm the heart of any serious gardener: a berm provides more planting space than would the flat area on which it rests.

Rock gardeners know that many choice alpine and dryland plants grow better on a sloping surface rather than on flat ground. The slope provides continuous, improved drainage around the crown of a plant, helping to prevent decay. In regions where spring comes as a series of rainstorms alternating with freezing weather, plants without this advantage can perish in the icy puddles trapped above frozen soil. Even without freezing temperatures, water pooled around the crowns and roots for any length of time is fatal to many plants.

PLATE 17. Berms for rock plants encircle the back yard of Gwen and Panayoti Kelaidis's former residence in Denver, Colorado. Photograph by Gwen Kelaidis

A berm's drainage cannot be equaled on flat ground. Think of a kitchen sponge thoroughly saturated with water. If you hold it horizontally, it retains the maximum quantity of water; but tilt the saturated sponge, and the water drips out rapidly. In the same way, a horizontal mass of soil retains more water than a mounded one. Like the sponge, the mound of soil remains somewhat drier at the top than at the bottom, creating a variety of micro-habitats. Moisture-loving plants can be placed near the bottom and dryland plants near the top. (Digging a hole beneath a plant and filling it with drainage material such as grit does no good if there isn't also vertical and lateral runoff: the hole fills with water, and eventually the plant drowns—a form of death often called the "teacup effect.")

A berm also offers more than one kind of exposure to the sun. A berm lying on an east–west axis has a southern and a northern slope; the northern slope is cooler, even if the whole berm is in full sun, because solar radiation falls there less directly. Snow lies longer on the northern slope in the winter, as well, and this can offer just enough protection to high-alpine plants adapted to long-term snow cover.

Some rock gardeners use the terms *berm* and *raised bed* interchangeably, but in this book we use *raised bed* to mean a more formal planting area with vertical or near-vertical sides. Like a berm, it is filled with a well-drained soil mixture and contains rock outcrops and a gravel mulch (see "Planted Walls and Formal Raised Beds"). The raised bed does not provide drainage as rapid as that of the berm because its surface is essentially horizontal and thus drains only downward, not laterally. In very wet climates, however, a raised bed may be preferred because it can easily be capped with a temporary roof.

Planning

Planning a rock garden ideally would be part of an overall landscape plan, but the truth is that most gardeners have no real idea of the eventual scope of their gardens, so they create them piecemeal, trying to blend new features with existing ones. In addition, rock gardeners progress in skills and tastes, growing different arrays of plants and using different styles of construction. The typical grower is always looking for the right site for the ultimate rock garden.

Integrating a feature as dominant and permanent as a berm into the landscape requires serious thought and perhaps the advice of a professional designer. The placement of the berm is also vital to the success of its plantings. To grow the widest variety of plants, consider all the microclimates that can exist in the garden. You might start with one rock garden in full sun and another in the shadier part of the garden, together providing suitable conditions for the majority of popular rock plants. A high berm or constructed outcrop with its axis oriented east–west offers a hot and a cool side, but many choice plants prefer the dappled shade of trees or shrubs, especially at midday.

Dimensions will be dictated by the shape and size of the available space and by the gardener's ambition, resources, and physical strength.

It is good to remember, though, that even the largest bed tends to fill up rapidly. The greater the height of the berm, the more pronounced are the microhabitat differences. However, very long, steep slopes can be difficult to plant (and to irrigate, if this is needed in your climate); berms between 3 and 4 feet (0.9 and 1.2 m) high are the most manageable.

Construction

Just because rock plants grow best in well-drained, well-aerated soil with a large proportion of rock and sand doesn't mean they won't benefit from good nutrition (see also "Soils"). Whether you are constructing a raised bed or a berm, the next step after planning and preparing a clear site is acquiring and mixing the soil components. Producing a suitable soil mix depends on the local climate and the materials available. A good basic recipe, however, is the traditional rock garden formula of 1 part good loam, 1 part sand, and 1 part pea gravel or washed grit, with a generous addition of humus. Not all gardeners have leafmold at hand to provide the humus. Very well rotted cow or horse manure can be used, but stay away from products containing bark or wood chips; the rotting wood and bark absorb soil nitrogen and encourage certain fungi. The additional nitrogen available from manure may be beneficial, as long as it has been composted long enough to kill weed seeds and prevent its being too hot.

In dry, hot climates, a heavier loam containing more clay may actually be preferable to a lighter soil, because the clay releases water more slowly, minimizing the need to irrigate and the disastrous effects of desiccation. By contrast, some growers in regions with heavy rainfall use soil that is half (or even more) gravel. Some top the basic soil mix with 1 foot (0.3 m) of sand. Those gardening on pure sand may add no loam—only humus, which holds nutrients and water that the sand cannot retain. Whatever formula you use, when it has been well mixed, you should be able to squeeze a handful of moist soil tightly, release it, and the soil ball should fall apart. If it sticks together like a snowball, add more gravel, sand, humus, or some combination of these.

It is easiest to concoct a soil mix that will suit a wide variety of plants. You can create small pockets of other soils within the rock garden, but these tend to become blended by earthworms. Of course, separate berms or beds can be built elsewhere in the garden, with different soils to host a wider range of more demanding plants.

Mixing the soil is the builder's first opportunity for serious exercise. It is very important to obtain a uniform mix before placing any rocks or plants. One method is to dump all the ingredients in a pile approximately the shape of the planned berm, and then turn the entire pile with a shovel, moving from the bottom to the top, tossing the soil across the top of the ridge, progressing all the way around the pile. It is often effective to move the entire pile several feet to one side, tossing the ingredients to mix them, and then shovel it back to the final position. Large berms can be mixed with a rototiller, and really mammoth ones—I have built them as much as 70 feet (21 m) long—with a backhoe or front-end loader and the help of an experienced, sympathetic heavy-equipment operator. If the materials are being delivered from a rock dealer, ask the supplier to mix the soil components as they are loaded into the truck. Some writers recommend using a cement mixer; but the ingredients must then be shoveled into the mixer, which is hardly labor-saving, especially if you are planning a large berm.

If you plan a berm of considerable height and length, it is tempting to use materials other than good rock garden soil at the center. Resist incorporating any material that you would mind digging out later! One useful possibility is sod removed from a former lawn and laid upside down. At least 1 foot (0.3 m) of soil mixture over the sod should prevent later disturbance and discourage the grass from reemerging. Using clinker, broken concrete, or stone rubble is not recommended, because alpines may soon extend their roots down into this unfavorable zone. Give them a good chance at health and long life by providing a root run of nutritious soil without large air pockets.

Once the soil is mixed and laid roughly into the desired shape, you can contemplate adding rocks. A *rockery* (a term of opprobrium when uttered by dedicated rock gardeners), featuring pretty rocks picked up on vacations around the country and perhaps a plaster gnome or two, is not our goal here. Use rocks of a single type to create a naturalistic scene. That is, we don't want our garden to look natural; we want it to look like a particular little segment of the natural world that was pleasing to us. The founders of rock gardening were fond of formulating rules about rock choice and placement that, they believed, reflected natural principles (at least as they knew them in their local regions or in the Alps), but a hike in the mountains shows you that nature can be quite careless, piling rocks helter-skelter, knocking them down, and then perhaps pouring mud or lava over the whole mess.

One thing Reginald Farrer and other early rock garden writers enjoyed was applying insulting names to every style of rock garden other than their own magnificent converted quarries and miniature Alps. They referred to a berm as a "dog's grave." A berm with rocks placed at random was a "plum pudding"; if the rocks were set on end, it became an "almond pudding." The latter is a bad design, to be sure, but the plum pudding is quite functional and can be artistic, too, especially if the rocks are arranged in concentric but asymmetrical terraces.

PLATE 18. The berm garden being extended. Photograph by Gwen Kelaidis

According to Farrer, an excessively regular stepped terrace was a "jack-o'-lantern." This, however, is perhaps the most functional of all styles for accommodating many small plants, and the regular lines are soon softened by foliage.

Rocks serve both practical and aesthetic functions in the garden. The type of rock you choose depends largely on what is locally available at a reasonable price. Choose what pleases you in terms of shape and color. One consideration is the type of gravel you will eventually use as a surface mulch; it should blend with the larger rocks in color and the reflective quality of the surface (see also "Rock Garden Design, Style, and Aesthetics" and "Soils").

The natural companions of alpine plants, rocks are beautiful contrasts to bright flowers and soft foliage. Large boulders vary the scale of a feature devoted primarily to low-growing plants. On the practical side, well-placed rocks hold the loose soil of the berm in place against weather erosion and the pressure of foot traffic. To hold soil on a slope, lay the rocks in a staggered pattern without long, continuous vertical crevices. Rocks can also be adjusted to direct water to or away from plants according to their individual needs. Finally, stone is a poor con-

PLATE 19. The author setting rocks into a new berm. Photograph by Panayoti Kelaidis

ductor of heat, so the soil below and behind a rock stays cool—a necessity for many alpines.

The primary advice on rock placement is, "Make the rocks look good to you, and make them stable." If you view and photograph rocks in natural settings and contemplate why and how the outcrops or rocky slopes are put together, you will have a solid foundation for success. Follow the traditional rule of placing rocks in a visually stable position, as if they had rolled into the spot; however, it is not necessary to bury every rock to one-third of its depth, as some writers have urged.

Test the stability of the rocks by stepping on them. If you can shift or tilt them with your foot, they are not stable enough. Plants like stability! A rock that shifts in the soil creates an open space that is a hazard for questing roots. Moreover, the gardener will have to step on the rocks while planting and weeding, and it is an unnecessary challenge to balance on a rocking stone. It's also a hazard for anyone else who may climb on the rock garden, with or without permission. If you are building a large berm, it's a good idea to arrange especially large, somewhat flat rocks as a staircase handy for ascending the slope; vary the sizes and shapes of these extra-stable rocks so they won't look too artificial. On the ridgetop, flat rocks look natural and afford platforms from which the gardener can tend the plants.

There are varying opinions in the rock gardening world on the subject of how much rock should be used in a rock garden. On one extreme, George Schenk, author of *Moss Gardening* (1997) and other works, has insisted that no rocks should be used in the garden, apparently because so few people are capable of using them with what he considers good taste. The other extreme is represented by the crevice garden (see "Crevice Gardens"), a style that has attracted almost religious devotion in some circles. Most gardeners prefer a happy medium with enough rocks to hold slopes and offer ornamental contrast to the plantings, along with plenty of planting space.

Here are some tips for working with rocks:

If this is a team effort, appoint one person to be in charge of design. It saves lots of time, temper, and negotiation. The boss need not be the physically strongest person, nor is the position of boss permanent. Another person may act as chief engineering consultant.

Start from the bottom of the berm or bed and build upward.

Each rock's center of gravity should tilt in toward the center of the berm. When necessary, dig out the slope under the rock so that it leans into the hill.

Where possible, use the lower rocks to support the upper rocks. This increases stability.

Shim the rocks as necessary with smaller stones to achieve the appropriate tilt, but don't let the shims show; fill any empty spaces created by a shim with good soil.

For the most natural look, don't space rocks evenly and let some of them touch. You don't need a specific amount of soil around each rock. The irregularity of the rocks themselves will create planting spaces of varying size.

Strive to make the rock slope look natural; forget about creating pockets for certain plants. It is fun to create a place where one rock overhangs, offering a special little microclimate, or tight crevices where some temperamental alpine can reside, but this should happen within the greater scheme of the rock garden.

Make moving rocks easier on yourself. A dolly or hand truck is very helpful, although it often takes two people to move large rocks this way. Use rolling pipes; strong steel bars as levers, winches, and ramps; and other devices. If you have an engineer in the family, court that person; plead, cajole, or feed him or her; present the project as a challenge to ingenuity!

Quit for the day before you are totally exhausted; fatigue makes injury more likely. Don't get too tired to feed yourself; this is supposed to be fun and creative, not drudgery! Forestall strains and swelling with an anti-inflammatory medication as soon as you quit. Get lots of sleep, too! Nonbuilders don't always understand, but it is very restful and refreshing for the builder to sit in a chair, perhaps with a drink, and just gaze at the day's accomplishments.

Planting and Mulching

Once the rocks are in place (this may take several sessions), the fun begins. You now have new homes for all those plants you have been accumulating. As you plant, remember that these plants like to have stone up against their roots. Tucking the plants close to the rocks also gives a more natural look to the garden, because niches like this are where seeds often lodge in the wild.

As the crowning touch, top the berm or bed with a mulch of pea gravel or grit from which the fines (the dusty, silty part) have been

PLATE 20. Flagstone steps flank a berm accented by a trickling artificial stream. Photograph by Gwen Kelaidis

PLATE 21. Mature plantings on the berm. Photograph by Gwen Kelaidis

washed. For the most naturalistic look, mix several sizes of the same kind of rock in unequal proportions, a few scoops of larger gravel to a wheelbarrow of pea gravel. Small saxatile (rock-dwelling) plants must be kept dry and free of the mud that can be splashed up during rainstorms. Tuck the mulch under the edges of the plant, right around the crown. Mulch also prevents erosion. To maximize this effect, use sharp, angular gravel that is less likely to roll down slopes; round river gravel is unsuitable. Gravel made up of stones less than ¼ inch (6 mm) across (sold as "one-quarter minus") is the easiest size to shovel, and it doesn't obstruct the gardener's trowel when it has become mixed in with the underlying soil. This mulch also prevents the germination of many weed seeds. Finally, the small gravel prevents a crust from forming on the soil surface, so that rainfall or irrigation water penetrate the surface rather than running off. It's easier to install the initial plants before mulching, because you don't have to scrape the gravel to one side to dig the planting hole; but don't wait so long that the next rain erodes all your work.

Moraine and Scree Gardens

RAY RADEBAUGH

Many choice rock garden plants are said to require scree conditions to survive over the years, flower well, and maintain a compact habit. Although writers of catalogs and books seldom mention it, some of these alpine plants do even better in a moraine garden—scree with a constantly renewed supply of moisture in the root zone. In the rock garden as in nature, most plants can tolerate a range of conditions; thus, in the construction of scree and moraine gardens, there is not just one best method or set of conditions. In this chapter, I discuss the important elements of these garden features and suggest what has worked well in my own experiments.

Scree is the lean, gravelly soil that many alpine plants prefer (see "Soils"). The only significant difference between a moraine and a scree garden is the steady supply of underground moisture in the moraine garden, which simulates the underground flow from melting snow or glaciers in the mountains. Engineering this water flow in the garden makes the construction of a moraine garden somewhat complex; only building surface water features, where appearance as well as function is important, is likely to be more difficult. Nonetheless, with care and a bit of hard work, any gardener can build a moraine.

Natural Moraine and Scree

Successful moraine and scree gardens closely mimic natural conditions, so it is important to examine these formations in nature to understand what makes them unique. A moraine is one of those choice spots that come as a delightful surprise to hikers above timberline. As we walk across a tundra area inspecting the plants, we may suddenly find ourselves on a slope where the plants are different and seem to be growing with little sign of struggling against their harsh environment. The

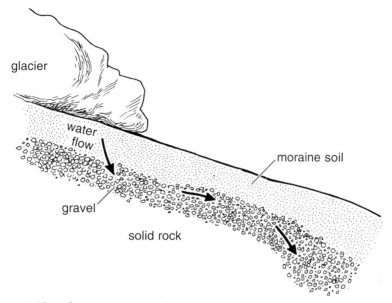

Figure 3. Flow of water in a moraine. Drawing by Sukey McDonough

reason is concealed underground: water flowing through gravel deposits on top of an impervious rock layer. The icy water comes from a melting glacier or snowfield somewhere on the slope above. Perhaps the same glacier moved through this area thousands of years ago, grinding the rock into gravelly debris and depositing it as it retreated. This combination—a flow of underground water through gravel— makes a moraine. Figure 3 depicts the structure of a natural moraine.

Even where rainfall above timberline is not reliable, plants growing on a moraine have a steady supply of water seeping into the soil from below. In the Northern Hemisphere, these areas are most often on north- or east-facing slopes, where glaciers and snowfields are more persistent. The cold underground water, flowing throughout the summer growing season, keeps the roots only a few degrees above freezing. This cool, moist environment is ideal for many alpine plants. The gravelly scree soil provides good aeration and drainage, yet remains constantly moist, while the cool temperature inhibits the growth of pathogenic fungi and bacteria.

The moraine is a unique and uncommon habitat. Much more frequent is the scree, which has the same gravelly soil but lacks underground water flow. Scree soil may be created by the grinding action of a moving glacier or by the breakup of large rocks by freezing and thawing of water in crevices. The limited supply of organic material above timberline has caused the plants that evolved here to adapt to lean soils with little humus.

Garden Moraine and Scree

After seeing the exquisite plants of the alpine tundra, whether in a natural moraine or a scree, many rock gardeners return with dreams of imitating these plant communities in their own gardens. The garden moraine can really bring the feel of alpine tundra into the garden. This type of garden should be reserved primarily for the more difficult alpines; it would be foolish to go to the extra work of building a moraine and then stock it with plants that can grow well without its special conditions. To enhance the overall visual effect, however, I may place some plants in the moraine that do well there but do not require these conditions. A scree garden, by contrast, is relatively easy to construct, and you need not be so particular in selecting the plants as long as they do well there.

In principle, duplicating a natural moraine in the garden is relatively simple, but successfully carrying out a principle is not always easy. Figure 4 shows the elements of a garden moraine. Water piped in from a faucet simulates the flow from a melting glacier. The impervious rock base is replaced by a plastic sheet. On top of that is the gravel through which the water flows. The plastic sheet and the gravel layer lie on a gentle grade, so that water dripped into the gravel at the top of the slope flows down through it, running into a drain line at the base of the slope. The planting soil on top of the gravel picks up the water by a capillary, or wicking, process.

The points to consider in moraine construction are location, drainage, water supply, water distribution, an impervious base, water flow

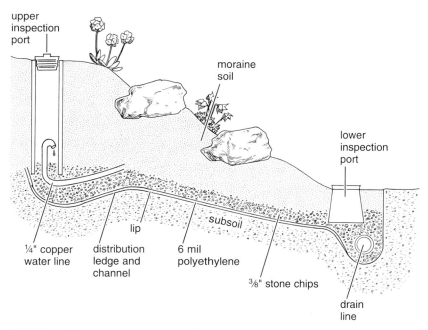

FIGURE 4. Schematic drawing of an artificial moraine. At top left and bottom right are open pipes with valve covers for checking water flow and drainage. Drawing by Sukey McDonough

medium, and moraine and scree soil. These elements are much discussed in books on rock gardening (including other chapters of this one), but I will go into more detail and point out some improvements that lead to reliable operation with low flow rates. When building a scree garden, we need only focus on three elements: location, drainage, and scree soil.

Location

The first step in constructing a moraine is to choose a site and decide on the size. A moraine can be as small as a few square feet. A large one for most home gardens would be 100 square feet (9 square meters). Mine is about 80 square feet (7.2 square meters). You can give the impression of a larger moraine by making the length greater than the width and incorporating a gentle meander.

The moraine may be adjacent to scree areas. The planting soil is similar, and the general character of the plants is the same. From a practical standpoint, it is easy to incorporate a bog area at the base of the moraine. All these things help to form a natural-looking landscape combination. Moraine and scree gardens should be in full or nearly full sun to provide the high light intensity required by plants from above timberline. The moraine should have a north- or east-facing slope to keep it cool and, in areas with snowfall, to hold snow cover longer. Situate it in a relatively open area with constant air currents to help cool it. In lowland gardens, we can never achieve the low summertime temperatures present on the natural moraine, but if the garden moraine is situated where there is natural air movement, this will enhance the evaporation of water seeping up through the soil and reduce both the soil temperature and the air temperature just above the surface. The cooling effect from evaporation is especially pronounced in climates with low atmospheric humidity in summer; in humid conditions, not as much moisture evaporates from the surface. The moraine must also be situated where water can drain away, naturally or via a pipe.

Once the site is chosen, the first step in construction is to contour the area roughly until you have the right visual effect. The entire area for the moraine or scree is then dug out to a depth of about 12 inches (30 cm). For my moraine and screes, I dug out about 20 inches (50 cm) at the top of the slope and about 10 inches (25 cm) at the bottom to produce a varying depth. As we will see later, soil depth affects the air and water capacity of the soil. The exposed clay area sloped 18 inches (45 cm) over a distance of about 8 feet (2.4 m). I divided the moraine into two parts and placed a bog at the base of one. The water level in the bog is held at the desired level by an overflow tube, and the overflow goes to a buried drain line. The other part of the moraine is long and meandering, and it drains directly into the same drain line.

Drainage

Drainage of a moraine or scree has two aspects. One has to do with the planting soil and how well water drains through it to leave the necessary amount of air for the roots. The other aspect pertains to what is underneath the soil and how well excess moisture drains away. In the moraine, this drainage carries away the excess water that is not wicked up to the soil surface and evaporated or taken up by plants. If your water supply contains minerals that can harm plants in excessive concentrations, it will be necessary to prevent salt buildup in the soil as the water evaporates at the surface; you can do this by watering the moraine from above whenever the rest of the rock garden is irrigated. This is not harmful: when it rains in the mountains, it rains just as much on the moraines as on the rest of the tundra. To prevent the soil from becoming waterlogged, the drainage system of both moraine and scree must be able to handle the heavy water flow during irrigation or rainstorms. This need for subsurface drainage requires that the base slope away from the rock garden, unless the native soil itself is very free-draining.

The best way to drain a moraine or scree built on top of clay soil is to provide a stone layer below the feature that continues onto the sloping clay base. The runoff can flow directly into a dry well at the base of the moraine or scree or into a drainpipe that leads to a dry well, lawn, or water feature elsewhere on the property. In the case of the scree, the dry well can be placed directly underneath the scree bed. A dry well is simply a hole in the ground, filled with rocks at least ¾ inch (2 cm) in diameter. The top 10 inches (25 cm) is covered with rock of steadily decreasing size, with coarse sand on the top few centimeters. A dry well outside the rock garden proper can be covered with soil and plants. It need not be large, provided it is not completely surrounded by heavy clay. To drain a 110-square-foot (10-square-meter) moraine, a dry well 3.3 feet (1 m) in diameter and 3.3 feet (1 m) deep should be sufficient; one for a scree bed can be much smaller, because it does not drain water continuously.

Water Supply

A concern for water conservation might deter the gardener from building a moraine. Certainly, a moraine takes more water than a prairie or desert garden of the same size, but it will grow many plants that cannot be grown elsewhere. Its water requirement may be a negligible part of normal household water use. For a moraine of 55 square feet (5 square meters), the water requirement for continuous flow is 5–10 gal (19–38 L) per day—about the same amount needed to flush a toilet. The plants in a moraine only need a fresh supply of water near the roots; they don't care how fast it flows.

The typical water source is domestic water piped from the house to the head end of the moraine. Because of the low flow rate, the diameter of the pipe need not be large. I use ¼-inch (6-mm) diameter soft copper refrigeration tubing. An alternative is vinyl drip irrigation tubing of the same diameter, which is cheaper and may be less susceptible to freeze damage. It is always safer to drain these water lines, especially copper lines, in winter where ground freezes to a significant depth.

In my system, the shutoff and drain valve are located in the basement, at a lower point than any other portion of the line. The flow control valve is one of the more important elements in the moraine and its reliable operation. After a couple of years of experimenting and after several failed valves, I finally found one that works: a stainless steel needle valve. I have two of them, one for each portion of the moraine, and they have been working flawlessly now for fourteen years. Before discovering these, I experienced the frustration of replacing valves about every two months after the valve seats wore out and could not maintain a low enough flow rate. They were like a dripping bathroom faucet, with the dripping becoming a steady stream even when the valve was closed tightly. I have found that brass valves erode in the presence of a steady flow of water; stainless steel does not erode, and the needle valve geometry provides a smooth, laminar flow across the valve seat. The two needle valves are located underground by the house, covered with a sprinkler valve control box. To drain the system in winter, I close the shutoff valve and open the flow control valves wide. I then open the drain valve and collect the water in a pail. The water flowing out the drain valve siphons out the two ¼-inch (6-mm) lines.

Water Distribution

There are at least two ways to introduce the water flowing from the copper or plastic tube to the top of the excavated slope. One method often recommended in books on rock gardening uses a perforated pipe across the top of the slope. However, this approach may not provide a very uniform water distribution for the low flow rates prescribed here. The water distribution technique I found to work best uses a combination of siphon and wicking actions. At the upper end of the exposed clay slope, I made a flat ledge about 4–6 inches (10–15 cm) wide that was very nearly level across the entire width of the feature. I dug out the ledge along the center to a depth of about 2 inches (5 cm) to form a channel (see figure 4). To test it, I dripped water into the channel near its center until it filled for its entire length. With water in the channel, I gradually lowered the front lip at the high spots until the water wet the lip edge uniformly along the entire length. As shown in figure 4, the lip edge has a very gradual curvature to keep it from being easily damaged. You may wish to lay a length of metal gutter in the channel once you have it right, so that after the moraine is finished soil movement will not disturb the lip.

An Impervious Base

The next step is to simulate the solid rock base below a natural moraine. After removing all protruding stones, lay a sheet of 6-mil (0.15-mm) polyethylene on top of the native soil slope. Pond liner material (see "Water") is sturdier, although much more expensive. The plastic lies over the ledge and covers the channel dug into it, and it extends to the bottom of the trench dug for the drain line. Place ⅜-inch (9-mm) stone chips in the upper channel. (For a larger moraine, you could place a small, perforated pipe in the channel and cover it with the stone chips.) The stone chips extend over the lip, and as the water level in the channel rises, water is pulled over the lip by a combination of the wicking and siphoning actions of the stone chips. The water then trickles down across the plastic sheet. Test this before proceeding. If some area does not show water flow, you can lower the lip of the ledge slightly at that spot. When water trickles out evenly all along the ledge, it is time for the next step.

Water Flow Medium

A layer of coarse gravel on top of the plastic sheet is the medium through which the water flows. Some descriptions of moraines mention using stones 1 inch (25 mm) or more in diameter for a depth of several inches at the base of the moraine to ensure excellent drainage. In nature, the medium through which the water flows may have stones that large, but the flow rates are large enough to keep the water level near the top of the stones. In the garden, where we have a slow trickle of water, the water depth is only about ⅛ inch (3 mm). The top surface of a deep layer of such large stones would remain dry as a bone, and the planting soil above it would never be able to absorb moisture; we would be left with excellent drainage but no way of feeding water to the soil above.

The stones on top of the plastic must be large enough to permit a continual flow of water through them but small enough to allow for wicking action of water to their upper surface. I find that ⅜-inch (9-mm) river gravel (that is, rounded stones, *not* crushed rock) is nearly ideal. This gravel is placed on top of the plastic sheet to a depth of 1.5–2.0 inches (38–50 mm). You should experiment at this point to determine the optimal depth for your slope and materials. As water trickles through a thin layer of gravel, the top surface becomes wet and darkens. As you increase the gravel depth, at some point wicking will no longer function, and the top surface will no longer become wet. At that point, remove the uppermost 0.5 inch (13 mm) of gravel. The entire stone base should now be wet. If there are any dry areas, you can adjust either the lip on the ledge or the slope itself.

To prevent soil from being washed into the stone chips and blocking the flow channels, spread a 1-inch (25-mm) layer of ¼-inch (6-mm) stone chips, followed by a 1-inch (25-mm) layer of coarse builder's sand. Again, trickle water through the stone base to ensure that the top surface of the sand is wet everywhere.

Before covering the area with planting soil, inspect the water flow rate at the upper and lower ends of the slope. To do this, install an inspection port that you can use throughout the life of the moraine. Bend the copper tube for the water supply near the end (see figure 4), so water will drip from the end without running back down the outside of the tube. Place a 2-inch (50-mm) diameter PVC or ABS plastic pipe with fittings for a plug at the end over the copper tube and extend it to where the final moraine surface will be. A similar arrangement can be used for the lower inspection port, but I chose to use a larger 6-inch (15-cm) diameter sprinkler valve cover. I found that the proper flow is achieved at about the rate where individual drops from the ¼-inch (6-mm) line become a continuous stream.

Moraine and Scree Soil

The planting soil for the moraine is now placed on top of the sand layer covering the stones. I chose to make it 8 inches (20 cm) deep near the lower end and 20 inches (50 cm) deep near the top. In general, moraine soil is the same as scree soil. In nature, these soils contain only a tiny amount of humus because of the small volume of plant life above timberline. The grinding action of glaciers and constant freezing and thawing results in an abundance of gravel in these alpine soils. This gravel provides many air channels, with excellent drainage and plenty of oxygen for the roots. Typical moraine and scree plants grow best in a soil that has at least 20 percent air space. In duplicating these soils for the garden, it is very important to maintain a high proportion of sharp gravel, lest the air pockets become filled with sand and humus.

I carried out a series of experiments with soils and their components to find out how the proportions of various components affect drainage as well as air and water capacities of the soil. These experiments were easy to do and a lot of fun—they reminded me why I became a physicist. They would make an excellent science fair project, and they cost almost nothing. The requirements are an oven and tray to dry out the soil; a piece of PVC pipe; an end fitting to hold the soil being tested; and a measuring cup to measure soil, the amount of water to saturate the soil, and the water drained from the soil.

Figure 5 shows the void volume (porosity), air capacity, and water capacity of a particular soil or a soil component. Table 1 identifies the various data points in the graph. The shaded region is the desired zone for most scree or moraine soils; that is, the soils should contain at least 20 percent air space and 10 percent water after draining. Typical regions for humus, solid particles (stone or sand), and porous particles (volcanic rock such as scoria, perlite, or vermiculite) are also shown in figure 5. The axes at 45° indicate the percentage of void space (porosity). A perfectly packed bed of solid particles will have a porosity of 38 percent if the particles are all one size and are spherical (approximated by river

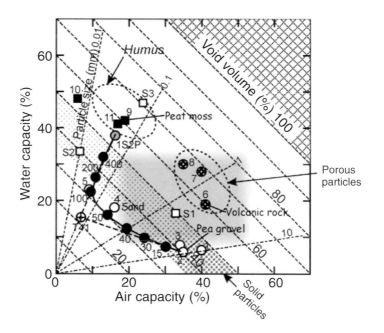

FIGURE 5. Air and water capacities of various 20-inch-deep (500-mm-deep) soils. The shaded region is the desired zone for most scree or moraine soils; that is, the soils should contain at least 20 percent air space and 10 percent water after draining. See the text and table 1 for details.

TABLE 1. Identification of soil or soil components in figure 5.

No.	Soil or soil component
1	⅜-inch (10-mm) crushed granite
2	⅜-inch (10-mm) river stone (pea gravel)
3	¼-inch (6-mm) river stone
4	coarse (concrete) sand
5	fine (masonry) sand
6	⅜-inch (10-mm) volcanic rock (scoria)
7	¼-inch (6-mm) vermiculite
8	¼-inch (6-mm) perlite
9	sphagnum peat moss
10	sedge peat moss
11	oak leafmold
S1	scree soil with scoria
S2	general garden soil
S3	Terrilite® potting soil
1S2P	1 part coarse sand + 2 parts sphagnum peat moss
15–400	*x* parts 1S2P + 100 parts pea gravel
T41	theoretical mix of 41 parts 1S2P + 100 parts pea gravel

stone). A packed bed of irregular particles (approximated by crushed rock) will have a porosity around 50 percent. The porosity is independent of particle size. In a mixture of two or more sizes in which the larger particles are at least three times larger than the smaller particles, the porosity can be decreased to 30 percent or less, because the smaller particles fill in the void space between the larger particles. It is this filling in of void space that we need to avoid when we prepare a soil mix.

Figure 5 shows how air and water capacity, as well as porosity, change when we combine 1 part coarse sand with 2 parts sphagnum peat moss. I refer to this mixture as 1S2P. We then add various amounts of 1S2P to 100 parts of ⅜-inch (9-mm) pea gravel or river rock. Because the pea gravel has a porosity of 41 percent, we expect theoretically to fill up that void space and reach a minimum porosity when we add 41 parts 1S2P to the 100 parts of pea gravel. That theoretical mix is shown as point T41 in figure 5. This composition has less air and less water capacity than one with *no* pea gravel. In practice, soil packing is not perfect, so I found that it requires about 50 parts 1S2P to reach a minimum porosity, but about 100 parts 1S2P to reach a minimum air capacity, as shown by the point labeled 100 in figure 5. To maintain a soil with at least 20 percent air space, then, for 100 parts pea gravel we should not have more than about 30 to 40 parts 1S2P, as indicated by points 30 and 40 in figure 5. These soils hold about 10 percent water after being drained. That amount of water should be sufficient for scree plants, but in dry climates it will evaporate quickly and need to be replenished every day or so, as in the mountains.

My suggested moraine or scree soil mix corresponds to points 30 and 40 in figure 5. In especially dry climates—for example, the Intermountain West, where I garden—more water capacity may be desirable. Replacing some of the ⅜-inch (10-mm) stones with ¼-inch (6-mm) stones and/or with porous or volcanic rock (crushed pumice or scoria) can greatly increase the water capacity without sacrificing air capacity. The formula I have used for my moraine and scree gardens in the dry Colorado climate consists of 1 part coarse sand, 2 parts sphagnum peat moss, and 8 to 10 parts ⅜-inch (10-mm) river stone. It is represented by point S1 in figure 5. I add somewhat smaller river stone to enhance the capillary effect of the soil and allow it to bring more water from the wet gravel up to the surface. (Note that for shallower soil depths, the points in figure 5 will shift toward higher water capacity and less air capacity, but with the same void volume.) The high gravel content of these soils tends to make them self-mulching; after a short time, the sand and peat moss settle out of the top few inches of soil, leaving nearly pure pea gravel as a mulch. My formula for moraine and scree soil using volcanic rock is 1 part coarse sand, 2 parts sphagnum peat moss, 3 parts ⅜-inch (10-mm) river stone, 2 parts ¼-inch (6-mm) river stone, and 3 parts ⅜-inch (10-mm) volcanic rock.

Figure 6 shows the drainage rate of a 20-inch-deep (500-mm-deep) column of soil composed of varying amounts of pea gravel and 1S2P.

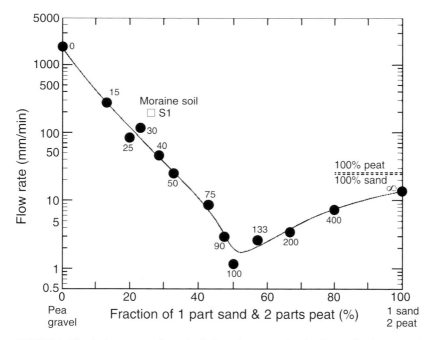

FIGURE 6. The drainage rate of a 20-inch-deep (500-mm-deep) column of soil composed of varying amounts of pea gravel and 1 part coarse sand with 2 parts sphagnum peat moss (1S2P). The numbers by the points refer to how many parts of 1S2P are combined with 100 parts of pea gravel.

The numbers by the points refer to how many parts of 1S2P are combined with 100 parts of pea gravel. Note the very large change in drainage rates when going from pure pea gravel to equal parts of pea gravel and 1S2P. This composition of 1 part sand, 2 parts peat, and 3 parts pea gravel should be avoided—not only because of its poor drainage (figure 6), but also for its very low air capacity (figure 5). Increasing the pea gravel to 7 to 10 parts greatly increases the drainage and air capacity while maintaining sufficient water capacity.

When the soil is in place, the moraine or scree is ready to plant. One choice plant grown in the upper, drier part of my moraine is *Dicentra peregrina*; the fascinating *Calceolaria uniflora* grows in the lower, wetter part. This moraine has functioned without any problems since 1988; the plant treasures it nourishes have given me much satisfaction.

Crevice Gardens

HARVEY WRIGHTMAN AND PHYLLIS GUSTAFSON

The term *crevice garden* came into wide use in the 1990s to denote a type of rock garden in which most of the surface is composed of closely set stone; the plants are inserted when small into the narrow crevices between the rocks. A style originated by Czech growers, crevice gardens are designed and built with an emphasis on providing conditions favorable for plants native to high alpine zones. Some climatic factors are beyond control, but the site, shape of the garden, soil composition, irrigation, and nutrients added can be modified to aid plant growth.

We garden in different regions: Harvey Wrightman in the continental climate of Ontario and Phyllis Gustafson in southern Oregon's Mediterranean climate. Harvey, a trained stonemason and nurseryman, works with sedimentary rocks, primarily limestone. Phyllis, who owns a seed business, gardens with the igneous and metamorphic stone found in the Siskiyou Mountains. Both of us have found the crevice style well suited to growing a range of plants from around the world. Phyllis first became acquainted with this style of garden in 1984, when Otakar Vydra visited southern Oregon. After watching him demonstrate the technique on a hillside in the Siskiyou Mountains, she tried to imitate it in a small section of a large garden she was working on. Years later, her initial effort was complemented with an addition by Vydra's own teacher, Josef Halda.

Halda, best known as an intrepid botanist-explorer, seed collector, and experienced mason, visited southern Oregon in 1986 and worked on a section of a new garden at Phyllis's home. This feature is constructed not of stratified rock but of native granite and other metamorphic rocks; it measures 24 × 30 feet (about 7 × 9 m) in extent. Halda used this work as a demonstration, showing an audience of rock gardeners how to place rocks close together on a tilted plane. The base of the feature is rich sandy loam, with large-diameter (3-inch minus [5–8 cm] grade) gravel under the rocks to keep drainage at a maximum while giving the plants the nutrients needed for the long period this garden will be in place. On later lecture tours in the United States, Halda returned to this garden and suggested new plants or other revisions. In 1997 he built a second crevice garden for Phyllis, this time based on pure sand. So far, both have supported a very healthy and colorful array of plants adapted to the mild winters and very hot, dry summers of southern Oregon.

Halda started to developed his style in the late 1960s. As a teenager, he was a rock-climber and also grew cacti and alpine plants in his mother's greenhouse. His great desire was to get his plants out of pots and into the garden, and he started building rock gardens to imitate places in the mountains where he climbed. In North America, unlike Britain, most rock gardeners grow their plants not in pots but outdoors, so this style suits their purposes well. Many Czechs now build beautiful crevice gardens, mostly of limestone but occasionally of granite.

PLATE 22. Natural formations like this are the inspiration for crevice rock gardens. Photograph by Harvey Wrightman

Gardens of this style range in size from no more than 3 feet (0.9 m) across and less than that in height to massive constructions resembling small mountaintops (an example of the latter, built by Halda at Siskiyou Rare Plant Nursery, is shown in plate 2). Crevice gardens can be tucked into a postage-stamp-sized yard, or they can be the central feature of a public display garden. In many rock gardens, crevice construction is combined with features such as berms and raised beds. A planted wall is essentially a crevice garden that also serves as an architectural element.

The Czech crevice garden was developed in a region where winters are cold and relatively dry and most rainfall arrives in summer. This type of climate prevails in most of North America except in the far West. In the Northeast, the crevice garden offers a combination of drainage and root protection well suited to the climate; it is, in a sense, a built-in overflow device in summer and in early spring. In addition, with enough rock mass, the soil temperature remains cooler in summer, when heat often damages alpines in the East (see "The Northeastern United States and Eastern Canada"). When summer heat combines with high humidity, there is little night cooling; the soil temperature can rise dangerously in such conditions if not shaded and insulated.

Planning and Building

In designing a crevice garden, we must consider three primary factors. The first is the growing medium: the composition of the soil with regard to fertility, drainage, and aeration. The second is the aesthetic effect of the feature. How well does it display the plants, and how pleasing is the stonework itself? Finally, it should be noted that this style deemphasizes human access to the garden, which is viewed as destructive, much like human intrusion on a natural ecosystem. The plants come first, and features such as pathways and seating must be very subtle or not present at all. If possible, choose a site well away from buildings.

Except for decorative statuary, most stonework in a typical garden (not a rock garden) consists of two types: vertical wall construction with ledge rock (broken pieces of stratified rock 4–6 inches [10–15 cm] thick), built to elevate a surface and retain the soil behind the wall, and flagstone paving using large, flat rocks. These concepts are as old as settled human society. They are practical means of, for instance, creating a flat terrace for crop production or a building site. Many people instinctively build their rock gardens on a modified wall-and-terrace system. It is an easy form to follow: simply start at the bottom and stack. Walkways are easily made of stepping stones. The plants are on an elevated plateau, thus easy to view. This design, however, impedes water movement. In a deluge of rain, the wall acts as a dam and the terrace as a sponge; in summer, they also retain heat. These conditions are tolerated by many large perennials but are lethal to most alpine plants.

One solution is simply to use more rock. Covering the surface with stone reduces evaporation loss. It also reduces soil temperature, because stone is a poor conductor of heat. Excess rainfall runs off a paved area that is set on an angle. Enough moisture for the plants enters the soil through the crevices between the rocks. There is no place for water to pool and saturate the soil.

PLATE 23. A crevice garden of stratified rock under construction. Photograph by Harvey Wrightman

The size of the rocks used should correspond to that of the overall garden. It is next to impossible to combine many fist-sized rocks into a natural-looking outcrop; these are better used in a scree garden. A small garden on a residential lot may look out of scale if built with gigantic rocks. Although getting rock of the right size to the site and into place may take more work than you imagined before you started, remember that a well-made crevice garden will not be altered for a long time. The joy of seeing the seasons change and the plants grow for years with little additional effort by the gardener is well worth the careful and strenuous work of construction.

Stone is used very effectively in this style: the actual tonnage employed may not be much more than is used in a wall-and-terrace garden of similar size. Many design variations and combinations are possible; indeed, there are so many different ways to select and set the stone that the task may seem daunting to the amateur. The designer, therefore, turns to nature for models. The following discussion describes two approaches to naturalistic design.

Working with Stratified Rock

Where stratified sedimentary rock is available, a convenient model is the sedimentary fold or uplift. Sedimentary rocks such as limestone and sandstone separate neatly on their lines of deposition (bedding planes), yielding relatively large, flat pieces that can be laid to resemble an original formation or natural pavement. The edge grain of such a formation often appears as a sloping wall; sometimes, owing to breakage, it appears stepped. Such a fold can emerge from the ground as an outcrop that can readily be imitated in the garden.

There is great inherent stability in this formation because the large, flat stones shed excess water and minimize erosive forces. This makes it a useful design for a crevice garden. The key to its construction lies in the angle at which the stone is set in the overall bedding plane. An outcrop is a simple piece of geology, but replicating one requires a kind of working backward.

The biggest problem is that all reference lines are off-kilter—not aligned with the normal horizontal and vertical planes. People are conditioned very early to think in terms of horizontal and vertical (remember those ancient terraced hillsides). It is a lot easier to work on a level surface, so tilting the plane of reference is disorienting. Much concentration and discipline are needed to maintain an overall plane of reference that lies askew, but the theory is disarmingly simple: combine a flat flagstone surface with a ledge surface.

Before starting to build, have an overall image of the outcrop firmly in mind. (If you can, make a drawing of your design.) You must decide beforehand how the outcrop will emerge, which will determine the basic shape of the soil mound that supports it. You will have to move soil and adjust stones to achieve the correct angles of the bedding plane. Almost any soil can be used for the underlying mound, but sandy loam is the easiest to work with. The soil should be firmly tamped before the stone is laid.

PLATE 24. Scooping away the scree soil to set rocks in the ledge face of the crevice garden. Photograph by Harvey Wrightman

Have a good selection of rocks on hand. Sort them roughly by shape and size. In general, flat stones with some surface texture and weathered edges are the most useful. Dolomitic limestone often exists in this form. Pieces as heavy as 200 pounds (91 kg) can be moved by a fit person of average size with the use of a heavy-duty dolly and a long pry bar. An 18-inch (45-cm) square, 4-inch (10-cm) thick stone will weigh about 100 pounds (45 kg). Round boulders are more difficult to set in a pattern because they have no single flat surface; flat or even angular stones fit together better.

Start with the broad, flat flagstone portion of the crevice formation. Beginning at the bottom, set a large stone so it lies with the slope of the mound. Stand back and check the angle (the bedding plane). If necessary, adjust the stone to match the angle. Set more stones, laying a pavement on the slope until the slope is covered. Check each stone for alignment. Stones can touch and even overlap, but spaces between them of up to 3 inches (8 cm) are fine. Eventually, a clear, straight ridgeline will emerge, higher at one end and sloping down into the surrounding

PLATE 25. The pavement face of the crevice garden with plants in place. Photograph by Harvey Wrightman

grade. This ridgeline is most important: together with the flat, broad surface just completed, it provides the overall sightline for creating a different pattern—the ledge on the opposite side, where the narrow sides of the stones are exposed.

Although you would normally expect to start at the bottom, you can begin the ledge side at the top, just below the ridgeline. This is possible if the angle of the slope is no steeper than about 60°. If beginning at the bottom is easier, be sure to maintain the bedding plane; stand back from your work frequently and check the alignment. The advantage of starting at the top is that it gives you a better view of the pavement side, making it easier to check the alignment and set the stones according to the bedding plane; however, it requires that you excavate a place to set each stone. After placing each stone, tamp the soil firmly around it to hold it in place. Set the rest of the stones to complete the crosswise course (or row). The course below can protrude farther, following the basic slope of this side of the mound. Be sure to set all the stones on the same angle.

PLATE 26. A pavement-and-ledge feature built with broken rock. Photograph by Phyllis Gustafson

Note that the broad, flat surface of each ledge stone is set in the same plane as the corresponding surfaces of the flag side. Here, however, this surface is mostly buried in the mound, leaving only a small part of the upper surface and the edge exposed. The amount of stone you are using is now two to three times greater, and the speed of the work slows correspondingly. This is another good reason to lay the flag portion first—you get immediate gratification.

The next courses of stone are set in a similar manner until you reach the bottom in steplike fashion. The whole mound will have a somewhat triangular form, like an off-center pyramid. The higher end of the mound, which terminates in the long direction, may be treated as part of this ledge and finished in the same style. Again, the broad surface of each stone is set in the same general bedding plane.

There are several types of formations that, in various combinations, give a great deal of character to the finished garden:

Depression: Make a recessed area by dropping a section of the stones by one layer, a depth of 2–8 inches (5–20 cm), depending on the thickness of the stone. A long-stemmed flower such as *Pelargonium endlicherianum* can be very effective peering out of this depression.

Projection: Conversely, an area can be exserted beyond the surrounding stones.

Overlap: Stone layers can be set stepwise, much like shingles on a roof.

Fold and break: Both sides of the mound can be set in a flag pattern, meeting in a break at the ridgeline. This method can be used to pave a slope quickly. The aesthetic effect can be improved by including some overlapping portions so the rock garden doesn't look just like a pile of dirt with a pavement on it.

Tufa Crevice Gardens

Where tufa, water-deposited calcium carbonate, is available, crevice gardens built from this porous rock are the primary choice of the growers of small, fussy, lime-loving plants (see "Working with Tufa"). The roots are able to penetrate the rock and find the nourishment left behind by the organic material transported by the depositing water, as well as calcium and other minerals. The lightweight tufa rock is a joy to work with. Even a small person can pick up large pieces and move them around to build ledges and valleys, and two big, strong people can handle gigantic pieces.

The soil mixture laid under tufa should hold some moisture but, like all well-made rock garden soils, it should still drain away excess water. Because the roots are in the rock itself, the absorbent tufa must lie in soil that will keep it moist. If the soil dries out, the rock will too, and the plants will wilt and die with lightning speed. A good mixture is composed of loam, sand, and crushed rock (grit) in roughly equal parts.

From an aesthetic standpoint as well as for the health of the plants, it is important that the rock be sunk well down into the soil, with the soil filling the crevices between pieces of tufa. If the tufa sits too high, it looks unnatural—and the little plant gems will become crisp and vanish. Phyllis Gustafson's small tufa garden rests on sand with rich, moisture-retentive soil under that. This supports a well-grown collection of saxifrages of the Porophyllum section, as well as other small plants.

Working with Nonstratified Rock

In regions where limestone, sandstone, and tufa are not available, it is still possible to build a natural-looking crevice garden. Josef Halda did this in Phyllis's garden and also, on a much larger scale, at the Siskiyou Rare Plant Nursery nearby. Base the nonstratified crevice garden on one or a few large rocks—as large as you can handle—to make it look more like a natural outcrop. In the Pacific Northwest, broken lava chunks are popular for landscape uses. These tend to have a flattened profile and

PLATE 27. Josef Halda and Phyllis Gustafson building a crevice garden of nonstratified rock. Photograph by Ramona Osburn

can be used much like the flags of limestone described above. Basalt fieldstone often exists in the form of angular (mostly five-sided) chunks, which can be fitted together in formations that mimic outcrops.

You can make nonstratified crevice gardens look more natural by incorporating sections that imitate talus, where the rock breaks up and tumbles down a slope. Use angular rocks ranging in diameter from 2 to 4 inches (5 to 10 cm) and pile them deeply in an inverted V between large, solid boulders. Certain plants like to creep around in this kind of formation, extending their crowns and flowering stems wherever they find the space. Their roots and self-layering stems find a cool, moderately moist run below the jumble of stones.

Planting the Crevice Garden

The crevice garden is the perfect place for many western North American plants as well as many from Turkey, central Asia, the Mediterranean region, and other areas of the world with very hot, dry summers and wet winters. If your climate does not favor this array, you can still use the crevice garden to grow the plants that will flourish in your area. There are crevice gardens full of ericaceous plants and others studded with tiny high-alpine ones; different soil substrates and a cool exposure—perhaps with shade from tall trees or on the northern side of a building—adapt the crevice style for these plant groups.

The triumph of this type of garden is drainage: not only of water, which flows down the rocks into the crevices and on down into the larger gravel below, but also of air. The air movement across the rocks removes excess moisture from the foliage so that mold and mildew are not as likely to set in. Plants such as lewisias, most eriogonums, and cacti that need to be high and dry to keep their crowns from rotting find perfect homes in the crevices.

Two favorite shrubs in Phyllis's garden are the Delphi form of *Daphne jasminea*, which snuggles tightly in the rocks in the hottest spot facing west, and *Daphne* 'Lawrence Crocker' (a hybrid of *D. arbuscula* and *D. collina*), which grows well in a deep crevice behind a larger rock where the roots have a cool run.

Phyllis's crevice garden built on sand is exposed to the sun for only half the day in summer and has proven to be a haven for many choice

PLATE 28. Phyllis Gustafson's crevice garden, four years after construction. Photograph by Phyllis Gustafson

alpine plants. A collection of a dozen small daphnes make every trip down the steps of this garden a delight. *Asperula boissieri* from the Parnassus Mountains of Greece forms a tiny, tight gray mound with pink flowers. Various campanulas, including *Campanula albovii, C. petrophila*, and *C. hercegovina*, enjoy the cooler spots with even moisture. The tiny but very bright blue flowers of *Veronica bombycina* var. *bolkardaghensis* spangle its silver mat of foliage in an almost vertical crevice. *Morisia monanthos* grows well here in the sand, a habitat much like its home on the Greek islands. In early spring, the buds of *Eunomia oppositifolia* open to the lavender-pink flowers set in little rosettes of round leaves. Just below it are the distinctive rosettes of various encrusted saxifrages; in some springs, the spectacular *Saxifraga* × 'Tumbling Waters' blooms. Among the saxifrages, *Clematis* ?*cartmanii* 'Joe' bears huge white flowers.

It is sometimes difficult to establish plants in the narrow areas of soil afforded by crevices, but the Czechs have a clever trick. Try to choose a plant that is still in a small pot—even a well-grown seedling. With a long trowel, stick, or similar tool, dig down in the crevice, removing the soil carefully into a container; then remove most of the soil from the plant's roots and drop the root mass down into the hole, keeping the roots as straight as possible. Carefully refill the hole with the soil removed from the crevice so that the roots will readily move out and down into the soil below. (As elsewhere in the garden, avoid creating abrupt horizons that will impede drainage and root growth.) Add water as you work, washing the soil down so no air pockets are left between the rocks. But, here is the unusual step: before you finish, add a second plant to the hole to moderate the soil temperature and protect the roots and trunk of the choice young specimen from harsh weather. For this purpose, the Czechs use easy-to-grow alpine succulents—sedums, sempervivums, and jovibarbas—which have shallow roots that do not interfere with the growth of the specimen plant and which can be removed later without disturbing the specimen. Other possibilities are *Teucrium pyrenaicum*, many of the small creeping veronicas, *Paronychia kapela* ssp. *serpyllifolia, P. argentea*, and *Artemisia pedemontana*. These mat-forming plants are used all

PLATE 29. A small crevice feature built by Josef Halda accents the display garden at Kurt Bluemel Nursery in Delaware and contrasts with ornamental grasses, a specialty of the nursery. Photograph by Pamela Harper

across the hot side of Phyllis's biggest crevice garden, where they also provide a unifying element.

Although the crevice garden is a wonderful place to show off a collection of choice plants, it needs the repetition of some species and foliage colors, or it becomes a visual hodge-podge. Repeat shapes, too: flat, spreading plants; mounding buns such as *Dianthus* and *Acantholimon* species; or rosettes such as *Townsendia*, *Gentiana acaulis*, and *Globularia*. Visual impact is also improved by repeating small conifers or other evergreen plants, which lend year-round interest.

In regions where the landscape can be enjoyed throughout the year, add plants that lengthen the period of interest. Turkish *Origanum* species have colorful bracts that hang down from stems 4–8 inches (10–20 cm) tall and remain attractive from late summer to Christmas. In early spring, *Iris pumila* and *Iris suaveolens* are among the first to bloom and love the long, hot summers. Phyllis divides the irises whenever they have filled a crevice and moves some to another area—an easy way to repeat the vertical element of their foliage and to obtain a better display of flowers.

Irrigation and Maintenance

Summer watering is carried out differently by every rock gardener. For gardeners who need to worry about water usage, the needs of a crevice garden are much smaller than those of more typical plantings such as perennial borders and lawns—and certainly more interesting. In regions where there is natural rainfall during the growing season, the gardener must monitor the crevice garden carefully for moisture needs. After a few years, you will become aware of how long it takes the feature to dry out between rainstorms.

Harvey can depend on Ontario's summer rainfall and high humidity for almost all the moisture his crevice garden needs. Phyllis gardens where there is no summer rain, low humidity, and hot daytime temperatures, so she has to irrigate her rock garden, usually early in the day. The crevice garden with soil under the rocks is watered about every third day for fifteen to twenty minutes from large overhead sprinklers installed when the garden was built; unfortunately, these large sprinkler heads are not very attractive. A nearby crevice garden has a micro-irrigation system so that she can move the tiny emitters to water areas that would dry out if the plants in front grow to block the spray. An alternative is a buried soaker hose, which keeps the water off the foliage, a special concern in climates with higher summer humidity where evaporation is not rapid. Any form of pre-installed irrigation is an advantage on midsized or large crevice gardens, where you don't want to drag a hose over the precious plants.

Phyllis waters her pure-sand crevice garden during the heat of summer every day for five minutes or less. She applies the water by hand because it needs so little, but she has to reach all the crevices. This sand bed is about 4 feet (1.2 m) deep, but she has lost only two or three plants from improper watering; sand this deep, with rock covering 90 percent of its surface, does not dry out very fast. Remember that it is easy to overwater established plants.

The small proportion of soil in the crevice garden soon becomes depleted of nutrients through uptake by plants and leaching in rainy periods. Replenish it in early spring with applications of soluble fertilizer, mixed at one-quarter to one-half the manufacturer's recommended strength

Over time, you may notice some subsidence of the rockwork. To minimize the effect of frost action in cold climates, use a fill mixture that does not contain clay. A crevice garden built with smaller stones is likely to need rebuilding sooner than one based on very large stones.

Working with Tufa

SHEILA PAULSON

Tufa rock is an evaporitic form of limestone that is essentially composed of pure calcium carbonate, often deposited around recent or ancient hot springs. (In some parts of North America, the word *tufa* is misapplied to volcanic tuff, another soft, light stone.) Tufa deposits typically form in layers, and
somewhat flattened pieces with a great deal of surface relief can be quarried. This picturesque light gray rock has long been recognized as an excellent medium for growing alpine plants.

For many years, European gardeners have prized this material and now pay high prices for it; tufa constructions feature in many fine European gardens. The use of tufa in North America has been limited by the scarcity of the rock and the fact that it is rarely offered by stone dealers. Following the opening and marketing of a large deposit at Brisco, British Columbia, however, western Canadian gardeners have eagerly adopted this material for their own gardens. Tufa can also be obtained in parts of New England, adjacent eastern Canada, and in a few geothermal limestone areas of the West. The best way to find it is to contact a state or provincial geological office for information on known deposits.

Tufa can be used to construct a prominent rock garden feature resembling a natural outcrop or to landscape a trough. A single specimen piece can be set in a gravel-mulched planting area surrounded by lawn. Some growers with alpine houses create table beds of tufa mounted on supports. An especially picturesque chunk of tufa can be affixed with mortar to a large clay saucer and planted, with water added to the saucer to keep the tufa moist. Some alpine plants that are difficult to grow otherwise do very well in tufa. This chapter focuses on the creation of a major garden feature, but the principles can be extended to its use in troughs or as a specimen rock.

Building with Tufa

A common desire among those building major rock garden features is to replicate the appearance of a mountain outcrop. The individual pieces used may be of various sizes, but tufa should be laid in parallel strata (see the section on using stratified rock in "Crevice Gardens"). Tufa is especially useful for this type of rockwork because it can often be obtained as slabs, or block-shaped pieces can be split to approximate slabs. The slabs should be closely placed and not set too much on end— otherwise, the rock garden may end up looking like a cemetery.

Prepare the site to remove unwanted vegetation, including persistent roots (see "Berms" for more tips on site preparation). Put down a layer of washed coarse gravel (3-inch minus, or 5–8 cm grade) about 8–10 inches (20–25 cm) deep to ensure good drainage under the mound. A dry well or drainpipe may be required to carry surplus water well away from the mound (see "Moraine and Scree Gardens" for construction details of these adjuncts).

PLATE 30. A tufa garden built by Harvey Wrightman and Josef Halda, in Ontario, Canada. Photograph by Harvey Wrightman

On top of the coarse gravel layer, raise a mound of good rock garden soil (see "Soils" and "Moraine and Scree Gardens"). Allow for settling: the mound should be slightly larger than the eventual desired height. It can be disappointing to watch your rock outcrop diminish to a rocky pasture. For example, a mound 15 × 30 feet (5 × 9 m) in extent and 4 feet (1.2 m) high required 5–6 cubic yards (3.8–4.6 cubic meters) of soil mix, as well as 3.85 tons (3.5 metric tons) of tufa rock. The base and soil mix are designed to provide the good drainage alpine plants require, as well as a medium in which plant roots flourish. My alpine mix consists of equal parts of washed sand (particles less than 0.12-inch [3-mm] diameter), loam, and washed gravel (about ¼ to ⅜ inch, 5 to 10 mm in diameter). The water retention of the soil mix should be sufficient to keep the tufa moistened through capillary action. Consider how much natural precipitation the rock garden will receive in your climate when choosing its composition.

Lay the tufa pieces out and examine them to visualize how to place them in the mound. It helps to have a strong back (or strong helpers), even though tufa is relatively light when dry. Decide on the slope you want the outcrop to have. You can suspend a string between two stakes in the mound to define the slope so the desired line does not become compromised during construction. Substantial plants such as dwarf conifers that are to be grown in the interstices of the rockwork should be placed during construction. It is very difficult to fit them into the garden after all the rocks are in place.

Start at ground level at one end and build upward and toward the other end to minimize the amount of digging needed after rocks have been set. You will be putting together a sort of jigsaw puzzle of your own design. Leave crevices (spaces 0.5–1.0 inch [13–25 mm] wide) between the rocks, and tilt the rocks back into the mound so rainwater will drain back into the soil. Stagger the vertical crevices as in brickwork to hold the soil; when they become filled in with plants, this will further reduce erosion.

Although it is not necessary to bury all rock garden stones in the soil, it *is* important to do this with tufa. Bury the pieces one-half to two-thirds their depth to ensure plenty of contact with the soil, which maintains the porous tufa's reservoir of moisture. When placing the tufa, tamp the underlying and surrounding soil very firmly, using a shovel and a tool handle of some kind. This reduces the chance of leaving air spaces, which can be fatal to plant roots, and it creates a stable mound that will not settle too much. If you find that a different rock would look better in a particular position than one you have already placed, change it, or it will always draw your attention. Don't rush this work; remember that nature took millions of years to create the outcrops that you are trying to imitate in a day or two.

Planting in Tufa

Some tufa rocks have natural holes formed during the deposition process or left by decayed vegetation. If your tufa has none, use a masonry bit to drill planting holes about 1 inch (25 mm) in diameter and 3–5 inches (75–125 mm) deep. (If the tufa is very soft, an ordinary drill bit can be used.) Save the waste tufa powder and chips for use in the mix to fill the planting hole.

In these holes, place young plants (up to a year old) or well-rooted cuttings. The root systems of older plants are too well developed to be jammed into the holes. Making bigger holes for bigger plants does not seem to work because the roots may be damaged, and mature plants take a longer time to recover, if they do at all. Older transplants starve because their root systems are too badly damaged and cannot absorb enough water and nutrients.

Partially fill the freshly bored hole with a mixture of 3 parts tufa waste from the drilling process, 1 part peat moss, and 1 part clay-free loam. Set the plant carefully in position and spread the roots very gently. Fill the hole with the same mixture and tamp it gently but firmly with your finger or a tool such as the head of a large nail. Remember

PLATE 31. This tufa cliff in the former garden of Margot Parrot in Massachusetts has a large collection of plants. Photograph by Pamela Harper

that roots are easily damaged. Anchor the plant by placing small bits of tufa around its neck (the subterranean part of the stem before the lowest leaves) to keep it from being pushed out by frost. As the plant becomes established, its roots penetrate the porous, permeable tufa, and it will mature into characteristically hard, compact specimens.

Certain plants (for example, saxifrages and ramondas) can be grown by sprinkling their seeds on tufa, followed by a sprinkling of tufa dust. This is an especially successful method in moist climates, such as that of the coastal Pacific Northwest. In drier climates and at higher elevations, seeds sown on tufa must be misted frequently.

Problems with Tufa

Moss can be either a problem or a pleasant addition to a garden, depending on the taste of the gardener and the vulnerability of the plants. If it begins to crowd out tiny alpines, it must be removed with tweezers from the immediate vicinity. Left alone, moss will eventually cover the tufa. Some gardeners report success in killing moss with products intended to kill algae in ponds, but these should not be applied where they might harm garden plants.

If water is allowed to collect in the porous tufa so that it fills some of the air spaces, the rock may begin to disintegrate from expansion under repeated freezing and thawing. The Brisco tufa I have used seems to have excellent permeability that allows the water to drain quickly enough to prevent this problem. My garden is on the eastern slope of the Rocky Mountains, where winter may include several temperature fluctuations from –12 to 50°F (–24 to 10°C) in the space of a few hours. In sudden thaws, the snow disappears and the ground dries out through sublimation. Nonetheless, in about six years the Brisco tufa has not evidenced signs of rock failure.

Few types of rock bring the appearance of age and weathering into the garden as effectively as tufa does. Its aesthetic qualities and its value as a substrate for difficult plant species make it worth the extra effort and expense needed to acquire it.

Planted Walls and Formal Raised Beds

JANE McGARY

The endlessly pleasing contrast of plants and stone draws many people to rock gardening. In the wild, some plants seem to grow directly from solid rock, trailing down boulders or forming flower-covered buns on vertical cliff faces. The desire to grow these highly specialized plants in the garden is one motive for constructing a planted wall. The planning, building, and planting of habitats for chasmophytes, or cliff-dwelling plants, is one facet of this chapter.

PLATE 32. This spectacular cliffside garden, designed by Harland Hand for Marjorie Harris of San Francisco, is the ultimate planted wall, using both stone and brick. Photograph by Pamela Harper

Another motive lies in the practical needs to support soil on a changing grade, divide the garden into pleasing and manageable areas, and incorporate architectural forms and textural contrasts. Most plant collectors try to introduce vegetation everywhere possible, especially in a small garden. Thus, I discuss here both the new construction of planted walls for the open garden and the reconstruction of existing retaining walls.

Walls can also be used to surround and support a freestanding elevated planting bed, termed a *formal raised bed* to distinguish it from the naturalistic raised beds described in "Berms." Such features combine the free root run offered by a berm with the more restricted spaces of the crevice rock garden. The second part of this chapter discusses how raised beds can be constructed once the principles of dry wall building are understood.

Retaining Walls

A retaining wall is a solid barrier, backed with soil, that supports a fairly abrupt change of grade. The type suitable for planting is the dry wall, which is set in place without mortar. The height limit for a dry wall depends on the degree of slope, the consistency of the soil, and the climate. Vertical dry retaining walls up to about 4 feet (1.2 m) high are feasible where the soil to be retained is fairly heavy, not sandy, and where frost heaving is not a severe problem. In regions with very cold winters, frost action is likely to unseat the rocks of a dry wall. A vertical wall higher than about 2 feet (0.6 m) is best built on a poured concrete foundation slightly below the basal soil surface to prevent excessive shifting. Vertical dry walls may be built with flat-surfaced stone (stratified rock, such as sandstone or limestone, is popular), recycled concrete paving, or concrete block, which is available in an increasing variety of attractive shapes and textures. Round river rocks are not suitable, but angular, irregular fieldstone is quite usable and provides ample vertical crevices (for the benefits of these, see "Crevice Gardens"). Retaining

PLATE 33. David Palmer
of West Linn, Oregon, built
this raised bed next to his
house using recycled broken
concrete slabs. The bed can
be covered for protection
from winter rains.
Photograph by David Palmer

walls made of railroad ties or logs can also be planted, although this is best done during construction of the wall.

A sloping retaining wall is easier to construct and plant (for a schematic example, see figure 7). Because the soil behind it gives it plenty of support, the wall can be made of almost any type of stone, although recycled concrete paving and concrete block are not appropriate for this informal, naturalistic feature. Sloped retaining walls can be higher than vertical dry walls and, in most climates, they do not need poured foundations.

The wall should have some barrier separating it from adjacent lawns and other features from which creeping plants may invade the stonework. At the base, a path is often laid that bars weeds and provides a place from which to view and tend the wall plants. The top of the

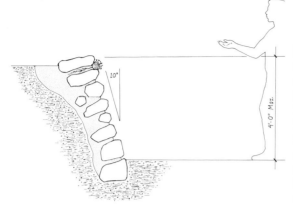

FIGURE 7. A planted dry wall. Note the area of specially mixed soil behind the wall, the angle of the face, and the angle of individual rocks. For easier tending by the gardener, a dry wall should be no more than 4 feet (1.2 m) tall. Drawing by Sukey McDonough

retaining wall is a good site for a scree bed, which also can be separated from an upper lawn by a gravel path. Sloped retaining walls more than 4–5 feet (1.2–1.5 m) high should be built with access in mind. When placing the rocks, test them for stability and spacing by stepping up into the wall area, and create an informal staircase of especially solid rocks.

Prepare the site for the wall by excavating it. Level the base as much as possible, and install a poured foundation if needed. Cut the face of the wall back to a distance equal to the depth of your larger rocks, plus 4 inches (10 cm) for backfill if this is to be used.

All retaining walls intended for planting should be backed and filled with suitable soil. If the site's natural soil is poorly drained, prepare a free-draining mixture of grit, sharp sand, good loam, and leafmold or compost for this purpose (see "Soils" and "Berms" for details). Place 4–6 inches (10–15 cm) of this mixture behind the rocks as you build up the wall, and fill the spaces between the rocks with it. To prevent the loose mixture from washing out, pack bits of gravel into the crevices on the face until the plants are mature enough to hold the soil.

If you have a choice of materials for your wall, consider these points. Choose stone that matches the gravel and sand you are likely to use in the rock garden. Don't build your wall of red sandstone if the only gravel you can get is pale gray. Light-colored stone reflects heat and provides a cooler root run for plants than does dark stone, and most flowers look more attractive against lighter stone. Matte stone surfaces blend more pleasingly with plants than do shiny surfaces. Stone in a variety of sizes makes a more interesting and naturalistic background for the plants. Recycled concrete looks best if the pieces vary in size.

As you build the wall, set the rocks at a downward angle back into the slope for stability (figure 7). Avoid long vertical crevices, which promote erosion, by staggering the rocks as you place them. Position the rocks naturally, as they would lie if they fell. Do not succumb to the temptation to gain height by setting them with their largest or longest faces outward—the result will be both unstable and unattractive. If you have a variety of sizes, use most of the larger ones at the base for stability, but save a few large ones to place higher in the wall, where they add visual interest and provide good backgrounds for special plants. Large flat rocks are useful to cap the wall. If the slope permits, create niches or ledges, which are especially suitable for dwarf shrubs.

It is usually recommended that plants be set in place while the wall is being built, and if you have a stock of container plants on hand, this is a good idea. Remove the plant from its pot, flatten the rootball gently, and set it at an angle at the junction of several rocks. Add more of the fill soil around it and place the rocks above it. Insert some small stones around the crown of the plant to prevent the loose soil from washing out before the plant becomes established, then water it with a gentle spray to settle the soil around the roots. If you don't have enough plants for the wall as you are building it, provide for future planting sites by inserting narrow rocks or pieces of wood lengthwise at appropriate spots in the wall. These placeholders can be removed later and the holes used for planting. Be sure the placeholder is angled slightly downward.

You may acquire a property with existing retaining walls. Unless the soil behind is very well drained, it is usually best to tear them down and rebuild them to accommodate plants. Remember the maxim: Take care of the soil, and the plants will take care of themselves. In this case, you at least have the advantage of stone or block with exposed surfaces that are already attractively weathered.

Specialized Walls

Almost any garden perennial of modest size can be grown in an open retaining wall, provided the moisture regime suits it. For the most challenging cliff-dwellers, however, enthusiasts have devised specialized planted walls that mimic the conditions of alpine cliffs and canyons.

Slabs of tufa (see "Working with Tufa") or other soft stone can be bolted to vertical concrete or brick walls and drilled to accommodate such plants as *Jankaea heldreichii* and *Dionysia* species. Backfill of almost pure grit—horticultural pumice is especially good—may be poured in behind the stone to provide a free root run and a substrate for the weak liquid fertilizer the plants may require. Such installations can be incorporated within an alpine house (see "The Alpine House"), as the German grower Michael Kammerlander has done, or they can be freestanding, protected against excessive winter rain by a small roof.

One of the most remarkable planted walls I have seen is not in a rock garden, but in the formal garden of Hever Castle in England. It is

PLATE 34. The Grottoes, or "dripping wall," at Hever Castle in England. Water circulates from the catch-basins to pipe outlets at the top of the stone wall, nurturing moisture-loving rock plants. Photograph by Rex Murfitt

constructed of artfully placed, mortared stones built up against a vertical freestanding masonry wall. The wall is the back of a paved pergola covered with flowering climbers that provide shade. Water circulates up through pipes from small pools at the base of the wall and trickles down from the top in many places. This encourages the growth of mosses and plants that love coolness and moisture, such as ferns, primulas, and certain saxifrages. This large installation might well be imitated on a smaller scale. Maintaining alpine plants that favor streamside habitats is notoriously difficult, but the drip and mist irrigation technology now available might give the gardener an edge.

The garden at Hever Castle features another unusual planted wall. A high stone wall of the kind common in England and much envied in North America has been embellished with architectural fragments, extended stonework ruins in the Picturesque manner, and statuary and then planted naturalistically. This rather surreal effect could be imitated on a smaller scale, perhaps in a city garden. Rock gardening need not be entirely serious!

Formal Raised Beds

In contrast to the naturalistic raised beds described by Gwen Kelaidis in "Berms," formal raised beds are architectural in design—rectangular or perhaps round, raised to a consistent level above the basic grade, and neatly finished. Formal raised beds may be more appropriate than berms when the rock garden planting must be done close to a house of traditional style, especially when the surrounding garden features other formal elements. This is a good compromise when the household includes two gardeners, one of whom is addicted to urns and topiary and the other to androsaces and eriogonums. Plants have no aesthetic perceptions, fortunately, and species from the wildest spots on earth are just as likely to flourish in a formal setting as in a naturalistic one, given a proper substrate and attention to the moisture regime.

The most common design for a raised bed is a rectangle formed by dry walls of dressed stone, exemplified by the display beds at Stonecrop

Nursery in Cold Spring on Hudson, New York. Gardeners without access to reasonably priced dressed stone can use recycled broken concrete or one of the many attractive cast-concrete products. The dimensions depend on the site, but if you restrict the width to about 4 feet (1.2 m), you will be able to tend the bed without climbing onto it and compacting it.

Construction is similar to that of the dry wall, except that the raised bed's sides are usually perfectly vertical; therefore, they should not be built higher than about 3 feet (0.9 m) without mortar. The easiest way to proceed is to add the interior fill in increments as the wall rises. If the bed is large, leave one short end open so you can bring in the fill with a wheelbarrow, and close it during the last stage of construction. If the bed is quite deep, the lower part can be filled with local soil, waste rocks, broken concrete, or any other nontoxic material that will not decompose. At least the upper 18 inches (45 cm) should be comprised of the mix in which the plants are to grow (see "Soils" and "Moraine and

PLATE 35. Walls of quarried stone, planted with hardy, easily grown species, surround raised beds in Frank Cabot's Stonecrop Garden and Nursery in New York. Photograph by Pamela Harper

Scree Gardens"). Surface rocks can be added as described in "Berms" and "Crevice Gardens."

A dividing wall can be constructed as two parallel walls with planting soil between them. This creates a narrow, formal raised bed that takes up very little space and can be tended easily—a good choice for a gardener with limited mobility. A feature of this type can separate a utilitarian nursery or vegetable-growing area from a perennial garden. Note, however, that this narrow feature affords little frost protection to the roots of the plants and might not be suitable in cold-winter regions.

When the raised bed is provided with a cover, it becomes an alpine frame (see "Bulb and Alpine Frames"). You can bury vertical pipes at intervals around the sides of the raised bed; in autumn PVC pipe hoops can be inserted to support a polyethylene cover that is removed in spring. Covers are useful in regions where winters are rainy or where snow cover is intermittent and wet thaws occur. They are not attractive, though.

Either dry or moist protected walls can be incorporated in an ornamental structure to make the best use of space in a small garden. A gazebo, arbor, or teahouse can serve double duty in this way. Ruth and Larry Korn created an unusual design in a very small garden near Portland, Oregon. Their caldera bed (named for its resemblance to a volcano with a crater) began as a conical berm about 4 feet (1.2 m) high and 12 feet (3.6 m) in diameter. The center was hollowed out to grade level and retained with an inner, circular, vertical wall. A hallway provides access to the interior. The outer slopes are planted with typical scree species, and the wall, with its shelter, perfect drainage, and varied exposures, provides a substrate for choice and demanding plants, which can be enjoyed from ornamental seats on the paved floor of this plant enthusiasts' garden room.

Dry Sand Beds

MICHAEL SLATER

Composing rock garden soils is a refined art, and almost every practitioner has his or her own formulas. The sand bed, by contrast, is a model of simplicity: it is composed entirely of sand placed on top of ordinary garden soil, with the plants set in the sand. Their roots grow down into the soil below to get the necessary nutrients. Rocks may be added—indeed, they are desirable—but only for decorative effect. A dry sand bed has good drainage, so the surface dries out rapidly after a rain. This specialized artificial habitat improves the chance of successfully cultivating small dryland plants and drought-tolerant alpines outdoors in wet climates. My experience with the benefits of sand beds has been in the Mid-Atlantic states, where hot, humid summers and wet

PLATE 36. Dryland plants are tucked among rocks in the dry sand bed. Photograph by Michael Slater

winters often combine to rot rock garden plants. For best results, sand beds should be built in locations that receive full sun for as much of the day as possible.

There are three major advantages in growing dryland and alpine plants in a dry sand bed. First, there is reduced incidence of fungal attack. As often happens when plants are brought into a wetter climate than the one in which they evolved, many alpine and dryland plants apparently are not adapted to resist attacks by unfamiliar fungi or the increased numbers of soil fungi that may attack root crowns, stems, and leaves. By reducing the amount of soil fungi to which choice rock garden plants are exposed, we should increase their health and longevity. The dry sand bed is designed to provide an acceptable habitat for rock garden plants that is also a poor habitat for soil fungi. The very low level of organic matter in the sand provides few nutrients to support the growth of soil fungi, and the low moisture level at the surface limits fungal growth. A second benefit is that the relatively low nutrient levels and bright sunlight keep the plants tight and hard. This is sometimes referred to as "alpine character," not stunted, just well adapted to surviving extreme conditions. Finally, weeding is much reduced. Unlike topsoil, quarried sand usually arrives free of weed seeds. After construction and planting, weed seeds that blow onto it may germinate, but most do not survive long because the surface dries out so fast. Those that survive are wonderfully easy to pull out: even dandelions are easily uprooted, and crabgrass comes out completely.

Sand beds are relatively easy to build. There is only one soil ingredient, so there is no need for laborious mixing of large quantities of expensive, difficult-to-find ingredients. A sand bed can be built on nearly any site that is sunny and not too steep. The sand can be placed in a hole dug out to the desired depth, although such a grade-level sand bed works only where the subsoil is very well drained. In most cases, a raised bed with a stone retaining wall is more effective and easier to build.

If the soil under the planned bed is very poor in nutrients, you can add a layer of composted leaves, well-aged manure, or other rich organic matter below the sand. The upper part of the sand bed, however, must hold as little organic matter as possible. From 6 to 18 inches (15 to 45 cm) of sand is the depth range that works best. Less than 6 inches may provide insufficient drainage; more can be too dry, and it may be too far for the plants to extend their roots into the underlying native soil for nutrients and moisture.

Hold the sand in place with a low wall built of stone, concrete block, recycled concrete paving, or treated timber. Before laying the sand, remove or kill the grass or other vegetation on the site. A week or ten days after applying a glyphosate herbicide, you can pile the sand on top. The main ingredient is builder's sand, the coarse sand used to make ordinary concrete. Masonry sand, the fine sand used in mortar, is less desirable because it drains poorly and can be unsightly when the fine grains splash up and stick to the plants during rainstorms (see "Soils").

Once the walls and sand are in place, add rocks according to your aesthetic preferences (see "Berms," "Crevice Gardens," and "Working with Tufa"). You can design a dry sand bed as a natural outcrop or a flat, stylized modernistic garden. If you are constructing the bed on a slope,

PLATE 37. The author placing rocks in the newly constructed sand bed. Photograph by Michael Slater

however, you must take care to prevent erosion caused by heavy rains and gravity. Placing rocks in irregular rows across the slope creates terraces to hold back the sand. With a little care, you can make them look natural by varying the height and depth of each terrace and the size of the rocks in a row. Placing plants in the vertical joints will keep sand from washing between the rocks.

Because the grain size varies quite a bit in builder's sand, a separate gravel mulch may not be necessary. Over time, rain and gravity cause the fine grains to wash down, leaving a thin layer of the largest particles on top—a self-developing mulch. In a properly drained dry sand bed exposed to daylong sunlight, this should be sufficient. However, if the bed is built on a pronounced slope or if there is not enough sun to dry the surface quickly after a rain, a thicker gravel mulch may be needed. Deeper gravel also discourages the growth of mosses, liverworts, and weed seedlings. Finally, the surface is a more attractive background for the plants if it contains particles of varied size, provided they are all the same kind of rock.

If the sand bed abuts a lawn, a barrier to prevent grass rhizomes from invading is essential. In the case of grade-level sand beds, a thick, impenetrable barrier must be placed on the vertical wall of the hole abutting the lawn. Fabric weed barriers fail to prevent the subterranean assault of grass and weed rhizomes; heavy black polyethylene, roofing felt, pond liner, or commercial nursery groundcloth are needed for adequate defense.

When planting in the sand bed, examine the potting soil in which the transplant has been grown. If it contains much organic matter, such as bark and peat, it should be washed off so as not to introduce fungi-hosting nutrients and so the roots will grow quickly into the sand. If the plant has been grown in a sandy, stony soil mix, the type favored by experienced alpine nursery growers, you need not disturb the roots and can just pop it into the bed. After planting, water and provide shade for the transplant. Because of the rapid drainage of the sand, I have had most success establishing plants set in during spring or autumn.

PLATE 38. A colorful spring display in the sand bed. Photograph by Michael Slater

Summer plantings usually fail—spend those months sitting in the shade and drinking iced tea, planning for autumn.

Maintenance is not a big chore in a well-planned dry sand bed. As noted, weeding is easy. You can broadcast a little timed-release fertilizer (look for the six-month variety) on the bed once every two or three years. Be wary of overfertilizing, however, as this can cause the plants to lose their character. Never add organic matter; that would defeat the purpose of the bed.

By definition, most dryland plants are likely to be xeric species, evolved for drought tolerance. Therefore, in most climates no watering is needed if you select only dryland plants. Here in western Pennsylvania, I do not water our three sand beds at all. Even a summer with sixty rain-less days was no problem for the dryland plants in our sand beds. In the far West, where two to three months without rain is common in summer, Jane McGary has built dry sand beds with a layer of fist-sized rocks buried about 2 inches (5 cm) below the surface. This technique helps retain moisture in summer without adding organic matter.

The only major trouble we have had with pests in our sand beds has been cats using them as a litter-box. Cats can be discouraged from this devastating behavior in several ways. The most effective one I have found is to place a few spiny cactus pads (*Opuntia fragilis*, for instance) in the spot they are using. Cats do learn quickly, and this halts their digging immediately. A heavy gravel mulch also makes the bed less hospitable to feline excavation. If you don't have a surplus of cacti, try setting mousetraps on the bed. Another successful method for discouraging cats involves grinding up hot peppers and mixing the resulting powder with diatomaceous earth; dust it on the bed when there is no wind, being careful not to breathe the irritating pepper powder. You need to repeat the application after each rainfall. There are also commercial repellents available at pet stores. Covering the garden completely with a layer of chicken wire propped a few inches above the surface works, but it is ugly. Whatever countermeasures you use, start them at the first sign of cat activity, before the cats acquire the habit of digging in your beds.

What plants benefit from a dry sand bed? For gardens in much of North America, the most obvious sources are cold-winter steppe regions such as Colorado and Wyoming, Turkey, and central Asia. In addition, many plants from dry microhabitats in wet regions may do well. Such habitats may include barrens, sandy areas, and rocky talus or glacial till with little soil and plenty of sunlight. Finally, certain high-alpine plants that like a lot of sun may do well. The list of plants that thrive in sand beds in eastern North America ranges from *Acantholimon* to *Zauschneria*. Success with many small species of *Dianthus*, *Echinocereus*, and *Eriogonum* is to be expected, but *Vitaliana primuliflora* and *Bruckenthalia spiculifolia* have surprised many people with their willingness to adapt to this habitat. A dry sand bed is not the only place to grow such plants, but it is often a very practical method for pleasing them.

Adapting a Natural Outcrop

ROB AND SHARON ILLINGWORTH

People come to rock gardening by many paths, but perhaps the most direct is purchasing a homesite that includes a natural surface rock formation. For example, Lincoln and Laura Louise Foster, the couple often regarded as the founders of modern rock gardening in the Northeast, built their garden, Millstream, on rocky New England land bisected by a rushing stream. In the West, Margaret Williams created a well-known garden on a steep site near Reno, Nevada, that is essentially a peak of unforgiving red sandstone. These gardens were not created merely by tucking plants into existing features, though. As anyone who has tried it knows, large rock outcrops usually require laborious modification to support more than a few plants.

PLATE 39. Millstream, Lincoln and Laura Louise Foster's garden in Falls Village, Connecticut, exploited a natural setting of stone and water to grow thousands of species. Photograph by Pamela Harper

Our own garden is situated south of Thunder Bay, just inland from the northwestern shore of Lake Superior and a short distance north of the Minnesota-Ontario border. The region is part of the Canadian Shield, a vast area underlain by ancient Precambrian rock, centered on Hudson Bay and extending from Alberta west to Greenland and south to the Great Lakes and beyond. The terrain features high ridges of diabase dikes separated by deep valleys filled with deposits of clay and gravel. The soil in our rock garden is meager, composed of sandy loam, heavy silt, and acidic forest duff. The garden site is a natural rocky promontory of more than 1 acre (0.4 ha), bounded by cliffs on two sides, with a stream and waterfall below. Tall spruces and pines form a perimeter and provide some shelter from the wind. The trees' roots spread a long way into the garden, drawing up excess water in periods of heavy rain but also competing with the cultivated plants.

In our early years here, the danger that the sheer cliffs posed for our young son made our visits to this wild place infrequent, even though it is less than 300 feet (90 m) from the house. It beckoned, however, and in 1989 we finally decided to make a rock garden. We had no model to work from in adapting this natural outcrop, because authors of books on rock gardening usually presume that these features are built entirely by artificial means. There was no soil to dig, and the site was completely covered by dense brush and brambles. Cautiously, we began cutting and left the stumps and roots to decay over time. The following spring, the stumps burst into growth with renewed vigor, and it became obvious that herbicide would be needed. Removing all the brush took three years.

The rugged features of the lichen-covered rock were revealed as we removed the brush. A chaotic tumble of rocks, split by frost and tree roots, lay all about. Natural stone walls and ledges created many planting opportunities. We were relieved to see that our cautious use of herbicide had had little effect on the mosses and lichens (they are not affected by glyphosate products, which are often recommended for use in moss gardens). Indeed, some wonderful native plants benefited from

PLATE 40. A small pool has been added to a natural outcrop in the Massachusetts garden created by Margot Parrot. Photograph by Pamela Harper

the removal of their rank competitors, and soon there were thriving clumps of *Cornus canadensis*, *Linnaea borealis*, and *Pyrola asarifolia*.

Initially, we decided to leave the rock as it was, feeling that tidying up any errant boulders would destroy the wild, random quality of the site. The usual rules regarding the design of paths and steps for safety and accessibility had to be compromised in favor of keeping a natural-looking garden. The logical places for paths gradually became clear; in the end, we had to move some stone to create access. The paths are narrow and topped with ⅜-inch (9-mm) crushed rock. We used rocks that had fractured into rectangular blocks to make rough steps. The ravine is still not easily accessible for those with limited mobility, and it is impossible to accommodate a large number of visitors at once. The cliffs have no barriers, so we discourage visitors from bringing children.

Once we had begun the paths, we also started planting; this has proceeded gradually. Container-grown plants can be set into the garden throughout summer, even into September. Where shallow soil covers

rock, we remove it and fill in the crevices, using the native soil amended
with sand, crushed rock, and peat in varying proportions. A crowbar is
a very useful tool at this stage. We try to group plants requiring basic
conditions together and add lime to their soil. In one area where the soil
is sandy and acidic, we have planted heathers (*Calluna vulgaris*) with no
soil amendment other than a heavy annual mulch of pine needles. On a
sunny slope on the edge of the garden, we made a scree by mounding
up rough gravel on top of the clay soil; *Paeonia cambessedesii*, a native
of the Balearic Islands in the Mediterranean, has survived there.

According to the hardiness zone maps, Thunder Bay straddles the
line between USDA zones 3 and 4 (Canadian zone 3a). The continental
climate is tempered by the moderating effect of Lake Superior, but winter lows can dip to −40°F (−40°C). More usual at our place are lows from
−22 to −32°F (−30 to −36°C). Most gardeners would consider this a
harsh climate, and we felt the same at first. We were naive and willing to
try everything, however, and the seed exchanges of rock garden societies gave us the chance to experiment. To our surprise, most of our
plants flourished, even those from warmer regions such as Turkey
(*Convolvulus compactus*) or Greece (*Haberlea rhodopensis*). The credit
probably lies in the fact that there is reliable, protective snow cover from
mid-November to late March, although damage can result if an early
spring is followed by a surprise cold snap.

The summers in our area are not terribly hot and humid, although
the air in the space directly above a waterfall beside the outcrop can be
full of moisture when the river is high. The mist in the air shimmers in
the slanting rays of the setting sun, and this mist may account for the
abundant lichens on the rocks throughout the garden. The shallow soil
can get very dry, so in times of drought we irrigate. If you are developing a large natural outcrop that cannot be irrigated, you will probably
want to choose xeric (drought-tolerant) plants.

Maintaining the natural outcrop garden is easy. The plants are
mulched with the same crushed rock used in the paths. Birch trees
(*Betula* spp.) are the most prevalent weed. We have now banished some

PLATE 41. Cushion phloxes spangle a natural outcrop incorporated in the garden of Rob and Sharon Illingworth. Photograph by Rob Illingworth

pernicious seeders like the spring bulb *Puschkinia* (an early mistake), and we have learned to deadhead others, such as the larger dianthuses and penstemons. Plants that are self-sowing, when not invasive, are welcomed. We may lose the occasional *Lewisia cotyledon*, but there are always more coming along. *Townsendia grandiflora* has kept itself going for years, even though it dies back after blooming. Small clumps of *Phlox subulata*, a standby in large natural rock gardens, have established themselves to happy effect on a vertical rock face that is next to impossible to plant.

It is difficult to say whether we would have become rock gardeners had we not had such a wonderful natural site at our doorstep. Yet, in the spring when we see the first flowers blooming through the snow, we realize that it's one of our greatest pleasures. We understand that the brush will quickly take over when we are gone, but, in an odd way, the ephemeral nature of our garden only heightens our present enjoyment.

Dwarf Conifers and Woody Plants

ROBERT FINCHAM

Conifers, the cone-bearing, needle-leaved, woody plants loosely termed *evergreens*, are among the aristocrats of the rock garden. The dwarfed and stunted conifers often seen in alpine regions are usually quite old; many conifer species have long life spans, sometimes more than a thousand years. In the garden, similar plants impart a sense of timelessness not offered by relatively short-lived flowering perennials. Unless the rock garden is very large in scale, however, such as those at the botanical gardens in Denver, Wisley, or Edinburgh, the gardener should select conifers that are true dwarfs.

In this chapter, the term *dwarf* denotes any plant that grows less than about 10 feet (3 m) in either height or width in twenty years. This definition excludes many of the plants presently sold as dwarf. A true dwarf plant requires a long time to develop any size, and this accounts both for their limited availability and their high price tags. Many plants labeled as "dwarf" in garden centers are better termed *compact*; these selections soon outgrow their sites if used in a design calling for dwarf cultivars.

In Japanese gardens, conifers represent age and stability; in many Western gardens, they form the basic framework or backbone of the garden. Conifers also provide focal interest in every season—especially in winter, when many other garden plants are leafless or entirely below ground. Many conifers change color with the seasons, and they can be found in a wide range of colors, textures, shapes, and sizes. Dwarf broad-leaved shrubs are not quite as effective as dwarf conifers in providing a feeling of age and stability, but they nicely complement the conifers. Genera such as *Berberis* (barberries), *Betula* (birches), *Buxus* (boxwood), *Cotoneaster*, *Salix* (willows), and *Vaccinium* contain a number of small species and dwarf selections appropriate for the rock garden.

Many of the plants mentioned in this chapter are rarely available at local garden centers. Specialty nurseries, mostly mail-order, are generally the most reliable sources for them. If you do not have a specialty nursery close by, contact those that advertise in *Rock Garden Quarterly* or do research on the Internet. Several websites list nurseries and even evaluate the quality of their products and service.

A Rock Garden for Dwarf Conifers

Many approaches to designing and building rock gardens are presented in this book. The forms most hospitable to dwarf conifers are the berm, slope with ledges, and the large crevice garden. The smallest conifers can be planted in more formal raised beds and in large troughs.

Rock garden soil should be very well drained and not rich in humus. Poorer soils stunt the growth of conifers and help keep them even more dwarf than they would be in ordinary garden soil, without affecting their health. My own rock garden is planted in glacial subsoil. The conifers are healthy in color and form, but they grow at about three-fourths their typical rate. This is not surprising, because many conifers thrive in organically poor alpine soils throughout the world.

Because I have collected conifers since the early 1970s, they have always made up more than 80 percent of my successive gardens in Pennsylvania, Oregon, and Washington State. Accompanying alpine plants provide contrast and interest. Most gardeners, however, prefer a more conservative assortment of conifers among a predominantly flowering plant community. In either case, be careful not to select plants that will outgrow their sites. Conifers need to be positioned before any companion plants, because most of them will be the longest-lived specimens in the garden. There are a number of ways to site conifers in a typical rock garden, whether newly constructed or long established.

Prostrate or spreading plants are best used on a site with varying elevations. A prostrate conifer planted on a slope directly above a large rock will grow downhill and form an evergreen mat around the rock. If

PLATE 42. Summer-flowering
rock plants combined with
dwarf conifers in the Platt
garden. Photograph by
Pamela Harper

there is a flat area on the top of the rock, the conifer can be encouraged
to grow over and down the front and sides, eventually covering most of
the rock. A deciduous woody plant can perform in much the same way,
but its branch structure is usually stiffer and the branches will be leafless in winter.

A wall of any height can be treated much like a flat-topped rock. If
the rock garden is to appear natural, a wall built along the base of the
slope needs an assortment of plants cascading over it. Plants growing
down a wall soften the hard boundary between wall base and path.
Where a path lies between two slopes, a grotto effect can be obtained
with plants flowing over the walls on either side. The vertical drop of a
waterfall can be enhanced with prostrate conifers among the rocks on
either side. If a prostrate conifer is staked to a height of 3–6 feet (0.9–1.8

m), depending on the height and breadth of the waterfall, and then allowed to cascade down, it can become a mirror image of the waterfall.

Good prostrate or spreading conifers that stay relatively dwarf and are well suited to these uses are *Cedrus libani* 'Sargentii', *Picea abies* 'Formanek', *P. abies* 'Frohburg', *Picea pungens* 'Pendens', *Pinus banksiana* 'Schoodic', *Pinus densiflora* 'Pendula', *Pinus mugo* 'Corley's Mat', *Pinus sylvestris* 'Albyns', *P. sylvestris* 'Hillside Creeper', *Tsuga canadensis* 'Cole's Prostrate', *Tsuga caroliniana* 'La Bar Weeping', and *Tsuga heterophylla* 'Thorson Weeping'. Broad-leaved shrubs that lend themselves to this sort of planting include *Cotoneaster cooperi, Genista pilosa* 'Vancouver Gold', and *Salix repens.*

Weeping or pendulous plants offer an alternative to prostrate selections, although the distinction between the two groups can be blurred.

PLATE 43. The Platt garden with *Picea pungens* 'Procumbens', a dwarf form of the Colorado blue spruce, in the foreground. Photograph by Don Howse

Pendulous plants can be broad and low, tall and narrow, or almost anything in between. There are few dwarf selections in this category, but several full-sized cultivars can be used as background for the smaller rock garden because they make a small footprint (require little ground surface area) in the garden. These plants often develop into broad, low (but not prostrate) specimens if not staked to the desired height. For example, a twenty-year-old plant of *Tsuga canadensis* 'Brookline' at the Arnold Arboretum was less than 3.3 feet (1 m) high when it was 6.6 feet (2 m) wide. Although not dwarf, 'Brookline' can easily be maintained at any desired size by annual pruning and shaping. A pendulous plant is attractive when allowed to grow naturally down the face of a wall. The mound it creates above the wall breaks up the straight rim and creates an effect that a prostrate conifer would. *Picea abies* 'Reflexa' will grow in this manner, as will *Picea pungens* 'Pendens'.

Weeping plants are quite effective near a small pond, especially one with a waterfall. Using a pendulous plant here creates a pleasing transition between the rushing waterfall and the stillness of the pond. The plant selected should have a spreading rather than vertical form. Weeping selections of *Tsuga canadensis* work nicely in this setting. If you are planting a very large rock garden, however, you may prefer more upright forms to match the larger scale of the waterfall.

If the garden contains massive rocks, a broadly weeping conifer can be complementary without altering the vertical dimension of the overall scene. Thus, *Abies procera* 'La Graciosa' planted near a boulder adds to the alpine feeling of the garden; this plant grows slowly upward while developing into a broad mound with strongly pendulous branches. *Picea pungens* 'Glauca Pendula' is not a true dwarf, but it grows slowly enough to be easily controlled, and its blue needles complement adjacent boulders. If a golden conifer is desired, *Picea abies* 'Gold Drift' provides a bright flow through summer and well into winter.

For the rock garden with a fence, especially a rail fence, weeping plants that exhibit some vertical development can be very effective. Their branches angling across the rails break up the straight, horizontal lines. The dwarf *Abies concolor* 'Gable's Weeping' works well, as would the larger-growing *Picea abies* 'Reflexa' or *Picea pungens* 'Glauca Pendula', either of which can be trained to knuckle over once they have reached the desired height above the fence.

Small, upright plants can be used in many positions throughout the rock garden, and large rocks make excellent backdrops for them. Upright plants soften the border between rock and surrounding plantings and balance the height of the rock behind. As long as the plant is dwarf, it will accent rocks rather than hide them.

An area studded with low alpine plants often benefits from the presence of one or more upright shrubs, which add variety to a landscape that could easily be uninteresting for much of the year. Such a vertical feature is useful to draw the eye upward and on to neighboring features. Dwarf conifers offer colors and textures that differ from those of alpines and have year-round foliage interest. Again, selection is the key: these plants must be dwarf so they will not overgrow the alpines and will remain in scale with the garden.

A conifer such as *Picea glauca* 'Laurin' or *Juniperus communis* 'Compressa' can be planted in a soil pocket within a group of small boulders to give the effect of a distant view of a tree near a massive rock outcrop. Even the compact *Abies alba* 'Pyramidalis' or *Abies concolor* 'Conica' can be used; they grow so slowly as young plants that it takes them twenty years to reach 6.6 feet (2 m) in height, especially if minimally fertilized. Dwarf broad-leaved shrubs for the same situation include *Salix ×boydii*, a gnarled, slow-growing, upright miniature willow, and *Ilex crenata* 'Dwarf Pagoda', a congested shrublet with tiny, dark evergreen leaves.

Selections that are not true dwarfs can be used as the rear border of the garden. Available space determines just how large these plants can be allowed to grow. Fastigiate (narrowly upright) plants have a small footprint, even though their height may be considerable. *Pinus nigra* 'Richard Reuter', the best columnar pine presently available, can be interplanted with *Picea abies* 'Columnaris' for a pleasing variety of

PLATE 44. This beautifully planted watercourse shows a judicious use of dwarf conifers and other woody plants together with perennials. Photograph by Pamela Harper

colors and textures. A few columnar beeches (*Fagus sylvatica*) mixed among the conifers creates a very interesting backdrop for the larger rock garden. Possibly the best dwarf fastigiate conifer for the garden is *Juniperus communis* 'Compressa'; another that grows slowly is *Taxus baccata* 'Standishii', which also provides color variation with its gold-edged needles.

Alpine meadows often have a scattering of stunted upright plants as well as some that have developed into tight little mounds, usually the result of a combination of harsh climate and grazing by herbivores. In the rock garden, these plants can be duplicated without importing a goat. Many dwarf plants never develop any strong shoots and naturally become cushions and buns. They can be scattered in the open areas of the rock garden, where their rounded shapes mimic round rocks or soften angular ones. Until recently, the only true cushion-forming conifers available were *Chamaecyparis obtusa* cultivars ('Intertexta', 'Nana', 'Juniperoides'), spruces (*Picea abies* 'Little Gem', *Picea glauca* 'Little Globe'), pines (*Pinus mugo* 'Mops', *Pinus strobus* 'Sea Urchin'), and many selections of *Tsuga canadensis* ('Minuta' and the faster-growing 'Cinnamomea'). Thankfully, there are many new selections of this type, including *Abies concolor* 'Pigglemee', *Abies koreana* 'Silberkugel', *A. koreana* 'Silberperl', *Abies procera* 'Blaue Hexe', *Picea abies* 'Hasin', *P. abies* 'Malena', *Picea omorika* 'Pimoko', *Picea orientalis* 'Mount Vernon', *P. orientalis* 'Tom Thumb Gold', *Picea pungens* 'Saint Mary', *Picea smithiana* 'Ballarat', *Pinus leucodermis* 'Smidt', *Pinus mugo* 'Jacobsen', *Pinus sylvestris* 'Jeremy', and *Pinus mugo* ssp. *uncinata* 'Offenpass'. Two of the best mounding to globose broad-leaved dwarf shrubs available are *Ilex* 'Rock' and *Buxus microphylla* 'Kingsville'.

A large number of dwarf plants become globose to broadly conical. They are good at filling spaces between the massive rocks of larger rock gardens. Used along a path to break up the straight line, they preserve the informal quality of the rock garden and also add interest by partially concealing a special feature from the visitor. *Picea abies* 'Will's Zwergform' is good for this use, becoming conical with age. *Pinus strobus* 'Bloomer's Dark Green Globe' is just what its name implies. *Pinus mugo* 'Carsten's Wintergold' has exceptionally good gold winter color. *Salix helvetica* is a small bushy shrub that stays small and globose; *Betula nana* is another with tiny, rounded, dark green leaves.

Dwarf conifers and broad-leaved shrubs should be part of every rock garden. They come in sizes, shapes, and colors to satisfy almost any gardener. If your garden does not contain some of these wonderful plants, consider adding a few—I am sure that you will be pleased with the results.

FURTHER READING

Robert L. Fincham, "Little-known Miniature Conifers"; Gerd Krussmann, *Manual of Cultivated Conifers*; D. M. van Gelderen and J. R. P. van Hoey Smith, *Conifers: The Illustrated Encyclopedia*

The Cactus and Succulent Specialist's Rock Garden

JOHN SPAIN

Most gardeners think of cacti and succulents as natives of the world's warmer regions, little suited to outdoor cultivation in temperate climates. In fact, hardy cacti and succulents exist, and they embody some of the best qualities to be found among rock garden plants. They are long-lived and easy to maintain. Most of them multiply rapidly and are easy to propagate from cuttings and offsets, and as a rule they require minimal fertilizer and watering. Cacti and succulents can be treated as alpine plants; indeed, certain species of cacti, sedums, sempervivums, and a number of other succulent groups are native to high mountains, sharing habitats with some of the most revered alpines.

A gardener who contracts this enthusiasm will probably need to provide specialized conditions, such as a raised bed, for the growing collection. I constructed such a rock garden in the front yard of my home in central Connecticut (USDA zone 6). At first intended to be an exclusive planting of cacti and succulents, it soon hosted every rock garden plant I could get my hands on. The earliest choices were buns, the small, dense, mounded plants that look so natural with cacti; later came dwarf bearded irises, dwarf conifers, Japanese maples, and spring bulbs. (It may seem surprising that the maples thrive in the rock garden; probably they are able to root deeply enough to get more moisture than the other plants do.)

To integrate cacti and succulents into the rock garden plant community, you must begin with a site that has ample sunlight and excellent drainage. Soil pH and other subtle factors seem to be of little consequence. You can provide the necessary drainage by constructing a berm, raised bed, or wall or by using a natural slope. I started with a slope, amending the native clay soil with peat and rotted manure. A

PLATE 45. A cactus and succulent collection need not look sparse, as this springtime scene in John Spain's rock garden demonstrates. Even Japanese maples grow well on its margin. Photograph by John Spain

good soil for hardy succulents consists of about 15–20 percent rich, friable loam mixed with an inorganic portion made up of 2 parts coarse sand and 1 part crushed rock in mixed sizes from ¼ to ¾ inch (6 to 18 mm). Almost any type of rock is suitable. I rototilled all the amendments into the slope to a depth of 8–10 inches (20–25 cm); in a raised bed or berm, a depth of 18 inches (45 cm) is good.

To form my rock garden after amending the soil, I brought in loads of boulders and rolled them down the slope into pre-dug holes, so that the finished design resembles a natural scree. Before planting, I covered the surface with about 1 inch (2.5 cm) of ½-inch (13-mm) gravel that came from the same quarry as the boulders, to preserve the natural appearance of the combined rock. The gravel mulch reflects heat toward the plants and discourages both rot and weeds.

I have also used troughs extensively to grow winter-hardy cacti. The small-padded opuntias (such as *Opuntia fragilis*) and all species of *Echinocereus*, *Coryphantha* (syn. *Escobaria*), and *Pediocactus* seem to

PLATE 46. This sun-baked scree bed was built by John Spain in Connecticut to host his collection of hardy cacti and other xeric plants. Photograph by John Spain

do even better in troughs than in the garden, probably because of the precise control of soil mix and moisture possible in containers.

The range of sizes, forms, and textures within the world of hardy succulents—to say nothing of the colorful flowers some bear—is remarkable. In my garden, upright, shrublike *Cylindropuntia* cacti have grown to more than 7 feet (2.1 m) in height. Ball-type cacti develop into 12-inch (30 cm) mounds with forty or more heads. Hardy succulent mats of *Delosperma* and *Sedum* may cover more ground than desired. Sempervivums hang over the stone borders of the garden, and small clumps of prickly pear *Opuntia* cacti mimic nearby buns of *Dianthus* and *Armeria*. Many of them have flowers of a brilliance and sheen rarely seen in other plant groups.

In the northeastern United States, a cactus and succulent garden needs no watering once established, although newly planted specimens must not be allowed to dry out too much. Fallen leaves, which may cause rot, can be removed with a shop vacuum, a task I do in spring (in regions with wetter winters, it would need to be done in autumn). A pre-emergent herbicide sprinkled on the garden in early spring helps

PLATE 47. Mat- and cushion-form rock plants complement cacti and succulents.
Photograph by John Spain

control weeds. Many succulent plants have low feeding requirements, but they should not be starved. A low-nitrate fertilizer can be applied once or twice a year. Pests that commonly attack succulents in greenhouses, such as mealy bug, are not much of a problem in the open garden. Many outdoor cactus growers experience problems with a form of black rot on *Opuntia* species, and no good cure is known; infected material should be removed.

Cacti hardy in cool temperate regions are found primarily in the genera *Opuntia, Echinocereus, Coryphantha* (syn. *Escobaria*), and *Pediocactus*. Less commonly grown genera, such as the South American *Maihuenia*, also deserve trials. The hardiest succulents are undoubtedly those basic plants of the rock garden, *Sempervivum, Sedum, Jovibarba,* and *Lewisia*. To these some gardeners add the smallest, hardiest *Agave* and *Yucca* species, which are wonderful contrasts in form to the other groups, as well as representatives from *Delosperma, Crassula, Orostachys,* and *Rosularia*.

Not all species in these genera can withstand winter temperatures below 0°F (−18°C), and other factors—available sunlight, precipitation

PLATE 48. A rock garden must be fairly grand in scale to host yuccas and large-growing hardy cacti. Photograph by John Spain

patterns, and wind—affect hardiness as well. Parts of western North America that have winter minima equivalent to USDA zone 6 or lower provide uniquely suitable conditions for hardy succulents. The climatic factors involved are the mountain and desert West's intense sunlight, low rainfall, strong air movement, and monsoon or thunderstorm precipitation followed by rapid drying of the soil surface. Many plants that cannot be grown in similarly cold regions elsewhere have been successfully grown in these regions. For example, *Delosperma cooperi*, a mat-forming succulent from South Africa, is quite hardy in Denver, Colorado, but it cannot live without protection in my Connecticut garden, where there is more than 40 inches (100 cm) of rain annually, compared with approximately 10 inches (25 cm) in Denver. At about

5000 feet (1500 m) elevation, Denver also receives 30 percent more insolation (calories of solar radiation per square centimeter) than Connecticut.

FURTHER READING

Edward F. Anderson, *The Cactus Family*; Claude Barr, *Jewels of the Plains*; Lyman Benson, *The Cacti of the United States and Canada*; Robert Clausen, *Sedum of North America North of the Mexican Plateau*; Mary Irish and Gary Irish, *Agaves, Yuccas, and Related Plants*; Brian Mathew, *The Genus Lewisia*; John Spain, *Growing Winter Hardy Cacti in Cold/Wet Climate Conditions*

PART 3

Structures and Containers

No matter how diligently and creatively you have built your rock garden, you may find that you want to grow plants that simply will not thrive there. Perhaps they need a very specialized soil or a particular combination of shade and sun that's not available on your rock garden site. Maybe even the sharpest drainage can't preserve them from your rainy winters or soggy summers. A plant may be so tiny, even when mature, that it would get smothered by its neighbors on the rock garden. Finally, not all who share the love of rare plants are property owners, and you can hardly create a scree or crevice bed on an apartment balcony.

The solutions to these problems are almost as old as the craft of alpine and rock gardening: growing sensitive plants in pots or in stone or concrete troughs, often in the shelter of a specialized greenhouse or cold frame. As the photographs in this section show, troughs are often incorporated in the design of the garden. Even a tiny alpine house (an especially well ventilated greenhouse) can host a remarkable collection on its benches. Frames protect moisture-sensitive plants and provide space for intensive propagation. All these devices can greatly expand your rock gardening horizons.

Making Troughs

JOYCE FINGERUT

To the rock gardener, a trough is not a place to water the horses—although that is the origin of the usage. In the early twentieth century, English gardeners began to salvage old stone watering troughs. They used these weathered, picturesque containers to create specialized sites for plants that needed extra drainage or protection from rain at certain times of the year. When the supply of stone troughs ran out—it was never very large in North America—gardeners turned to imitating them in concrete. Over the years, rock gardeners have developed materials that are lighter in weight than conventional concrete, along with ways to finish the troughs attractively and make them hospitable to plants. This chapter describes how to make troughs, and Rex Murfitt's subsequent chapter gives suggestions about planting them.

There are two approaches to using troughs: (1) creating a miniature landscape within the confines of a trough; and (2) using planted troughs as elements of the wider garden landscape. It's all a question of scale. No single definition of a "correct trough planting" exists. There are, however, what might be called "classic troughs," if only because they represent the initial attempt at defining the art. Most trough-making instructions assume that the gardener will be building small troughs to fill odd corners in the garden or terrace, but a collection of several smaller troughs (for our purposes, less than 18 inches [45 cm] in any one dimension) can be a significant landscape feature. Large troughs offer options for siting and planting, but they also require additional considerations in construction.

Larger troughs have certain horticultural advantages: a greater root run, better buffering against rapid changes in soil temperature and moisture, and natural drainage based on gravity. Choosing a size also involves aesthetic considerations. Too large a trough may resemble a casket liner (attempting to imitate the Saxon coffin is not necessarily a wise landscape decision). The trough should not be too deep in relation to its length and width. Although extra depth makes sense horticulturally, when the trough is set in the garden, it will look perched on the surface rather than blended into the landscape. If you need the deeper root run, you can minimize the trough's visual height either by placing in-ground plantings around its base or by sinking the trough partway into the ground (in the latter case, remember that the soil below must not be so impervious that it blocks drainage).

Gardeners who make troughs today are not restricted to any particular size or shape; nevertheless, it is wise to make them deep enough to hold at least 6 inches (15 cm) of soil. This depth is sufficient to sustain a healthy number of plants and to provide enough soil volume to delay rapid fluctuations between wet and dry. Small or shallow troughs are better regarded as pans, pots, or planters, and they demand a greater level of care and attention. They can only sustain a few shallow-rooted plants—but that may be just what you want.

PLATE 49. This collection of newly made troughs by Betsey Knapp of Rochester, New York, shows a smoothly finished style; note the ornamental hypertufa spheres in the background. Photograph by Roslyn Bliss

Preparing the Mold

Small troughs can be molded inside household containers such as dish-pans, baking pans, and bowls, but the molds for large ones have to be built. Forms for larger troughs must have thicker walls to withstand the extra forces of the larger mass of hypertufa and the extra pounding needed to place and compact it.

The best material for trough forms, even for larger troughs, is extruded polystyrene foam insulation board. All major brands are equally good. The boards are lightweight and portable, easily cut with a kitchen knife, and easily assembled into a form by pushing (not hammering) nails at the four corners. The forms can be reused, too. Here are the materials and tools needed to make the forms:

Rigid foam board, 1.5 inches (38 mm) thick for most trough forms, 2 inches (50 mm) thick for troughs larger than 18 inches (45 cm) in any dimension

Straight-edged or serrated knife

Yardstick

Pencil, pen, or marker

Nails 3–4 inches (75–100 mm) long, depending on the thickness of the board

Duct tape

Forms for the drainage holes, such as tin cans with the tops and bottoms removed or short lengths of 3-inch (75-mm) diameter PVC pipe

Pieces of hardware cloth (rigid wire mesh) or landscape fabric to place over the drainage holes before planting

Sheet plastic (polyethylene film)

A sturdy board, slightly larger than the trough, is handy if you are making a smaller trough and need to move it from the work site while it's curing. Lay sheets of plastic on the board, beneath the trough form, before beginning construction. Allow a generous amount of plastic to wrap each trough completely and securely, to hold in the moisture while the hypertufa is curing. You may want to protect the floors and surface of your work area with additional plastic.

To build the mold, cut the foam board into the sizes needed for sides and bottom. Remember when measuring that the ends will overlap, so you need to take the thickness of the board itself into consideration. For instance, a form to make a square trough that is 12 inches (30 cm) on a side will require each 1.5-inch (4-cm) thick piece to be 13.5 inches (34 cm) long. Next, center the drainage hole forms within the walls. Fix the foam rectangles together with the large nails, using three nails at each overlapping corner. Finally, reinforce the whole thing by wrapping duct tape around the sides (see figure 8).

Although often suggested, forms with both inner and outer walls do not work well. It is difficult to construct the corners so that the nails will be exposed for easy disassembly after the first curing, when the trough is partially hardened. There are also problems in compacting the hypertufa mixture tightly enough in the narrow space between the double walls. To eliminate all air pockets, you would need either a

FIGURE 8. A foam-board trough mold being completed, held together with heavy nails and duct tape. Drawing by Sukey McDonough

wetter mixture that pours easily or a tamping tool. The wet mixture would compromise the strength of the trough because it would be excessively diluted; while the tool is a better possibility, you could not see the results of your packing or test its firmness.

Mixing the Hypertufa

Hypertufa is a highly adaptable, easily produced material, perfect for use by the gardener and amateur (even beginning) craftsperson. The following is only one of several formulas for hypertufa, but it is both durable and lightweight. The modifications of color and finishing are the creator's aesthetic choices. Often, however, the greater visual impact of a large trough calls for altering the basic light gray color of the hypertufa material used to construct it, unless the trough is to be set among pale limestone rocks. A slight tint in a darker or warmer shade does much to reduce the trough's visual size and to blend it with its surroundings.

Hypertufa is based on the classic proportions for mortar: 1 part Portland cement to 3 parts aggregate (stone and sand). In this case, however, lightweight aggregates such as peat and perlite replace the heavier stone and sand, greatly reducing the overall weight of the mixture. The minor loss of strength resulting from this substitution is offset by the addition of acrylic fibers and/or liquid acrylic (in any case, structural strength is not as crucial in a garden container as it might be in other concrete constructions). My formula for hypertufa is 3 parts Portland cement, 4 parts peat, and 5 parts perlite. (Notice, as a memory aid, that they are in numerical and alphabetical order.) The parts may be a measure of any size—cups, pints, liters, or coffee cans; the important consideration is the proper ratio by volume.

Handling any concrete product requires attention to safety. The reaction of lime-laden cement with moisture—even a sweaty palm— can lead to burning and blistering. Wear household rubber gloves, and keep a spare pair on hand; disposable, thin rubber gloves are not strong enough for this purpose. To avoid the irritating dust raised by preparing, measuring, and combining the cement, peat, and perlite, always wear a dust mask. Plastic safety goggles are helpful, especially for contact-lens wearers.

Purchase the following ingredients:

Portland cement, Type I: This is a type of cement, not a brand name. Do not use concrete mix, which is a blend of cement, stone, and sand.

Peat (peat moss or milled sphagnum peat): This needs to be sifted and cleaned of all solid chunks of undecomposed peat and sticks before it is measured.

Perlite: This mineral product is white and very lightweight. It can be measured straight from the bag, but its fine dust is very irritating, so wear the dust mask. (Gardeners in areas where crushed horticultural pumice is available often use that instead of perlite.)

Synthetic reinforcement fibers: These can be acrylic, polypropylene, nylon, or a combination of these; all work equally well.

Liquid acrylic bonding agent: This is a liquid form of the material used in the fiber, and it is easier to incorporate uniformly throughout the mixture. It seals the pores and makes the trough walls more impervious to water. (The subsequent freezing and thawing of captured water breaks down the walls of the container.) Do not use the rewettable type of liquid acrylic, which will go back into solution each time the trough becomes wet.

Cement colors: These powdered oxides of natural minerals are available from light tan through browns and reds to black. You need to use very little; most people prefer their troughs merely tinted to mimic the local rock, rather than deeply colored.

To mix the hypertufa, you will need these common garden items:

A convenient water supply and a hose with a shut-off nozzle. Failing this, fill several watering cans ahead of time.

Mixing containers that are wider than deep; mortar pans are the obvious choice, but wheelbarrows work equally well.

Shovels and trowels for mixing, appropriate to the mixing container; use long-handled tools with mortar pans on the ground and short-handled tools with wheelbarrows.

Measuring containers, selected with an eye to the amount of hypertufa you will be mixing. I use a 1-pound coffee can or a container of equivalent size; a measuring container larger than that may be unwieldy.

The total amount of hypertufa you will need for a given project is difficult to estimate, but here is a recipe for enough to make a small sample trough 12 inches (30 cm) square and 6 inches (15 cm) high. Novices are best advised to start with a small trough. The advanced (or risk-taking) trough-maker can rely on experience, or mathematics, to multiply this recipe for a larger one. Use a 1-pound coffee can as a measure and mix:

3 scoops Type I Portland cement

4 scoops well-sieved or hand-cleaned peat

5 scoops perlite

Optional coloring: ¼ cup will produce a noticeable tint

The dry ingredients can be measured and mixed well ahead and stored in heavy plastic bags for some time. Be sure to double-bag it for storage in an area with temperature fluctuations, so that any condensation forms between the two plastic bags, rather than on the inside of the bag, thus wetting the mix and ruining it. (This also holds true for storing cement: double-bag it as soon as you bring it home, if it will not be used immediately.)

Building the Trough

Choose your work site carefully, especially if you will be working on larger containers. In general, no matter what size trough you are making, you will need: (1) good lighting, from several directions if possible; (2) good ventilation, because the dry materials generate a fair amount of dust; and (3) plenty of elbow room (allow room for friends—it's a rare person who has the initiative to get started alone, especially the first time). When you have gathered all the ingredients and tools at your work site, ready the trough mold. If you are making a small, movable trough, lay down the base board, cover it with plastic sheet, and set the foam-board form on top of the plastic.

Once you are certain that everything necessary is at hand, you can mix the hypertufa. Because hypertufa is a cement-based mixture, working with it is very time-sensitive. Once the cement is wet, the process *cannot* be delayed or halted. Measure and thoroughly mix the dry materials (cement, peat, perlite, and colors) in the mixing container and begin adding water. The first addition should be just enough to wet the mixture and lower the level of free dust. Mix it in thoroughly. Then add a good handful (or two, depending on the size of the batch of hypertufa being mixed) of fluffed-up reinforcing fibers, sprinkling them over the surface of the cement mix, and liquid bonding agent. Add a little more water and mix thoroughly. Continue adding water in small amounts until the hypertufa mix is thoroughly moistened, but not so wet that excess water shows on the surface. Hypertufa is ready to work when a squeezed handful of the mixture is moist enough to hold together but does not produce excess water on its surface. Adding any more water beyond the amount necessary to create a plastic medium only dilutes the strength of the cement bond.

When the hypertufa reaches the proper consistency, begin packing it into the trough form. Start with the floor, packing the hypertufa by the handful, starting in the corners and working toward the center, until the floor is level with the drainage hole form or perhaps slightly higher in the corners. The drainage hole should be the lowest spot in the floor. Be certain to tamp very hard, compacting the floor as tightly as possible for added strength.

Next, raise the walls. Make the walls a thickness in proportion to the overall size of the trough: 1.5 inches (38 mm) is adequate for a trough 12 inches (30 cm) square, but larger troughs need the stability of walls 2–3 inches (50–75 mm) thick. Adding only 1 inch (2.5 cm) of height at a time to maintain the integrity, work around the walls of the trough, connecting the corners to form the base of the four walls. Do not complete each wall separately. Again, begin in the corners, using your fist to compact handfuls of the hypertufa tightly into the angles of the mold. Be certain that the corners are firm, well-packed, and slightly flared into the floor at their base to provide a good foundation for the walls above. Compact the hypertufa as tightly as possible, pushing both outward against the form wall and downward.

When you have built the trough walls as high as you wish, give the upper edge an extra measure of pounding, and you are finished—for the day. Wrap the plastic sheet up and completely around the trough and seal the cover with duct tape. Leave the trough to settle in for the first curing. If possible, move it to a spot out of direct sun for a slower cure.

Curing and Finishing

The curing time depends mostly on the size of the trough. A smaller trough, surprisingly, takes longer to cure than a large one. The initial (not total) curing time of a large trough is reduced to about twenty-four hours because of the greater heat generated by the chemical reaction within its larger mass and the better insulation of its thicker form walls. A skin forms on the outside of the walls relatively quickly, but the cores

PLATE 50. Rough-surfaced and free-form hypertufa troughs created by Roberta Berg of Wenham, Massachusetts, age and gather moss in the shade. Photograph by Joyce Fingerut

of the walls are still unconsolidated, so the trough must be handled with care even after it feels set on the surface.

The next step can take place anytime from two days to one week after the construction of the trough, depending on its size and the time you have available. When you are sure the trough is fully consolidated, unwrap the plastic sheet, but do not remove it from under the trough. Unwind the duct tape from the form and discard it; pull out the nails from the corners and save them. Carefully remove the form walls, which may be cleaned and reused. Do not remove the drainage hole forms—they are permanent.

Texturing the smooth walls will make your trough more closely resemble natural stone. This can be done with a wide variety of tools, as simple as a kitchen butter knife (the hypertufa is just that workable at this stage) or a garden weeding fork; my favorite combination is a screwdriver and a wire brush. Begin by rounding the sharp edges of the walls at the top, corners, and bottom. Work on the side walls by scoring

PLATE 51. A hand-built, free-form hypertufa rock made by Roberta Berg incorporates planting pockets; it can be used much like the natural tufa discussed in "Working with Tufa." Photograph by Joyce Fingerut

or gouging the surface in an even, steady rhythm; do not pull the walls outward or apply too much pressure on any one spot. Create fissures or scouring marks, pocking or pitting: the more you work it, the more naturally weathered and aged the trough will look. Save the crumbs of hypertufa scraped from the walls for a coordinated top-dressing (mulch) after the trough is planted.

When the trough walls are suitably worked and distressed, completely rewrap it, secure the plastic with duct tape, and leave it for its final curing. The ideal curing time, from the first wetting and mixing of the hypertufa, should be a full four weeks, although a day or so less will not make much difference. After the final curing is complete, unwrap the trough and use a small propane torch, or even a butane lighter, to burn off the protruding acrylic fibers. Keep the flame moving constantly so as not to overheat any one spot that may still contain bubbles of moisture. Finally, hose the trough down—and you're ready to plant!

Planting Troughs

REX MURFITT

Now that you have built a trough, you need to decide where to put it. Unless the trough is quite small, it will be very heavy once planted, so the filling and planting is best done in the final position. Small troughs should be protected from hot sun and drying winds; you will have to maintain a careful watch on the soil to be sure it doesn't dry out. Many alpine plants cannot tolerate fluctuations between wet and dry, and any prolonged period of total drought is fatal to all but a few xerophilic (drought-adapted) genera. Larger troughs, whose mass moderates such fluctuations, can be placed in sun or shade. Troughs designed for plants that need protection from rainfall can be situated under the eaves of a house. If you will need to move a trough into a building during winter, place it where you can easily move it with a wheeled hand-truck. A

PLATE 52. A classic British style of trough display sets them in gravelly spaces opened in pavement, with complementary plants growing around the base. Photograph by Joyce Fingerut

trough positioned by a frequently used doorway is a constant pleasure as you come and go, observing the slight daily changes in the plants.

Most alpine plants prefer to grow in open sunlight, where plenty of light ensures that they remain dwarf and compact and produce plenty of flowers. If you have plants that require some shade, put the trough in the lee of a tree or shrub. Do not put them directly under trees and shrubs or—unless drought is required—under overhanging roofs.

I usually set my troughs on four sturdy square masonry blocks to raise them a few inches above the ground. There is no horticultural reason for this: they just look more attractive, and they are certainly easier to enjoy when closer to the eye. Critics suggest that elevated troughs dry out more quickly or freeze more solidly, and roots may well gain a modicum of frost protection if the troughs are sitting on the soil surface during winter. If I lived in a region with hard winters, I might drop my troughs down for the winter. Protection from wind chill, too, is advantageous.

Soil Mixtures

Soil mixtures are constantly debated by gardeners. Indeed, so many recipes have been published that it can be confusing to the uninitiated reader (for more information, see "Soils"). Rock garden soils need to have just two essential qualities. First, the soil must drain fast, permitting excess water to run away rapidly. Second, the mixture should contain enough topsoil, or loam, to provide the basic nutrients needed for successful plant growth, along with some organic matter to serve as a sponge, retaining and regulating a reserve of moisture.

Soil drainage is increased by the addition of coarse sand and crushed rock, or grit. Coarse sand is usually available from building supply stores, but you will probably have to screen out the fines, the smaller particles and dustlike grains. (I use a sieve made with a mesh the size of window screen.) Add some crushed rock, grit, or gravel to the mixture. The actual size of these components is not critical, but I suggest a mixture of sizes from $\frac{1}{8}$ to $\frac{1}{4}$ inch (3 to 6 mm). A range of grits, nicely cleaned and bagged, can be obtained from feed stores and sometimes from suppliers of decorative rock. To increase acidity and fiber content, incorporate coarse peat moss, if you can get it; otherwise, rub block peat over a ¼-inch (6-mm) mesh sieve and use just the larger chunks left on the screen.

Use a good natural topsoil or loam that is not heavily enriched with manure or with organic or chemical fertilizers. Commercial soil mixtures are likely to contain amendments such as peat, manure, sand, lime, or fertilizers, as well as cheap organic materials such as bark, which can host fungi. Remove large stones and debris, preferably by hand rather than by forcing the soil through a screen. Breaking the clumps of soil by hand is an old-fashioned practice that retains beneficial fibers that would be lost in a screening process. It's not a big job with the quantities of soil needed for a trough.

A good basic soil mixture contains 4 parts topsoil, 2 parts sand, 2 parts gravel, and 1 part peat. If the topsoil is especially heavy clay or sandy, light loam, you may need to adjust the amount of sand and gravel. To avoid the danger of using too much peat, which is bad for drainage and air content, add it slowly to the mixture.

The confusing subject of lime in the soil often arises, especially if you study British and European books on rock gardening. Unless you wish to grow rare, choice, finicky ericaceous plants—tiny *Cassiope*, *Gaultheria*, or *Vaccinium*, for example—the presence or absence of lime is not a major problem. Many alpine plants are indifferent to it and thrive with traces of lime in the soil. However, if you live in an area with lime soils and limestone, you should avoid using your local topsoil, sands, gravels, and even the water for your lime-hating plants, and take care not to landscape the trough with limestone.

Some writers advocate spreading a layer of drainage material, or crocks, evenly across the bottom of the trough. A large, flat stone is placed over the drain hole to prevent soil from washing through. A thin mesh screen can be installed over the hole to bar undesirable creatures such as earthworms. This drainage material is then covered with a layer of something to prevent the soil mix from filtering into it, such as landscape fabric. One drawback of this drainage method is the space it takes up, leaving less room for nutritive soil. More important, however, research on container-grown nursery stock indicates that this drainage layer is neither necessary nor desirable. If the trough's drain hole becomes obstructed, stagnant water in the drainage layer can be very bad indeed for the plants. In fact, it is only necessary to provide exit holes that allow the free passage of water but not soil. I have several troughs of exactly the same size, each drained using one of these methods, and I cannot see any difference in the results. This suggests that you skip the extra step of a drainage, or crock, layer and simply fill the entire trough with the same soil mixture.

The Trough Landscape

Once you have filled your trough with soil, it's time to build the landscape. There is a great temptation to fill a new trough with all the plants and ideas you have bottled up inside. Traditionally, alpine trough gardens are designed to suggest a windswept mountainside, a fissured rock

PLATE 53. Sempervivums and other easy-to-grow plants quickly produce a pleasing trough landscape (made by Betsey Knapp). Photograph by Roslyn Bliss

outcrop, or perhaps a simple scree slope. All are excellent ideas as long as the design is kept simple, using as few design elements as possible. The pioneers of rock gardening used to build models of entire mountains, complete with snow painted on the summit. The scale was not convincing, however, so the whole idea was spoiled. It is easy to ruin the scale of a landscape in miniature, so steel yourself and limit your design to re-creating just one tiny feature.

A simple group of stones or even a single rock can evoke the alpine atmosphere, particularly if the stone is fractured with age and coated with lichen. Troughs can be landscaped effectively with one large porous stone, such as a piece of tufa or pumice. The plants are set in holes drilled into the rock (see "Working with Tufa"). Many alpine plants love this treatment and reward us with compact, iron-hard growth and copious flowers.

The main object of a trough garden is to display and enjoy the plants, and there can be no wasted space. I have developed a method I

PLATE 54. Flat rocks are often set in crevice fashion in troughs, as in this example made by Betsey Knapp. Photograph by Roslyn Bliss

call the "hamburger sandwich." To make this feature, select two stones of similar size that are flat on one side. Fit them together like a sandwich, with soil in between, and bury the lower part in the trough soil, deep enough to be securely in place. Now is the ideal time to set the plants between the stones, with their roots deeply into the sandwich soil and their heads just peeping out. Once they have made a little growth, they will form a natural-looking crevice planting. This technique is effective with saxifrages, drabas, and androsaces.

Many rock gardeners venerate landscapes that have weathered several seasons. The patina of age lent by mosses and lichens is considered the sign of a successful trough garden. Yet this is not necessary. Plant up a garden, enjoy it for a while, then redo it when you see fit. Just because the trough itself is made of concrete, the landscape does not have to be cast in stone!

Selecting Plants

Recommending plants suitable for trough culture makes me uneasy. It is not difficult to write up a list of plants based on qualities such as ultimate size or flower color. The trouble arises from two considerations: (1) the ability of a given species to survive in the many different climatic zones in North America; and (2) the unpredictable skills of individual gardeners. Local weather can be the limiting factor, regardless of the care lavished on the plants. A third concern is availability; it is maddening to read about a wonderful plant, only to find no nurseries offer it for sale. Nonetheless, it may help you if I recommend a few ideal trough subjects.

Scale is the first important factor, assuming that you have already considered your climate and the exposure of the site. A smaller trough nicely frames the little cushions of classic alpines, whereas a larger trough calls for bolder strokes in plant selection to create a scene in keeping with its setting. Dwarf woody plants—miniature trees and shrubs—are aesthetically pleasing and do well in a large trough. There are dwarf forms in just about every genus of plants, but be sure you

PLATE 55. Troughs incorporated into the garden landscape among dwarf conifers in the garden of Ernie and Marietta O'Byrne, Eugene, Oregon. Photograph by Nicholas Klise

know the ultimate size (or, more likely, the size to be expected in ten years) of every plant you consider: *dwarf* or *compact* does not necessarily mean trough-sized. A conifer can attain 10 feet (3 m) in height in as many years and still be considered dwarf in comparison to its 100-foot parent species.

The simplest trough planting showcases a single species or genus, such as *Gentiana verna* or a group of *Saxifraga* cultivars. In a more complex design, it is desirable to tie the planted trough into its surrounding landscape. Use a group of troughs rather than just one perched in isolation. Plant around the troughs, not just in them, using some of the same species or related ones. Plate 53 shows an often-used technique in which an open space in stone pavement hosts low plants surrounding a trough. Repetition creates a natural rhythm. Combine plants and appropriate rocks, local either to your site or to the native home of the plants, within and around the trough to create a naturalistic connection.

It is not always necessary to grow rare and difficult alpines. Why not stock your trough with a few easy plants and have some fun? A trouble-free planting can be made by purchasing a few sempervivums (commonly called "hens and chicks") from the garden center. Choose the smaller kinds and those with lots of red and purple coloration. The cobweb houseleek (*Sempervivum arachnoideum*) appeals to all and is a fairly fast grower, forming mats of compressed pink and green rosettes heavily netted with a web of fine white hairs. Sempervivums are content in shallow soil and follow the contours of the landscape, eventually flowing over the sides of the trough. The different varieties soon grow together in a carpet of red, brown, purple, gold, and apple-green. Add a couple of the less rampageous sedums and perhaps one of the easy smaller *Dianthus* species for variety. I use *Sedum hispanicum* and its forms that have gray leaves tipped with pink; *Sedum lydium*, domes of bright green that take on bronzy hues in summer; and *Sedum spathulifolium*, a western American species with several color selections.

If I were restricted to one genus for my trough gardens, I would certainly choose *Saxifraga*. Saxifrages offer a very wide range of shapes and sizes and, if anything epitomizes an alpine plant, the saxifrages do. Some are small plants with silvery foliage, carrying lots of large, bright flowers on tiny stems or in graceful arching plumes of white, pink, or yellow. They are perennial and evergreen, the silvery rosettes there to be admired all year. Flowering begins in early spring with the cushion saxifrages (section Porphyrion, formerly called Kabschias), hard mounds of silvery needlelike leaves clothed with flowers in shades of primrose yellow, gold, rose-pink, shell-pink, red, purple, or gleaming white, often enhanced by bright red stems. They do well in troughs, particularly in close association with rocks, where the roots can delve into the cool depths. Many do well planted directly in holes drilled into tufa.

The silver or encrusted saxifrages (section Ligulatae) are great rock garden plants, and the smaller-growing ones are wonderful in troughs. Despite their hard, leathery foliage, however, the silver saxifrages cannot tolerate blazing midday summer sun. They are generally winter-hardy except when caught by unseasonable cold spells. Absolute drainage is a must where there is much autumn and winter rain.

PLATE 56. A flat, graveled area at the Berry Botanic Garden, Portland, Oregon, displays a large number of troughs; some were made and planted forty years ago. Photograph by Bonnie Brunkow Olson

The *Saxifraga paniculata* group provides 'Minutifolia', a very old cultivar reputed to have been discovered by Reginald Farrer on Monte Baldo in the Dolomites of Italy around 1913. It is fairly undemanding. Each rosette is composed of blue-gray toothed leaves that become heavily lime-encrusted and, depending on cultural condition, may grow to 0.5 inch (1.3 cm) across. Once established, the plant flows across the miniature landscape over the rocks and soil to the sides, where it will hang down in the most natural manner. An ideal companion is the bright green leaf of *S. paniculata* 'Venetia', which have a noticeable red reverse. Look for *Saxifraga cochlearis* 'Minor' or any forms and hybrids of this species.

FURTHER READING

Joe Elliott, *Alpines in Sinks and Troughs*; Joyce Fingerut and Rex Murfitt, *Creating and Planting Garden Troughs*; Duncan Lowe, *Growing Alpines in Raised Beds, Troughs, and Tufa*

The Alpine House

LEE RADEN

The hearts of rock gardeners beat faster when they first learn of the alpine house, a vision of specialized gardening to surpass all others: row after row of rare miniature plants, blemish-free, bug-free, picture-perfect in every respect, with minimal maintenance and expense. I have been in thrall to this myth for forty years, and I have found that, in fact, the alpine house is an unforgiving master that takes all the effort one can give and rewards largely by whim. If you are now sufficiently discouraged, we can get on with this chapter.

An alpine house is a greenhouse that has been customized for the cultivation of plants that flourish in conditions of ample light, cool summers, and winters that are dry and barely above freezing. The features that must be added to a basic greenhouse include extra ventilation in the roof (probably aided by a powerful electric fan), some kind of shading, and, in colder climates, heating (see figure 9). Popular in Britain and Europe, alpine houses are little known in North America, where most rock gardeners who have them are specialists in genera such as *Saxifraga* and *Androsace*. Nevertheless, anyone who has ever walked into a well-stocked alpine house in late winter is likely to want one.

Most North Americans who have hobby greenhouses build them from kits. If you are starting with a kit, pay special attention to ventilation and light penetration. In hot-summer areas, a large, high-roofed greenhouse may offer advantages for controlling air circulation and keeping humidity low; if your summers are cool or if the alpine house will receive some afternoon shade, however, a small one with a big fan is perfectly adequate. Most good greenhouse suppliers can provide extra roof vents, which can be thermostatically controlled (although the sensors are prone to failure).

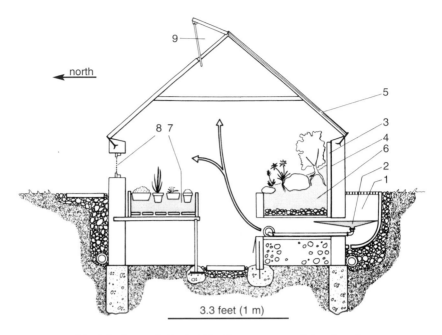

FIGURE 9. This alpine house design by Fritz Kummert, a noted Austrian plantsman, shows a structure set partially below grade to maximize heat retention in winter and coolness in summer. It has many special features designed for challenging alpine plants. (1) Outside air is drawn in on the south side through a grate-covered trench and a row of breeze blocks, passing through (2) a mist sprinkler that acts as an evaporation cooler. (3, 4) A solid south wall is insulated with moisture-proof membranes and a small wall built against it. (5) Shade cloth can be rolled down the south-facing roof in summer. (6) A scree mix fills the bed on the south side of the alpine house, which is landscaped with rocks and has plants set directly in it. (7) On the north side is a plunge bed for potted specimens. (8) Vents extend along the north side above the bench; the vents are covered with wire mesh in summer to keep out cats and birds and with glass in winter. (9) Vents in the roof may be automatic or manually operated. Drawing by F. Kummert. From F. Kummert, *Pflanzen für das Alpinenhaus*.

The classic British alpine house is glazed with glass, which offers maximum sunlight penetration. Greenhouse designers, however, are constantly developing new alternatives that are lighter and less break-able (for a discussion of glazing materials, see "Bulb and Alpine Frames"). The amount of light you will want depends on the range of plants grown: cacti and other western North American desert plants will require very high light levels, but Himalayan androsaces and Kabschia saxifrages need lower levels.

Royton E. Heath, in his masterpiece *Collectors' Alpines* (1983), makes several important points. he writes, "An alpine house is a place to flower plants that bloom early in the year," so both the gardener and his or her friends can enjoy flowers in a season when the garden is still sleeping. Moreover, "Some plants require individual attention if there is to be any reasonable chance for their successful cultivation," that is, the gardener must spend much time researching the plants' native habitats and cultivating them.

Heath concisely defines an alpine house as "a place to eliminate alternating cold and warm spells with attendant rain or icy conditions." He notes that "Many alpines have covering of fine hairs on their foliage. Sometimes this can be very woolly in appearance, giving protection against loss of moisture in their home environment. Here they have ever-moving air and hot sun ... [In the alpine zone] humidity is always at a premium during the growing season." This characteristic of exposed alpine zones is reversed in the lowlands of England, Europe, and eastern North America, however, where summer humidity is the norm and woolly plants rot before our eyes.

In the alpine zone, "plants are protected in the winter months by snow which keeps them at a perfect 32–33°F (0–1°C), dry, and in a state of suspended animation." Lowland gardens in winter are more likely to experience repeatedly melting snow, cold rain, or ice; all this moisture is absorbed by the plant, which dies from the surfeit. An alpine house that has dry heat (for example, from a propane heater) alleviates this problem and provides the buoyant atmosphere necessary to keeping alpines healthy over winter. Not all rock garden specialties grow near the eternal snows, however, and Heath points out that "plants of borderline hardiness can be brought along."

I have had two alpine houses. The first was a freestanding glass-to-ground structure measuring 24 feet (7.2 m) long, 15 feet (4.5 m) wide, and 10 feet (3.0 m) high. It was framed in redwood and single-glazed glass and oriented east–west on its long axis. It had no roof vent. A propane forced-air heater warmed it in winter. To control humidity in summer, the alpine house had two window-type air conditioners, which kept humidity around 40 percent; the temperature never exceeded 80°F (27°C). Shade was provided by black ash trees that leafed out in early May—this was perfect climate control. The air conditioning fans kept a small gale blowing through the house. I kept night temperatures in winter between 34°F (1°C) and approximately 45°F (7°C). Minimum temperature controls winter dormancy. Circulating hot air in the winter months provides the very low humidity essential to plants in dormancy and semi-dormancy.

In 1976, I built a lean-to, glass-to-ground, aluminum-frame greenhouse. It measures 26 feet (7.8 m) long, 10 feet (3.0 m) wide, and 10 feet (3.0 m) high. Against its solid wall is a bench (the wide table that holds potted plants) and two shelves, one above the other, each measuring 22 feet (6.6 m) long and 20 inches (50 cm) wide. This setup offers the same bench area as one would have in a freestanding alpine house with benches on either side of a center aisle.

This alpine house faces due south on its long axis. There are no trees nearby, so from May to October it is shaded with 63 percent shadecloth

PLATE 57. A classic European alpine house at the Würzburg Botanic Garden, with curator Michael Kammerlander. In essence, a tufa rock garden has been built directly on the benches. Photograph by David Hale

(a woven plastic material available in various densities). Without the shadecloth, temperatures inside might reach 120°F (49°C). An 18-inch (45-cm) diameter exhaust fan runs continually all summer, day and night, in the upper northwestern corner of the alpine house. The air inlet shutters are placed in the southeastern corner at ground level. This arrangement sweeps the complete alpine house and exhausts the air content every fifteen seconds, supplying the buoyant atmosphere and evaporative cooling essential to the plants. In winter, the rheostat is turned down so fan speed is much reduced, but on sunlit winter days the temperature is kept to a maximum of 50°F (10°C). A propane heater is placed 5 feet (1.5 m) aboveground in the western end so that hot air is blown the length of the house. A ceiling fan set at very low speed is used to equalize circulation from top to bottom.

The benches have steel frames filled with treated wood slats, covered with gravel. (Greenhouse suppliers now offer PVC grids for use in benches; although expensive, they require no maintenance.) The benches run east–west on both sides of the alpine house and are 3 feet (0.9 m) wide. They are somewhat higher than standard greenhouse benches, 31 inches (78 cm). This is a good level for someone my height—I don't have to bend down as far to water, fertilize, look for bugs, and groom the plants. The extra height also provides under-the-bench growing and storage space for tall plants and dormant pots. I garden in central Pennsylvania, at latitude 40°7' N; winter sun floods into the space under the bench, but no sun reaches the area during summer.

Alpine house growers often debate the question, "To plunge or not to plunge?" In this context, plunge means to fill the bench with a medium such as coarse sand and sink the pots to their rims in the medium. Doing this moderates soil temperature; if the plants are grown in clay pots, this technique also moderates moisture so well that dormant plants need not be watered, receiving enough moisture from the slightly watered surrounding plunge medium. I have been plunging pots for about ten years now. The plunge bed on one bench is filled 6 inches (15 cm) deep with builder's sand. I have not noticed much difference in survival and flowering with identical plants grown in or out of the plunge, but summers are very humid in central Pennsylvania; growers in dry-summer regions find that pot-grown alpines do far better if plunged.

Watering is the most important aspect of gardening under glass. With alpines, one must understand the moisture requirements of the individual plants through the growing and dormancy periods. Indiscriminate, uninformed watering spells doom to many plants. If you want to have an alpine house, you must make some arrangement to water the plants when you are traveling. Some growers rely on plunged pots and an automatic watering system that keeps the soil and plunge medium just moist enough. Most, however, try to find a plant caretaker who can listen and learn. Otherwise, the grower is a slave to the alpine house: no long weekends, no vacations. The house must be checked

PLATE 58. The alpine house at Stonecrop Garden and Nursery in New York, created by Frank Cabot and Rex Murfitt. In a large alpine house, a four-sided bench can be built in the middle, as shown here. Photograph by Pamela Harper

once a day in winter, and twice a day (if the sun is out) the rest of the time. I check every pot for moisture content by lifting and weighing it in my hand to determine if it is too heavy (too wet) or too light (too dry). In the pots, a free-draining medium with plenty of air space must be used (see "Soils"), or you will certainly lose many plants in the winter when they are semi-dormant or dormant.

It is a myth that one should not fertilize alpines, especially those in pots. If you use a fast-draining, open soil, you need to fertilize. Most growers prefer soluble fertilizers, which should be low in nitrogen relative to phosphorus and potassium; products formulated to increase flowering should be suitable, but you should mix them at half the strength recommended for annuals and food plants. It's where and when you fertilize that can get you into trouble, however. I apply half-strength liquid fertilizer twice a month during the period when plants are in active growth but have not set buds. After they set buds, I stop fertilizing until after bloom, and then resume fertilizing until the plants show signs of going dormant; these signs appear in the foliage, which starts to change color and become dull on the surface, or in the case of bulbs, withers completely. When growing alpines in pots, you must be keenly aware of when they break dormancy. Color, active growth, a subtle show of buds, and elongation of stems are all signs telling you to start fertilizing. It is this initial fertilizing that leads to brilliant results and healthy plants.

Why go to all this effort? For the joy of viewing a plant grown to perfection. Months and even years of research and patient care brings you to the wonderful moment when the plant breaks into bloom. In the alpine house, even if a storm is raging outside, you can pick up a pot and savor the perfect plant.

FURTHER READING

Royton E. Heath, *Collectors' Alpines: The Cultivation in Frames and Alpine Houses*; Fritz Kummert, *Pflanzen für das Alpinenhaus*; Robert Rolfe, *The Alpine House: Its Plants and Purposes*

Bulb and Alpine Frames

JANE McGARY

A frame is a low, covered structure designed to protect plants from extremes of weather. The plants within a frame may be grown directly in a soil medium filling the frame or in pots set directly on the ground or raised above the surrounding soil level with some sort of fill. The most familiar term is *cold frame*, typically a simple box with a glass or other light-transmitting cover (called a "light") set at a rain-shedding angle. Here seedlings can be raised while protected from frost and rain. Adding soil-heating cables makes it a *heated frame*.

For growers of specialized plant collections, the frame can be more than a propagating area. Where winters are not too severe, most of the plants typically grown in alpine houses (see "The Alpine House") can also be maintained in a frame. Collections of rare bulbs, especially in winter-wet climates, are often kept in frames, either in plunged pots or planted directly in the soil fill. The term *bulb frame* thus denotes a structure designed to control moisture first and temperature second. Most rock gardeners will want some sort of frame for propagating and growing plants until they are ready to be planted out in the garden, and any of the structures described in this chapter can be used for those purposes (see also "Propagation Facilities"). The main intent here, however, is to describe the use of frames as permanent growing sites.

Frames are often constructed adjacent to greenhouses or alpine houses, but they can also substitute for them. Frames are much cheaper and easier to build. Because they take less space and are less visually obtrusive, frames may be permitted in planned developments where greenhouses are not. Compared with alpine houses, frames are easier to ventilate thoroughly and seem to have fewer problems with fungus and insect infestation; however, it is far more comfortable to work inside an alpine house than to stoop over a frame, and visitors can see the plants

PLATE 59. Bulb frames and raised propagating beds used by the author in northwestern Oregon. Photograph by Jane McGary

better when they are displayed on a bench. The alpine house provides more protection against night cooling, but this does not necessarily benefit the plants.

Site

On a small property, the gardener may not have the luxury of choosing an ideal site, but success is more likely if exposure to sun and wind is considered. For almost every class of plants, good air circulation is necessary, so the frame should be situated where the prevailing breezes blow through it when the lights are partly open. Many bulbous plants and alpines revel in full sun during their growing season, but some high-alpine genera such as *Saxifraga* and *Androsace* need protection from hot lowland summer sun, and bulb species from woodland or scrub habitats tolerate partial shade. It is easiest to place the frame in full sun and then shade parts of it for those plants that need it. Avoid the northern side of a building or the shade of conifers, unless the frame is to be used primarily for starting cuttings or growing woodland plants. Narrow frames are often built along the outside of a greenhouse.

Place the frame as far as possible from large trees to avert two catastrophes: damage from falling branches and invasion by squirrels and chipmunks. It also makes maintenance easier in that leaves do not fall onto the lights or blow into the frame. Tree pollen and honeydew from insect-infested trees are difficult to clean off the panes.

A flat site is most convenient for both construction and gardening. Where only a slope is available, it can be terraced to accommodate the frame. If the frame is set transverse to the slope and sunk to the rim on the uphill side, it should be narrow enough to be tended from the downhill side alone, because reaching into it from the uphill side would be awkward. Prepare the site by grading it flat. Use a string and stakes to check for unevenness where the sides will rest. A long frame can have a slight degree of slope from end to end. If the site is poorly drained, install drainage tiles or perforated pipes or plan for an extra layer of stone at the base of the fill. On light or deeply disturbed soil, use a lawn roller to compact the ground before starting to build.

Allow plenty of room for walking and working around the frame. The path should accommodate a large wheelbarrow or garden cart and should be wide enough for a small group of visitors to view the plants or for the gardener to wield long-handled tools. The minimum adequate space between parallel rows of frames is 4 feet (1.2 m). The path surface should provide safe, comfortable footing in wet weather. If possible, surround the entire frame with a zone of weed-proof material such as woven groundcloth (which can be topped with a mulch if desired) to prevent infestation by running grasses or other pests; alternatively, use a gravel path sprayed with herbicide when necessary (see also "Paths and Hardscaping").

Design

A frame is just a box with a lid. To plan the box, you must decide on the dimensions. Remember that a larger frame moderates temperature better—and you will *never* have more frame space than you want. Length is determined by site size, available funds, and the gardener's ambition. Depth depends on the types of plants to be grown and how deep a root run they need. For most bulbs and alpines, allow 2–3 inches (50–75 mm) of drainage material (if used) and at least 12 inches (30 cm) of plunge medium above it, with a few inches of frame foundation above the surface of the plunge. Two railroad ties stacked with their wider sides facing out or three boards measuring 2 × 8 feet (0.6 × 2.4 m) provide adequate depth for most purposes. Width must permit the gardener to reach all the plants. If access is possible from both sides, the frame can be 4–5 feet (1.2–1.5 m) wide; if from only one side, half that.

Several general frame forms exist. In the shed frame (shown uncovered in plate 61), one long side is higher than the other. The lights can be attached to the higher side and open at the lower side, the only access, or completely removable to permit access to both sides. This form is feasible for even the least handy of builders. It has some disadvantages, however. The shed frame must be quite narrow if the lights are permanently attached. If they are removable, it is awkward to work

PLATE 60. Colorful display of *Erythronium*, *Narcissus*, and *Fritillaria* in the bulb frame. Photograph by Jane McGary

from the high side, and the lights must be stored somewhere when removed. Finally, air circulation is not as good in a shed frame as in one with full cross-ventilation.

The A-frame form (figures 10 and 11) incorporates a structure that is set on the sides and supports the lights, which are permanently attached with hinges at the ridge. Building this style in wood requires good carpentry skills because of its many angle cuts. The A-frame must be sturdy and well braced so that it does not warp. The span between the A-shaped trusses should be no more than 4 feet (1.2 m), a handy measure because glazing materials come in 2- and 4-foot (0.6- and 1.2-m)

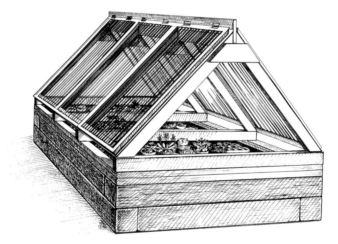

FIGURE 10. A-frame with permanently open vents below the lights, which are supported when open by aluminum conduit. Drawing by Sukey McDonough

FIGURE 11. A-frame with attached supports that permit the lights to be adjusted to a wide range of openings. Drawing by Sukey McDonough

widths. Calculate the necessary height of the support and the width of the box by using the length of the light as the hypotenuse of a right triangle. (Recall that $c^2 = a^2 + b^2$, where c is the length of the hypotenuse [the longest side] and a and b are lengths of the other sides.) This form has many advantages: good air circulation, wind resistance, and strength under snow load. Taller plants can be grown in the center and shorter ones toward the edges.

A rectangular support structure is framed like a miniature building and glazed both on top and the sides. This design is used in the commercial Access, frames. A bit easier to build than the A-frame, it offers good air circulation when both sides are open. Tall plants can be grown even at the outer edges, although this is not a need of most rock gardeners. The sides, being vertical, can be glazed with lighter, cheaper material, even sheet polyethylene. However, rectangular frames are prone to wind damage, and the flat roof cannot support much snow. Working around the side lights can be awkward unless they are removable.

A fourth possibility is the tunnel frame, a support structure made of PVC pipe hoops anchored to base boards and covered with polyethylene film. This requires no carpentry skills at all—just a hacksaw, a hammer, and a can of glue. This design is suitable primarily for a small frame, oriented so air circulates lengthwise over the plants through the open ends. The support should be made in separate sections no more than 4 feet (1.2 m) long, which can be removed and stacked when the frame is open. Such a cover is very susceptible to wind damage and must be anchored firmly to the box, but it sheds snow well. It is tedious to remove the covers every time you need access to the plants, and the polyethylene is short-lived, can't be recycled, and does not transmit light as well as other glazing materials. Therefore, the tunnel frame is suitable only as a temporary measure.

Several methods have been devised for supporting hinged lights at various heights. Galvanized steel conduit, which is cheap and easy to cut with a hacksaw, is a good material for the support poles. In most climates, much of the time the frame is left open at a level that maximizes

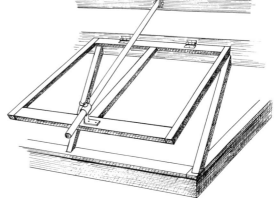

FIGURE 12. Detail of the attached supports. The conduit pipe is attached at the top bracket with a cotter pin on which it rotates and at the bottom with a pressure bolt and wingnut. Drawing by Sukey McDonough

air circulation and minimizes exposure to rain and snow. If the frame is not more than 20 feet (7 m), leaving the ends open to the prevailing wind can be adequate; a removable endpiece can be installed during severe cold periods. Gardeners in milder climates may prefer a design with permanent ventilation (figure 10), protecting the plants during severe cold spells with a removable plug or an insulating row cover.

Figures 11 and 12 depict a system in which the lights are supported from above at any desired height by a rod held by a pressure bolt mechanism. The tube-and-bolt fitting must be custom-made by a metal fabricator. This design works very well but is a bit fragile, and care must be taken not to leave the lights raised above the horizontal in windy conditions. The upper ridge piece must be strongly braced and rigid.

Materials

All materials used in the frame must be resistant to moisture: wood should be pressure-treated and hardware specified for outdoor use—galvanized steel, aluminum, or brass. The glazing material has to be heavy enough to withstand anticipated weather conditions, such as high wind and snow. The base, or box, must be sturdy enough to support the lights and contain the fill without collapsing or warping. The box can be built of any of the following materials:

RAILROAD TIES. Pros: sturdy, reasonably long-lasting, need little or no maintenance, good insulators, quick to assemble. Cons: difficult to move very far by hand, difficult to cut to length, uneven surfaces require shimming, shed smelly creosote and splinters. Railroad ties (known in the United Kingdom as "sleepers") are treated with preservatives, but no adverse effect on plants has been documented. When purchasing ties, examine the stock carefully and buy the best grade available; otherwise you may end up with splintered, decomposing, or very uneven ties. Useful tools for working with ties include logging tongs, a chain saw, and a heavy-duty drill with a long bit. Stacked ties should be connected by steel reinforcing rod inserted into drilled holes, or (more easily) by short lengths of waste lumber nailed or screwed to the inner surfaces.

PRESSURE-TREATED WOOD. Pros: reasonably long-lasting if treated periodically, easy to carry, saw, and assemble, available in standard sizes. Cons: warps and shrinks, requires repeated preservative treatment, too thin to insulate effectively. Consider this option only for small frames with lightweight superstructures, such as the shed frame. To prevent loss of fill material when the boards shrink, line the inside with woven groundcloth before filling.

CONCRETE BLOCKS. Pros: last indefinitely without maintenance, fairly easy to move, available in standard sizes, fair insulating properties. Cons: require excellent site leveling and masonry skills, attaching wooden or metal superstructure may be difficult.

POURED CONCRETE. Pros: can be relatively inexpensive, lasts indefinitely without maintenance. Cons: intensive site preparation, requires specialized skills and equipment, difficult to remove, poor insulator. Poured concrete frames are used for commercial production of alpines at Scotland's famed Ardfearn Nursery and are an economical choice for large, permanent installations. The construction is similar to pouring a foundation for a small building and should be easily accomplished by any concrete contractor. Angle iron or other permanent metal supports for the lights should be installed with bolts at the time the concrete is poured.

The frame superstructure can be made of wood or metal. Commercial frame covers are usually made of aluminum. If you intend to use aluminum covers, buy them before you build your foundation to ensure a good fit. A metal fabricator can weld together a custom superstructure. Most home gardeners, however, will probably build their frame supports of lumber, either pressure-treated or rot-resistant woods such as red cedar.

Do not skimp on the quality and sturdiness of the lumber and hardware. The frame must be relatively rigid and must withstand wind and perhaps snow. All hinges, bolts, screws, and other metal parts should be galvanized steel or brass, intended for outdoor use. Extra rigidity can be added by reinforcing corner joints with toothed metal plates that are simply hammered in.

After the supporting structure is in place, the glazing material is fitted into its frames, and these are attached to the support with the hinges. (If high winds are a problem, you may wish to add U-bolts to the lower part of the light frame and to the base, so you can tie the lights down with shock cords when necessary.) A variety of glazing materials is available. The very cheapest is the clear sheet plastic (polyethylene film) used to cover commercial greenhouses. It should be at least 6 mil (0.15 mm) thick and can be tacked or stapled onto the frames, where it will survive a year or two. More permanent choices are described below. You may find other materials in a visit to a greenhouse manufacturer, but none are inexpensive.

CORRUGATED FIBERGLASS. Pros: inexpensive, lightweight, easy to cut, no danger of shattering. Cons: relatively poor light transmission, becomes opaque and brittle with age, not very rigid. A good choice for removable covers that are used only in inclement weather.

POLYCARBONATE (LEXAN®). Pros: lightweight, tough and resilient, easy to cut, no danger of shattering, excellent light transmission. Cons: expensive, not very rigid. Polycarbonate is an excellent material for permanent lights.

PLEXIGLAS. Pros: rigid, excellent light transmission, medium weight. Cons: expensive, difficult to cut, tougher than glass, but can still shatter on impact.

GLASS. Pros: rigid, excellent light transmission, resists scratching, moderate price. Cons: difficult to cut, shatters on impact, heavy.

If it is necessary to shade the plants in your frame, the best solution is nursery shadecloth, which comes in a range of shade percentages. It can be tacked onto the inside of the frame (where it will be more effective than it would be on the outside). If the lights are removable, the shadecloth can be draped over a lightweight support made of PVC pipe. In the large frame shown in figure 10, shadecloth is hung from the ridge pole to shade the northern half of the frame in summer, providing good conditions for woodland bulbs, lily seedlings, and other plants that prefer cool conditions. Low-growing shade-lovers and seedlings can also be accommodated by placing them against the southern side of the frame, where the rise of the foundation offers a few inches of shade.

Plunge Medium

Plants grown in pots almost always do best if the pots are plunged—sunk to their rims in a sterile medium. The best plunge material is coarse, gritty sand. If only fine sand is obtainable, mix it with fine crushed rock to improve its drainage. Do not make the material too loose, however, or you will have trouble excavating holes for the pots.

Before filling the frame with the plunge material, line the bottom with a barrier to tunneling rodents: hardware cloth, aviary wire (similar to chicken wire but with a smaller mesh), or woven plastic nursery groundcloth are suitable. If groundwater is likely to be a problem, place a layer of large-diameter round (river) gravel or a similar drainage material on the base to prevent too much water being sucked up into the level holding the plants. A layer of woven plastic groundcloth above this will keep the gravel free of fines from above.

If you have potted plants ready to place in the new frame, it is easiest to lay down 2–3 inches (50–75 mm) of plunge sand, set the pots in place, and fill in around them with sand. A large scoop is handy for this operation. After adding the sand to the level of the pot rims, run a hose on the sand to settle it (provided the plants can tolerate moisture at this time).

Frame Management

For best results, the ventilation of the frame should be adjusted in accordance with ambient temperature: fully closed during severe cold; slightly open most of the time; and fully open in mild, dry weather. Air circulation is much better in two-sided frames, where the lights on both sides can be raised slightly. The frame shown in figure 10, designed for

PLATE 61. Spring bloom in the bulb frame. Photograph by Jane McGary

cold-hardy bulbs in a cool temperate climate, has permanent cross-ventilation openings below the lights; extra frost protection, needed only a few nights a year, is supplied by laying sheets of microfoam plant blanket directly over the plants. A handy device for monitoring frame temperature is a wireless remote thermometer, which broadcasts temperature readings to a base unit in the house; the base unit records maximum and minimum temperatures and may have a frost alarm.

Frames with lights that cannot be removed need to be irrigated. Gardeners with an extensive range of frames may prefer to install drip irrigation, but I find that hand-watering—even with more than a thousand pots—is a good opportunity to observe the individual plants closely and to micromanage their moisture regimes.

Frames housing a large collection of plants are easier to use with some accessories nearby. These might include a potting bench with tool storage; a place to store fertilizer and chemicals; a sturdy kneeling pad or low gardener's seat; a bin for mixing compost; a plastic garbage can for mixing liquid fertilizer; and a moisture-proof container for notes, pencils, seed envelopes, and spare labels.

FURTHER READING

Brian Mathew, *Growing Bulbs: The Complete Practical Guide*; Roger Phillips and Martyn Rix, *The Random House Book of Bulbs*; Martyn Rix, *Growing Bulbs*

Rock Gardening on a Balcony

LAWRENCE THOMAS

For those who aren't blessed with the space to create an in-ground rock garden, there is an alternative: contained gardening. Think small—but in a big way. I garden on an eleventh floor, 13 × 40 foot (3.9 × 12 m) terrace in the heart of Manhattan. The long exposure faces east and the short south, which gives the terrace full sun from sunrise until midafternoon. This exposure effectively protects the terrace from the prevailing northwesterly winds, a major consideration for this type of gardening. Some terrace or balcony gardeners, particularly those with southern or western exposures, find heat build-up to be a problem. Late-afternoon sunshine can both overheat and burn plants. Makeshift shade of some sort, usually a canopy, is then a necessity. Other gardeners with exposures similar to mine have trouble with wind. This must be dealt with, usually with hedge windbreaks to deflect strong prevailing winds. If you know you want a balcony garden, try to find an apartment with an eastern exposure and in the lee of the building.

The flooring of my terrace consists of 1-foot (0.3-m), square concrete blocks mounted at each corner on plastic supports that elevate the blocks off the underlying waterproof membrane. Although the building is constructed of steel and concrete, there are restrictions that require that the weight of any large planter box be spread evenly over several blocks. Because all large containers must be elevated 2 inches (5 cm) above the deck, sections of 2 × 4 lumber serve well. Elevating the containers also protects the underlying roof from invasive roots. Don't forget, you are responsible for any leaks below. (If that doesn't cause a shudder or two, you're not cut out to be a terrace gardener.)

Everything I grow is in planter boxes, troughs, pans, or pots. There are virtues as well as drawbacks in such gardening constraints. Many choice alpine plants, once taken away from their rigorous native habitats, adapt better to life in containers than in the open ground. You can customize the growing situation to cater to each plant's basic needs, manipulating the size and depth of the container and specifics such as soils and microclimates. You can also protect vulnerable gems such as *Campanula zoysii* from the predators that bedevil ground-level gardeners. No deer and fewer slugs and other critters! Landed gardening friends will envy the apartment-dweller for that.

Alpines are tough little high-mountain plants that have adapted to rigors of wind, solar radiation, and exposure that would kill many other plants; yet, if you can meet their basic needs, many alpines adjust readily to lowland conditions—slumming, as it were, with their lowland kin. Knowledge of the plant's growth habit and native conditions is essential, requiring some homework on your part (see the section

PLATE 62. Hand-thrown pots and strawberry jars add interest to Lawrence Thomas's balcony rock garden. Photograph by Lawrence Thomas

"Plants for the Rock Garden" in the bibliography for books offering information on this). Choosing the proper container requires some thought. Some plants have very small, shallow root systems; others have long, fibrous roots that can run several feet in rocky crevices. Hence, the size of the container is important. Overpot an alpine primula, for instance, and it simply will sit and sulk, whereas choice campanulas require deeper pots (the English call them "long toms") for their extensive root runs, and they still need to be repotted every other year.

Don't crock your pots with shards as older books often recommend; this merely encourages ants, slugs, sowbugs, and similar pests to take up residence. Instead, use wire or plastic screen mesh, which keeps the pests at bay and also ensures the good drainage crucial to success with these "miffy" plants.

A standard soil mix should incorporate at least 50 percent grit (such as poultry grit or aquarium gravel) to promote quick drainage and allow sufficient oxygen to reach the roots. This is critical: alpines drown quickly in soggy soil. Most lime-loving plants accommodate to acid soil, but the converse is not true. Acid-lovers such as rhododendrons and azaleas are likely to fail in alkaline soil, so be sure your grit is not limestone. Once again, container gardening provides an easy solution. Simply tailor the soil to the plant's needs. Check your pots periodically and renew the soil as needed, adding compost, leafmold, or peat moss to rejuvenate it. Most campanulas respond to this, because they exhaust the soil after a year or so.

When planting, it is wise to bare-root most new plants by dipping them repeatedly in water, rolling the roots in sand, and replanting in your own soil medium. They'll establish more quickly, and removing the soil prevents the introduction of the slug eggs, grubs, and weevils that sometimes arrive in nursery soil. Top-dressing with gravel, chicken grit, or a fired clay product such as Turface, benefits the plant by keeping its crown dry, something many alpines appreciate; it also adds a decorative touch.

Establish a regular watering and fertilizing schedule. Learn to tell when a plant needs water by hefting the pot and feeling its weight. In a terrace or balcony situation, most clay pots require daily watering, particularly in summer; plastic pots are less likely to need such frequent watering. Fertilize regularly (every two to three weeks) during the active growth season with a quarter-strength dose of soluble fertilizer. I normally use a popular chemical fertilizer with a 20–20–20 formula and sometimes supplement this with a smelly but highly effective organic fermented fish fertilizer in a 1.4–0.2–0.2 formula. (An exception is penstemons in pots, which need only one weak dose early in the growing season.) Stop fertilizing in late summer to give the plants an opportunity to harden their new growth before the onset of frost.

When I first began terrace gardening thirty-five years ago, soft coal and oil with high sulfur content were the main fuels for our power plants. This made city gardening—even city living—a particularly dirty business. Because these fuels have been phased out in favor of natural gas, the situation has changed dramatically. Still, as part of my daily watering routine, I spray all my plants, giving them a daily shower. Besides minimizing pollution effects, this helps cut down on insect predation.

Some plants need a bit of winter protection—not from the cold, but from moisture. Plants such as dryland ferns or *Campanula raineri* should be kept dry from first hard frost until they break into active growth in the spring. Putting them under a potting bench, shelf, or table should suffice.

Hypertufa troughs are an ideal container for terraces and balconies (for details, see "Making Troughs"). Their medium, a cement-based mixture laced with perlite, peat moss, and plastic fibers instead of stony aggregate, effectively reduces the weight of the container while strengthening it. Raised on upended cinder blocks, troughs become the focal point of any terrace garden, and most alpines and rock garden plants thrive in them. Adding sizable chunks of tufa or other rock can

PLATE 63. Even on a balcony, complementary plant combinations can be devised: *Platycodon grandiflorum* and small hostas. Photograph by Lawrence Thomas

simulate natural outcrops and provide the crannies and crevices in which many alpines love to grow.

A real virtue of container gardening is portability. You can stage-manage your terrace by shifting containers to display whatever has "star power" at the moment. You also can screen specimens that have bloomed out behind other plants, or confine those that predators have chewed on to sick bay for a period of recuperation. And in the unlikely event that something actually dies, you can quickly conceal the sad event and fill the gap.

One of my gardening friends says, with much truth, that we city folk garden in spite of the odds. Everything conspires against us, yet we labor on, determined to tame the asphalt jungle with our patches of civilized greenery. Our breed are natural-born scavengers, accustomed to making do with whatever is at hand. If that means picking it up on the street, so be it. Some of our best finds are street finds—road kill, so to speak, somebody else's trash—that we simply can't pass up. Some friends found a splendid antique lead planter sitting on the street, waiting to be picked up by the trash collector. The fact that they were on their way to a formal reception was no reason to pass up such a treasure, so, dressed to the nines, they walked home lugging a handsome piece that became the centerpiece of their terrace garden.

Obtaining supplies is often a problem in the city because prohibitive rents have driven most nursery or garden-supply operations out to the suburbs. Without a car, the problem is compounded. Hence, suburban friends and their autos are often pressed into service to help the urban gardener truck in heavy bags of topsoil, sand, grit, peat, leafmold, manure, containers, and plants. You name it, we covet it and we tote it up stairs, or, if we're lucky, in a service elevator. If you're not so lucky, be prepared for neighborly sniffs and snubs when you conscript the front public elevator to transport your horticultural necessities.

Soil, of course, is the backbone of gardening, and the terrace gardener quickly becomes expert at recycling precious soil again and again, repeatedly enriching it with whatever he can scrounge. One gardening friend attributes his considerable success with alpine clematis solely to the beech leafmold he gathers furtively in Manhattan's Central Park. Another hounds his neighbors into saving scraps—garbage, mind you—which he takes regularly to a local green market, where they are composted and returned periodically to him as rich, black gold, the ideal soil enhancement. A compost pile may be a given for most gardeners, but the urban terrace gardener must improvise in any way possible. The same is true of such niceties as bulb or cold frames, for which there simply isn't room. As a substitute, I've begun using the heavy-walled Styrofoam containers in which frozen meat is shipped, covered with frosted glass salvaged from the vegetable crisper of a discarded refrigerator. This make-do cold frame has worked beautifully for wintering over tender bulbs and plants that require protection from winter wet. Such measures may amuse the in-ground gardener; for us aerial alpinists, they are a way of life.

The Broadway moppet Annie sings, "It's a hard-knock world." Any terrace gardener can respond to that, for ours often seems a strictly uphill climb. Still, the red-headed orphan also offers us the promise of "Tomorrow," to which any gardener worth his tilth would agree. The pessimists may say gloomily, "You should have seen it last week." For us optimists, there's always next week.

Propagation Facilities

RICK LUPP

Plant propagation is an integral part of rock gardening. First, many of the plants you may wish to grow are simply not available in the nursery trade; the only way to get them is by growing them yourself from seeds or cuttings obtained from friends, seed exchanges, professional seed collectors, or other sources. Another compelling reason to propagate your own plants is to ensure that once you obtain a plant, you can produce more, so that if your original plant dies, all is not lost. Many rare plants that come into cultivation from seed or plants collected from the wild are not collected again for many years, and even after they reach gardens, the plants may not be available from a commercial source for many years, if ever. A small supply of starts of your best plants is also invaluable as trading material for other desiderata for your own collection or simply as gifts to bring a smile to the face of your rock gardening friends.

The typical rock gardener or alpine-house owner uses three principal methods of plant propagation: growing from seed, propagating cuttings (including root and leaf cuttings), and division. Grafting may also be used for such plants as the smaller *Daphne* species and certain dwarf conifers.

Growing from Seed

Growing from seed is a wonderful undertaking, filled with suspense and gratification. Will the seed germinate? Will the plants be true to name? Will you get a new color form or a worthwhile hybrid? All these possibilities and more face the seed grower and add interest to the undertaking: every seedling is a new entity with its own potential. Another good reason to grow from seed is that you will not be bringing some other garden's pests and viruses into your garden, as you might with cuttings or plants.

Many different methods of seed growing have been devised by legions of gardeners, from simply sowing the seed in the open garden to elaborate systems of lights and heating cables. The seeds of many plants of interest to the rock gardener require stratification, a process in which seed sown in pots is exposed to low temperatures until the minimum chilling requirement for the species is met. Gardeners in temperate climates have no problem meeting these requirements by keeping their seed pots outdoors over winter. Temperatures around 40°F (4°C) or lower for a prolonged period will do the job. The seed should be sown in a free-draining, moisture-retentive, relatively sterile soil mix and covered with a thin layer of fine grit. Typical components used in seed mixes include peat moss, coarse sand, ground pumice, perlite, and vermiculite; poultry grit or aquarium gravel may be employed as the top-dressing.

Many experienced seed growers leave their seed pots outside until the seed begins to germinate. In this case, the pots should not be simply placed out on the ground to fend for themselves—the seed is likely to

PLATE 64. Rick Lupp starts hundreds of pots of seed annually on shelves in a simple polyfilm hoop house. Photograph by Rick Lupp

be scratched out by birds or washed out by heavy rainfall. The emerging plants are also likely to be attacked by slugs and snails or forced out of the soil by castings of earthworms that find their way into the pots via the drainage holes. Most of these problems can be overcome by building a simple shelf or bench, placed in a well-lit spot, to hold the seed pots above ground level. Cover them with a large piece of cheesecloth, and you will eliminate the problems of birds and heavy rain. The cheesecloth allows water and light to pass through and is easy to lift to check for germination.

Some seed growers prefer to start their seeds under the benches of an alpine house or unheated greenhouse. Here, the flats holding the seed pots (or sown directly with seed) can be placed right on the floor, as long as the light is ample and there is adequate air circulation. Poor air circulation and high humidity cause damp-off, a fungus that kills many new seedlings. A simple cold frame or a small plastic hoop house works just as well as an elaborate alpine house for the purpose of starting seed, as long as the structure offers bright light, good air circulation, and protection from predators.

I start all the seeds for my alpine nursery operation in a simple 20 × 15–foot (6.0 × 4.5–m) hoop house (sheet polyethylene stretched over metal or PVC pipe arches; see "Bulb and Alpine Frames") that has been fitted with benches on one side to accommodate the seed trays. The lowest shelf (made of 2 × 4 slats) is about 4 feet (1.2 m) above the floor, and the upper shelves above it are at 30-inch (75-cm) intervals. This allows enough light to reach all the pots as long as the shadecloth is off. The house is open on both ends most of the time to expose the seeds to outdoor temperature fluctuations and excellent air circulation. The roof of the house is covered with 50 percent shadecloth from mid-April to October. Care must be taken in watering the pots under these circumstances: too much water, and the pots become overrun with mosses and liverworts; too little, and the seed loses its viability. I let the pots become just dry on the surface before watering. Top watering should be done with a relatively fine spray to avoid washing out the grit and seed. A misting wand that can be attached to a garden hose is a wise investment.

The very fine seeds of plants such as *Rhododendron* and *Shortia* require different conditions than those of other alpine plants. The young plants need constant moisture for at least the first year after germination, and the seed needs constant moisture to germinate. Therefore, I start this kind of seed in covered pots or seed trays. Any type of clear plastic works fine for covering the pots or trays; I often just pop a plastic sandwich bag over a 3.5-inch (9-cm) pot that has been filled with the standard potting mix and topped with 1 inch (2.5 cm) of sterilized peat. The pots can then be placed in a bright position that does not get direct sun and left until the seed has germinated. The seedlings can be left in these pots for a full year, after which the plant and soil should be gently tipped out and moved without root disturbance into a larger covered pot to grow on for one more year. You can also prick the seedlings out into individual pots at this time or line the plants into a covered propagating bed (see the following section) to grow for another year before moving them into individual pots. Seedlings that have been moved up to individual pots after only one year require careful attention to ensure that they do not dry out, because their root systems are still very small.

Cuttings and Divisions

Probably the most common means that rock gardeners use to increase their plants is taking cuttings of various sorts: green top-growth cuttings of herbaceous plants; hardwood and semi-hardwood cuttings of shrubs; root cuttings from *Phlox*, *Viola*, or *Pulsatilla*; and leaf cuttings from members of the Gesneriaceae. This method ensures that the new plants will be genetically identical to the parent, an important consideration in the case of hybrids and named cultivars.

A simple way to handle green, hardwood, and semi-hardwood cuttings is to build an old-fashioned Nearing frame, named for its inventor. The box, or base, should be about 12 inches (30 cm) deep and can be any size you wish. Use pressure-treated wood to construct it, sunk so that about half of its depth is below ground. Be sure to build on a well-drained site so that there is no standing water in your frame. Line the bottom with permeable plastic groundcloth or weed barrier (for more details, see "Bulb and Alpine Frames"). The frame is to be situated so that its open side faces north. On the eastern and western sides, the frame is fitted with triangular endpieces that slope at a 45° angle. The southern side is rectangular and 2–3 feet (0.6–0.9 m) high—tall enough to exclude direct sunlight. Some growers line the frame with a reflective material such as aluminum foil or paint the interior white to increase the brightness of the indirect light that enters the frame from the north. Once the cuttings are installed, the frame is covered with clear polyethylene to maintain enough humidity to keep the cuttings from drying out by normal transpiration.

The propagating frame can be fitted with heating cables, if you wish. These are laid when the frame has been half filled with a sterile, well-drained potting mix, coarse sand, or finely ground pumice—all work well to root cuttings. Heating cables are a great help to root cuttings out of season or to speed up the rooting process at any time. They are available at almost any garden center or through mail-order garden catalogs, and they are much cheaper and more reliable than they were in the past. The benefits of using them are well worth the minor extra expense involved.

Growers who already have an alpine house, hoop house, or unheated greenhouse can use even simpler facilities to root cuttings. Many sorts of inexpensive propagators for the home grower are now offered, from simple clear plastic domes that fit over a standard seed flat to clear plastic mini-propagators with built-in bottom heaters. There are even mini-propagator systems available that are fitted with water reservoirs and capillary mats that feed moisture to the cuttings as needed, eliminating the need for regular checks to see if the cuttings are drying out.

I make heavy use of domed clear-plastic seed tray covers when starting cuttings for my nursery. After sticking the cuttings in a suitable

PLATE 65. Starting alpine plant cuttings in flats with clear plastic caps. Photograph by Rick Lupp

mix in flats, I cover the flats with the plastic domes and line them out on the floors of my open-ended hoop houses in bright light, but not direct sun. Because the hoop houses are open to the breezes, I fasten the plastic covers in place with inexpensive binder clips, available at office supply stores. These clips keep the tops from blowing off and allow a tighter seal that keeps humidity at the proper level. Clear plastic seed flat covers are also available in high-top styles, which are excellent for covering flats containing fresh grafts, which need high humidity for the first few weeks to succeed.

Domed clear plastic flat covers are also excellent for covering fresh divisions until they have recovered from the trauma of being torn apart and have initiated new growth. Small divisions with just a little root should be treated the same as cuttings for at least a few weeks, which means that they should stay in a closed propagator until new green growth resumes. Divisions with plenty of healthy roots can simply be placed in a cool, bright area such as the opening of a north-facing shed or the northern side of a building for a week or so until they have recovered and resume growth.

Another simple way to root small quantities of cuttings is to fill a 6-inch (15-cm) pot with a suitable rooting medium, stick the cuttings in the pot, and cover the pot with a plastic bag. Be sure that the bag fits tightly enough to keep the humidity in the pot at a high level. I bend a piece of wire into a hoop and place the hoop just inside the rim of the pot to keep the plastic bag from lying on the cuttings; rot often results if the plastic comes in contact with the plant.

Many growers use rooting hormones to increase the take of their cuttings. I very rarely use these hormones on green cuttings of herbaceous plants, although I use them occasionally on plants that just do not want to root otherwise. The overwhelming majority of green cuttings root readily without hormones; they are, however, very useful with hardwood, semi-hardwood, and conifer cuttings. Rooting hormones are sold as powders, liquids, and gels. The powders have a tendency to be wiped off unless you make a hole (for instance, with a pencil) for each cutting as you stick it (the technical term for inserting a cutting in the rooting medium). The liquids work well, but you must soak the cuttings in the liquid hormone for a couple of minutes to get the best results. I use gel hormones for my most difficult-to-root plants. The gel adheres well to the cuttings and is generally of higher strength than other hormone solutions. Most of these hormone solutions also contain antibacterial and antifungal agents, and some even contain vitamins and mineral nutrients to feed the young roots for accelerated growth.

As mentioned earlier, bottom heat is very useful for speeding up the rooting of cuttings and for starting cuttings in the cooler months of late autumn and even winter. Heavy-duty rubber propagating mats are now widely available at reasonable prices and are just right for use with domed clear plastic flat covers or with cuttings stuck into covered pots. These mats are waterproof and impervious to most chemicals and fertilizers that you might use. The heating cables are embedded in the mats, and the mats can be plugged into specially made heat-mat thermostats to maintain just the right temperature for the cuttings at any time of the year. The temperature range provided by these mats runs from about 40 to 100°F (4 to 38°C), and the better ones come with temperature sensors on long capillary tubes that allow the grower to control the temperature at the roots of each individual flat.

A shock protector is a sensible investment for the grower who uses heating cables or propagating mats. These are quite inexpensive and provide protection against shock if the cables or mats become damaged. In these units if an electrical current leaks to the ground, the ground fault interrupters, thus immediately disconnecting the power to the cables or mats.

Mist and fogging systems are often used to provide the proper conditions for rooting cuttings. I have found that the only purpose for which they provide better results than a closed propagator is in rooting conifers and certain broad-leafed shrubs and in maintaining the high humidity needed by fresh grafts. However, satisfactory results can be obtained with a closed propagator even in these applications. A wide range of mist and fog systems are now made with the amateur grower in mind. Inexpensive fogging systems are available at most farm supply stores; these are actually made to cool livestock during the heat of summer, but they also work quite well in a small greenhouse. Another simple and relatively inexpensive option for small areas is a portable misting system, which is little more than a metal box with a connection for water and a fogging nozzle with a fan mounted behind the nozzle. These devices broadcast mist about 6–8 feet (1.8–2.4 m) and have the advantage of needing only to be hooked up to a hose faucet, with the power cord plugged into a standard 120-volt outlet. They can also be attached to a timer to control their operation.

More elaborate fogging systems made for use in commercial greenhouses include a booster pump, which increases the water pressure to about 160 psi, along with precut tubing, nozzle fittings, and nozzles. Other requirements include a nozzle cleaner and calcium filter. For automatic control, you need a solenoid valve and a humidistat or cyclestat (timer). You can set up these systems over one portion of the greenhouse or alpine house bench by enclosing the area with polyethylene, or you can build a freestanding miniature hoop house to contain the system.

Good sanitation is an important factor if you want to obtain good results from your propagation systems. All propagators and propagation areas should be washed and cleaned after each use, and cuttings and seedlings planted in clean pots or trays. Do not allow mosses and liverworts to become established in your propagation areas, where they spore freely and are difficult to eradicate. A few minutes a day of housecleaning can prevent many problems down the road.

PART 4

Regional Styles and Techniques

The most dangerous thing about reading about gardening is that books can lead us to apply recommendations formulated for one climate region to our own very different situation. For instance, a vast number of English gardening books are sold in North America, yet almost no part of our continent matches the climate of the British Isles. Canadian and U.S. publishers in recent decades have attempted to remedy this problem by producing many books on regional gardening, such as the *Sunset Garden Book* series.

Almost all rock gardening books before this volume have come to us from England, so few of them address the climatic extremes that are found by gardeners in places as disparate as Calgary, Vancouver, Tucson, Kansas City, Raleigh, and Boston. Books on the subject published in the United States have focused on the Northeast (Kolaga, *All About Rock Gardens and Plants* [1966]; Foster, *Rock Gardening: A Guide to Growing Alpines and Other Wildflowers in the American Garden* [1968]), the Northern Plains (Barr, *Jewels of the Plains: Wild Flowers of the Great Plains Grasslands and Hills* [1983]), or the Rocky Mountains (Springer, *The Undaunted Gardener* [1994]).

To make the information in this volume meaningful in local contexts, this part includes chapters devoted to regional rock gardening. We begin in the Pacific Northwest, a region of mild, very wet winters and dry summers, where growers of rock and alpine plants need primarily to moderate the moisture regime in the garden. A chapter on Alaska, the site of burgeoning interest in rock gardens, can also apply to northwestern Canada. California rock gardens have a special style that accommodates drought-tolerant, mild-climate plants. In the Intermountain West and Rocky Mountain region, low precipitation, limited water resources, cold winters, and hot summers have brought the response known as xeriscaping, a perfect match to rock gardening. The major challenge to rock gardeners in eastern North America is the moisture and humidity of the summers, with winter cold also a consideration. Judicious choice of plant material and sites and particularly good drainage to divert summer precipitation are important here. In the Southeast and Mid-Atlantic region these strategies are magnified, and many southeastern rock gardeners turn to the shade and to woodland plants. Many of the points made in these latter two chapters can be applied in the Midwest as well. For more region-specific ideas, see part 5 and its descriptions of public rock gardens around North America.

The Pacific Northwest

LOREN RUSSELL

The temperate Pacific Coast of North America is known for its fine gardens, and many consider it a rock gardener's paradise. Moderate temperatures, generally ample water, clearly defined seasons, and varied topography make it possible to grow plants from most parts of the world here. In gardening terms, the Pacific Northwest is often compared with Britain. However, this comparison is misleading; there are important differences, particularly in the rainfall regimes and temperature extremes. In Britain rain is likely to fall at any time of the year, whereas in the Pacific Northwest 90 percent or more of the precipitation falls between October and June. Moreover, the most densely populated areas of the Northwest regularly experience lower winter minimum and higher summer maximum temperatures than most British gardens. In this chapter I primarily consider rock gardening in the area west of the Cascade Mountains. The information is based on my personal experience gardening in northwestern Oregon and my visits to gardens throughout the area. Much drier and more continental climatic conditions prevail on the eastern side of the Cascades; the chapter "The Xeric Rock Garden" is a good guide for that region.

Most gardeners in the region reside in Washington's Puget Sound lowlands and the interior valleys of western Oregon's Willamette, Umpqua, and Rogue Rivers. In this area, winters are wet and mild (usually USDA zone 7 or 8), the summers are dry and mild to hot, and annual rainfall generally ranges from 32 to 50 inches (80 to 125 cm). As little as 18 inches (45 cm) falls in rain-shadow areas in the Puget Sound islands and the southern Oregon valleys. The average winter minimum temperatures vary little from north to south (ranging from about 10 to 20°F [−12 to −7°C] in most years), but summers are much hotter (with

PLATE 66. A moisture-sensitive cactus and succulent section of the Leach Botanical Garden's rock garden in Portland, Oregon, is covered for winter with a simple roof of fiberglass sheets mounted on galvanized steel pipe rails. Photograph by Bonnie Brunkow Olson

many days over 90°F [32°C]) and the summer drought period is longer in the southern part of the region.

The Mediterranean rainfall pattern of the Pacific Northwest (including northern California) stands in striking contrast to the other areas where rock gardening is popular. Rock gardeners in eastern North America, in northwestern and central Europe, and in temperate eastern Asia experience evenly distributed rainfall or (more often) a decided maximum during the growing season. Summer rainfall maxima are also typical of most of the source areas for hardy rock plants, (for example, the Alps, Himalayas, and Rocky Mountains). Most of the areas with Mediterranean rainfall patterns are nearly frost-free (for example, coastal areas of California, the Mediterranean basin, Chile, and South Africa's Western Cape). Closer approximations to the Pacific Northwest climate exist in uplands in the arc from the western Mediterranean, through the Balkan Mountains, to the southern coast of the Black Sea. Many of the best-adapted rock plants for the Northwest are native to this region.

PLATE 67. The author building with lava rocks. Photograph by Louise Parsons

On both sides of the Cascades, the Pacific Northwest is distinctive in its geology. The surface geology of Washington and Oregon is dominated by Miocene to Recent volcanic rocks (basalts, andesites, and ash deposits) and by sediments derived from these volcanic rocks. More complex geology, characterized by the presence of granite, limestone, and ultramafic (serpentine) rocks, is found in Washington's northern Cascades and Wenatchee Mountains and in the Siskiyou and the Blue Mountain regions of southwestern and northeastern Oregon. As would be expected in a region with volcanic geology and high rainfall, the soils on the western side are moderately acidic and usually heavy in texture, often clay loam. Tracts of gravelly, sandy loam or peaty soils are also found in association with glacial drift (as far south as Tenino, Washington) and as river alluvium and lake-bed deposits. Some lucky gardeners will find that their soils are derived from basaltic bedrock. These reddish brown, shot-clay soils appear to be heavy textured, but they drain freely in winter; many rock plants grow well without addition of drainage to the soil.

Is there a style or methodology appropriate to or typical of the Pacific Northwest? Despite the vast range of plants that can be grown

PLATE 68. The granite crevice garden built by Josef Halda at Siskiyou Rare Plant Nursery. Photograph by Phyllis Gustafson

and the variations both in the garden situations and the personal taste of gardeners, both limits and opportunities are imposed by the region's climate and geology. The only book available on rock gardening in the Pacific Northwest is by George Schenk (1964). The many texts based on the experience of British and eastern North American authors are useful for ideas about rock garden construction, although some stand-by suggestions do not apply well to conditions in the Northwest. In particular, such soak-away structures as French drains rarely solve winter drainage problems in the region. These texts are farther from the mark when dealing with the cultural needs of the plants. Soil pH and zone hardiness, the physical factors usually emphasized in rock gardening texts, are not important considerations for gardeners in the maritime Northwest. If they were, gardeners in the region could grow almost any hardy rock plant in the open garden. The most vexing problems with rock plants in the Northwest are caused by the winter rains, the heat and drought of summer, and the armies of slugs, rather than the infrequent 5°F (−15°C) freezes or some problem of soil chemistry.

PLATE 69. David Hale's garden, within 600 feet (180 m) of the Pacific Ocean in Arch Cape, Oregon, offers the opportunity to grow many rare but not very cold-hardy rock plants that can tolerate the occasionally salt-laden atmosphere. Photograph by David Hale

A regional geology dominated by volcanic rock obviously determines much about rock garden construction. Most texts encourage the use of local rock, then present a choice of sandstone or limestone, and go on to illustrate an idealized reconstruction of an outcrop of the chosen sedimentary rock. (Graham Stuart Thomas [1989], however, gives a useful and nonderivative account that does acknowledge the existence of igneous rock.) As a beginner, I read Reginald Farrer's counsel (*The English Rock Garden*, 1919) that "All granite, flint, porphyry, syenite or calliard is only to be used as a resource of despair. These rocks are lifeless, arid . . . unfriendly to beauty whether of conformation or plant life." Of the rocks in Farrer's list, I'd be lucky to obtain even granite. I can grin at my concern now, but I find that new rock gardeners continue to ask where they may find the limestone or sandstone they need. In the Northwest, the few sedimentary rocks available are usually not useful. Many local sandstones and mudstones weather rapidly into fine particles when exposed. (Volcanic tuffs, and many submarine [pillow] basalts also disintegrate rapidly in the garden.) Limestones and marble exist locally in the north Cascades and in the Siskiyous, but are usually available only as irregularly shaped, unweathered quarry rock of no great utility or appeal.

The best rocks widely available here are basalt and andesite, each in a variety of forms. The most attractive and useful types of basalt include the porous (vesicular) surface rock that covers much of the Columbia River Basin and massive (often columnar) basalt, where weathered rock can be found, as in abandoned quarries. Most Forest Service stations issue personal use permits and directions to suitable quarries for this and other rock products. These rocks are also available from landscape suppliers in the region. Columnar basalt, where it has weathered in the soil to a reddish color and rough texture, is especially attractive, and some rock gardeners in the area have been able to gather such rock on their own properties. Andesite, lighter in color and weight than basalt, is usually found in irregular shapes, although columns and slabs do exist. Thinly split sections of andesite are referred to locally as "slate" and much used as paving. Granite or granodiorite, usually available as angular quarry rock, has been used in several rock gardens in northwestern Washington and southwestern Oregon. A few gardens in the area use ultramafic (serpentine) boulders or quarry rocks. These generally resemble massive basalt in their dark color and lumpy shapes. Despite the toxicity to many plants of soils derived from serpentine rock, the rocks are hard and weather very slowly, so there is no problem with their use in rock gardens.

A rock garden can consume a massive amount of sand and gravel, and the geology of the Pacific Northwest constrains choices even for these unglamorous materials. Clean quartz sand can be harvested from decomposing granite in a few places, but the usual sources will be commercial sand and gravel mines or rock crushing plants. In northwestern Washington, much of the sand and gravel is extracted from glacial drift; this material is generally cleaner (with less silt) and sharper (the particles are more angular) than that mined in rivers. In western Oregon, most commercially available sand and gravel is neither clean nor sharp, because the sources are generally low-gradient reaches of the bigger streams, and environmental regulations limit the availability of silt-free (washed) sand and gravel. Rock crushing plants operating at these gravel mines and quarries are the best sources for grit and gravel. It's worth looking for an operator who can sell crushed sand—the fines (about ⅛ inch [3 mm] and finer) from a rock crusher. When washed free of silt, this sharp grit is excellent both for drainage and for use as top-dressing.

Two types of porous volcanic rock, both widely available in the Northwest, are valuable as rock garden drainage materials. The first, pumice, is widely used in horticulture as an ingredient of specialized potting composts. In the Northwest it is so cheap and widely available that it can be used widely in the open garden. It is useful for drainage in rock garden soil mixes, although, like perlite, it has the fault of conspicuously washing to the surface. The other porous material, scoria, differs from pumice in its red or black color, higher density, and chemical composition, which is similar to that of basalt. Scoria is found in the Pacific Northwest and northern California and is mined from volcanic spatter cones for use as highway sand. Scoria weathers rapidly, and rock plants grow vigorously in soil mixes containing it; the Sebring Rock Garden in Eugene, Oregon, used about 30 percent scoria grit of ¼-inch (6-mm) diameter in a loam-based soil. My source of sand-sized scoria is the waste pile at a highway department quarry; I obtain the ¼-inch grade from a local landscape supplier.

Every imaginable type of rock garden has been constructed in the Pacific Northwest. Raised beds, dry walls, dry-sand gardens, crevice gardens, and designs combining these approaches all work well (refer to chapters on these specialized features in part 2). Note, however, that traditional screes constructed with below-grade drainage, when situated on flat sites with heavy soils, are often not successful as a means of growing alpines. Winter rains in the Northwest overwhelm the drainage layer in these screes, while in the summer, the limited water-holding capacity of a scree is challenged by prolonged drought.

PLATE 70. The author's slope rock garden, partially finished. Photograph by Loren Russell

PLATE 71. Within three years, the slope rock garden offers a panoply of western American and Mediterranean flowers. Photograph by Loren Russell

Most rock gardens in the Northwest are complexes of low raised beds on flat sites or outcrops, terraces, or walls built into a slope. Many are not really naturalistic and could easily be called rockeries. *Rockery* is not a nice word in the rock garden literature; it conveys the idea of a garden feature that uses rocks and plants informally and is built without explicit reference to natural rock formations and generally without a great deal of engineering. I build rockeries where my goal is to use the lumpy volcanic rock in an attractive manner and to cultivate a wide variety of easy-growing rock plants. I rarely try to grow high alpines in the open garden; these are happier in troughs with winter protection.

My first rockery, built before I had seen a rock garden or met another rock gardener, was a success. It was small and easily rearranged and replanted. My first rock plants, which included some alpines, mostly grew and flowered well in it. I describe that first rock garden and two later, very different, projects.

A Small Raised Bed

A garden feature may originate with a plan in search of a place or an empty place begging to be filled. Mine was the latter, a narrow rectangle between a concrete walk and the back of my garage. I built a raised bed on a flat site with eastern exposure, 4 × 16 feet (1.2 × 4.8 m) in extent. I used weathered, angular granodiorite rocks weighing no more than 25 pounds (12 kg) each. The soil mix was 2 parts silty clay loam, 3 parts discarded peat-perlite potting compost, and 1 part sand-sized scoria. Because I wanted to use dwarf shrubs, a magazine article on the subject led me to, among others, *Daphne cneorum* and a source for it, Siskiyou Rare Plant Nursery in southern Oregon. The nursery's catalog opened the world of rock plants and their basic cultural requirements and led me, in turn, to Lincoln Foster's *Rock Gardening* (1968).

I dug the bed to a depth of 12 inches (30 cm) and forked in about 2.6 cubic yards (2 cubic meters) of the peat-perlite and 1 cubic yard (0.8 cubic meters) of scoria. The resulting mound of soil reached about 12 inches above the grade. I shaped the mound into a long barrow and arranged my smallish stones to my satisfaction, using Foster's description of a "rocky outcrop" as a guide to set chevrons of rocks. I ended with terraces peaking near either end of the bed and with vertical crevices for planting. Much of my arrangement was suggested by rocky outcrop sketches in the Foster book. A surprising number of plants, almost all new to me, went into the bed. Many grew well, including daphnes, campanulas, dianthus, lewisias, and penstemons; a few alpines prospered initially, but disappeared in the first winter.

I did several things right, but my best decision was to proceed without much planning. My raised bed was small enough and the rockwork loose enough to be easily reworked. Fortunately, there were no overhanging branches or invasive roots from nearby trees and shrubs, anathema to most rock plants. Over the four years that I enjoyed this garden, I moved things around as I learned more about the cultural needs of my plants. Thus, I learned (against what I had read) that lewisias thrived when planted on the horizontal in full sun, and that dryas and globularia formed denser mats and flowered better when trained over the rocks. I learned to propagate my plants to fill several similar beds I built later.

A Terraced Wall Garden on Public View

Some rock gardeners manage to buy a natural stone ledge, with a house or lot thrown in on the deal. Ledges, or suitable bedrock of any kind, are rare in built-up areas in the muddy maritime Northwest, so a northeast-facing, ivy-covered embankment along the driveway was a good enough reason to buy my present home. The bank seemed to have "capability" for a rock garden.

Two years later, I began to build a dry-stone wall with terraces, 60 feet (18 m) long and 6–10 feet (1.8–3.0 m) high, into the driveway embankment. The rockwork is slabs of porous basalt rocks weighing 20–90 pounds (9–41 kg). The soil mix throughout was 35 percent clay loam (excavated from the site), 15 percent composted oak leaves, 15 percent municipal compost, and 35 percent scoria and sand.

While planning this project, I made several photographs of the slope, then taped these into a composite. I enlarged the composite on a photocopier and used this to pencil in designs for the rockwork. I also compiled an album of snapshots of stone retaining walls on similar slopes nearby. These vernacular walls gave me my basic concept of terracing the slope with a series of curved walls that I could backfill with rock garden soil. I decided that each section of wall should be low, usually of two or three rock courses, with none exceeding 3 feet (0.9 m) in height; the terraces then would be narrow, generally 12–18 inches (30–45 cm) wide. I chose to terrace the slope in this way for both practical and aesthetic reasons. A wall with higher sections would entail removing a great deal of soil and would require deep footings and added drainage. Varying the height of the terraces and making them curved made this a more naturalistic and attractive feature. Finally, this design allowed me a maximum of planting sites for rock plants, especially the dwarf shrubby ones that look best on the level pockets afforded by the terracing.

I started the project by cutting a series of horizontal terraces about 16–24 inches (40–60 cm) wide, inclining slightly into the slope. Excavated soil was passed through screens and some of the screened soil was reserved for use in the backfill soil mix. After clearing and terracing a 10- to 16.5-foot (3- to 5-m) section, I began to set the rocks into ¾-inch (19-mm) crushed rock and garden sand laid on each terrace. Because the rock surfaces were irregular, it was helpful to find the best fit by first laying a section of wall, then reassembling with layers of sand and gravel between the rock. I generally used the largest rocks in the first course, and set the more irregular face of these into the drainage material. As I reassembled the section one course at a time, I back-filled with soil mix, wetting the soil and tamping it behind and between rocks until each rock was firmly set. I planted crevices as each course was laid.

During construction, I cut into the lawn at the top of the slope to decrease its angle from 45° to nearer 30° at the highest part of the bank. This shallower incline made the wall more stable and allowed more variation in width of the terraces. No footings or specialized drainage systems were installed, although these would be necessary in a higher, more vertical wall or any wall structure in a climate with heavier frost.

This wall is certainly a rock garden, but not especially an alpine rock garden. Small rock plants would be lost in the scale of the wall, and it is somewhat difficult to irrigate as well. I also wished it to be attractive at a distance and over a long season. As a result, I chose from among the many medium-sized plants (20–30 cm in height) that are adapted to rock garden conditions, but too large for the average rock garden. Even taller perennials and shrubs could be planted above the wall. This emphasis on drought tolerance and a long period of bloom led me to a garden that was dominated by plants from the Mediterranean basin and western North America. Among the plants that have thrived in the wall are dwarf shrubs including halimocistus, helianthemum, teuchrium, daphne, and dryas and mat-forming rock plants such as aubrietas, campanulas, dianthus, geraniums, phlox, pterocephalus and phlox. A long season of bloom is provided by, among others, scutellarias, *Gentiana paradoxa*, inulas, linums, onosmas, erodiums, and self-seeding annuals and biennials (for example, silenes, *Campanula incurva*, and *Campanula rupestris*). North American plants used include penstemons, lewisias, eriogonums, *Ageratina occidentalis*, and zauschnerias. The bloom peaks in May and June, but the wall is colorful from early March through late October. An excellent source for lists of rock plants with particularly long bloom is Foerster (1987). Lowry (1986) describes some of the western North American plants that do well in low-elevation rock gardens in the Northwest.

What have I learned from this project? Primarily, that it is very difficult to amend the soil without rebuilding the entire wall. After nine years, the leafmold is gone, and the soil has reverted almost completely to the heavy clay that I started with. If I were to start a project like this today, I would incorporate a geotextile (woven plastic groundcloth) behind the wall to prevent infiltration of the underlying clay. I would also use purchased sandy loam as the base for the soil mix and incorporate soaker hoses for summer irrigation.

A Pool, Bog, and Shaded Rock Garden

Although water features are covered elsewhere (see "Water"), I include this section as an example of how to use an awkward site in the landscape. Our house is set near the top of a hillside, and one corner of the back yard the junction is formed two 45° banks of exposed subsoil and mudstone. Over four decades, several previous owners were unable to make anything grow in this site. The record rains of November 1996 sent water cascading down the hillside to flood my back lawn. This forced me to install drainage, and I took this opportunity to regrade the embankments and build a shade garden. At the corner of the yard, where the winter flooding was worst, I decided that a small pond with an artificial stream coursing down the slope was a natural solution for the flooding. My pond and bog were modeled on one in a garden

PLATE 72. The author's shaded, moist rock garden. Photograph by Loren Russell

visited in Massachusetts; the stream, trickling down an amphitheater of stepped columnar andesite, was a good copy of a small natural stream in the nearby Cascades. Overflow from the pond runs into the bog, and overflow from this drains directly over an oak log into a dry stream overlying the main drainage line. I have emphasized elsewhere that my gardens are not explicitly naturalistic, but this garden is situated so that I'm often asked if the stream source is natural.

In this chapter I explored ways of thinking about rock construction and how to visualize the potential of different sites. You would have come to my sites with a different eye, and your gardens would have developed differently from mine. For any beginner, I can recommend starting with a small, inexpensive project, as I did. As you become more interested in rock gardens, take every opportunity to see other people's expressions of this avocation, both first-hand and at garden lectures. Rock gardens in the Pacific Northwest can be as different as the maze of high Chinese walls built from rounded granite boulders by Terry Terrell and the low raised beds built from large basalt columns in Christine Ebrahimi's garden. Rock gardeners in the Northwest have the advantage of working within a milieu where naturalistic, or at least informal, gardens incorporating walls, stone, and native or wild-looking plants have long been an established style. It's common to see residential districts with decades-old rockeries and retaining walls that are overgrown with aubrietas, iberis, and arabis. Adding the vast range of plant material available to specialist gardeners is both a natural step and a rewarding one.

FURTHER READING

Karl Foerster, *Rock Gardens through the Year*; Betty J. Lowry, "In the Northwest"; George Schenk, *How to Plan, Establish, and Maintain Rock Gardens*; Graham Stuart Thomas, *The Rock Garden and Its Plants*

Alaska and the Far North

JAIME RODRIGUEZ

The most densely inhabited part of Alaska, the region around Cook Inlet known as south-central Alaska, is a rock gardener's paradise. The combination of climate and geology make it possible to duplicate alpine tundra in the garden at sea level. It is puzzling, then, that rock garden construction is a relatively young art in Alaska. There were a few notable pioneers, including Alene Strutz, Helen White, Lenore Hedla, and Verna Pratt (Hedla and Pratt wrote books about Alaskan gardening and wildflowers, respectively), but rock gardening remained the specialized hobby of the most enthusiastic plant lovers. After the winter of 1995–1996, however, when the temperature in Anchorage dropped to −20°F (−29°C) in mid-November, with no snow cover, and stayed that cold or colder until the first snowfall in mid-February, traditional perennial gardens were devastated. After noticing that alpine plants had fared better, Les Brake propose starting an Alaska chapter of NARGS. Thus, the Alaska Rock Garden Society was born, and soon rock gardens were springing up all over Anchorage and the Matanuska-Susitna Valley just inland.

Winter temperatures are the most obvious factor to be considered by Alaskan gardeners. It is much colder here than in most places where rock gardening has been long established. Moreover, temperature variation shows no convenient consistency. Alaska is a huge state with a vast coastline, extending from 55° N latitude in the south to above 79° N latitude. Many climatic regimes can be found here, although most of Alaska receives some precipitation, both snow and rain, throughout the year. Kodiak Island's climate is moderated by the warm Japanese Current, a Pacific equivalent of the Gulf Stream, producing conditions similar to those along the Strait of Magellan in southern Chile; winter lows are typically around 32°F (0°C) but have dipped to −20°F (−29°C).

Fairbanks, in interior Alaska, can experience summer days of 90°F (32°C) and winter days of –60°F (–51°C) or colder; precipitation is low in the interior's continental climate. The town of Homer is 250 miles (400 km) south of Anchorage. Both communities are coastal and surrounded by mountains, but summer temperatures average 10°F (6°C) warmer in Anchorage. Homer gets more rainfall, and its winters have significantly more snowfall and milder temperatures, rarely below 0°F (–18°C), whereas Anchorage's winter lows are regularly around –30°F (–34°C). Many cold-sensitive plants, thus, survive better in Homer; on the other hand, warmer summers allow Anchorage gardeners to succeed with some plants that may survive in Homer but not bloom well. Southeastern Alaska, the southern coastal strip and its islands, hosts a temperate rain forest continuous with that of British Columbia and the Pacific Northwest. Its maritime communities see milder winters with more snowfall than in the interior, but the summers are cooler, rarely exceeding 70°F (21°C).

At these high latitudes, seasonal variation in day length has dramatic effect on gardening. The closer one gets to the Arctic Circle (66°34' N), the longer are summer days and the shorter are winter days. In the Anchorage area, sunrise on June 21, the summer solstice, is around 2:30 A.M. and sunset about 11:00 P.M., when the sun sets just dips below the horizon into a long twilight that blends with dawn. Sunrise on December 21, winter solstice, is about 10:30 A.M. and sunset about 2:00 P.M. These day lengths can have intense effects on plants from lower latitudes. Some simply refuse to bloom because they get too much light during summer; others bolt in the spring almost immediately after germinating; still others try to bloom too late in autumn, and the flowers freeze in bud.

A less obvious consequence of day length is its effect on soil temperatures. According to the Alaska Agriculture Statistics Service, in the Matanuska Valley soil temperatures go from freezing to 40°F (4°C) in April and up to 55°F (13°C) by the end of May; temperatures stay between 55 and 65°F (13 and 18°C) during June and July before cooling begins. Cool soil temperatures throughout Alaska can be both an advantage and a disadvantage. Many high-alpine plants can thrive at low elevations; cool soil is a blessing for plants such as *Meconopsis* and *Delphinium*.

Deep frost penetration in winter, however, severely challenges some species. When spring arrives, it is a long, slow tease. Constant cycles of freeze and thaw play havoc with woody plants. When temperatures reach –50°F (–46°C) and snow cover is thin, frost can penetrate to depths of 10 feet (3 m). In really cold years, the soil does not thaw completely until June. While the ground is still frozen, meltwater or precipitation pools on the surface during the warm days and at night freezes into deadly collars at the bases of woody plants. Even in mild winters the soil stays cool, and the long days do little to warm it. The angle of sunlight in the far north means that less solar energy reaches the surface, so it warms more slowly. As a result, heat-loving plants wake up

PLATE 73. Florene Carney's rock garden exemplifies both the range of plants that can be grown in Alaska and the breathtaking wilderness background. Photograph by Florene Carney

very late in spring. If a species is triggered to break dormancy by a particular day length, the plant may be cut down by spring frost because the proper day length is reached too soon. If the plant's dormancy is broken by warmth, it may not appear until late June.

Plants adapted to cold environments, whether at high elevations or high latitudes, emerge quickly from dormancy as their growing season begins—as though they know there is not much time. An almost tropical lushness seems to appear overnight. Local folklore says that when birch leaves are as big as a mouse ear, it is safe to plant bedding annuals because the frosts are over until autumn. This is usually in mid to late May.

Unlike the drawn-out spring, autumn comes suddenly. Killing frost can occur any time after August 1, although it's usually in early to mid-September. Once hard frost has occurred, it is often only two weeks before the first snowfall. In such a rapid autumn, many introduced woody plants don't get the signals they need to harden off and attain dormancy. Day length is still too long, and the plants go right on growing until they freeze. This dooms many beautiful trees, shrubs, and herbaceous perennials, but alpine plants are better adapted to rapid changes of season.

Much of Alaska is a natural rock garden. Southeastern Alaska is basically a layer of humus on top of bedrock, a perfect base for a rock garden, and in some Alaskan communities *any* garden has to be a rock garden. Drainage and excessive rainfall are the major challenges to rock gardening there. South-central Alaska has mountain ranges that create rain shadows; thus, parts of the Matanuska-Susitna Valley have too little rainfall for some gardeners. Ice age glaciation has left a bounty over much of Alaska: deep layers of sand and gravel. For rock gardeners, the mountains provide endless inspiration and examples of natural rock gardens, along with an infinite supply of construction material.

Road construction through Alaskan mountains allows easy rock-picking. (It is a good idea to check with the Department of Transportation before taking rocks.) The low-tech method is to pick rocks that can be carried by one or two people, loading them into a pickup; this can require several trips to get enough for a small rock garden. Volunteers collected rocks for the rock garden at the Alaska Botanical Garden from a highway construction site, eventually moving more than 20 truckloads. A few larger boulders were brought in by heavy equipment. Using heavy equipment to place very large rocks is expensive, but the resulting gardens are impressive.

Basic rock garden construction in Alaska or Canada's far north is pretty simple. Find a slope, preferably with a base of gravel and sand. Failing a slope, build up a berm of desired height with pit-run gravel or any other well-drained material (see "Berms"). Add boulders to fit your own aesthetic sense. Spread a shallow layer of topsoil over the boulders and base gravel. How you mix soil and gravel depends on the requirements of the plants you hope to grow (see "Soils" and "Moraine and Scree Gardens"). The rocks should be buried deeply enough to secure them against frost action—usually one-third to one-half of the rock's depth. The planting areas must be arranged so that snowmelt and rain runoff don't cause troublesome erosion. A good way to ensure this is to build the rock garden and then allow a sprinkler to run on it for several hours to reveal potential runoff troubles. A mulch of fine, sharp gravel, scree, or pea gravel finishes off the basic construction. The real art lies in the placement of the stones.

Alaskan rock garden construction often appears to be based on breaking the rules. For example, Susan Lemagie's rock garden on Lazy Mountain in Palmer, built in 1989, is designed in the traditional style on a natural slope. Somewhat untraditional is the direction the slope faces. The standard books suggest that a southeastern slope is most effective, but the Lemagie rock garden faces due west. Two stone stairways curve through the garden, leading to a small bench at the top with a pleasant view of the garden and a distant vista of the Chugach Mountains and the Knik Arm of Cook Inlet. This garden requires no watering. The only regular maintenance is weeding, mostly of overenthusiastic garden species. Susan's experimentation with plant varieties and placement has shattered a horticultural myth that in the harsh Alaskan climate, only a limited number of exotic plants would grow. One experiment that succeeded here is *Gentiana sino-ornata*; this late-autumn-blooming gentian has proven very winter hardy, bringing important color beginning in September. The flowers are often covered by the first snow, and it can be shocking to see them still blooming during a November thaw.

Verna Pratt has been rock gardening in Alaska for many years and was instrumental in designing the new public rock garden at the Alaska Botanical Garden. Because this garden is in a clearing surrounded by herbaceous perennial beds and native forest, it was not possible to bring in heavy equipment. All the material was delivered in pickup trucks. To build several berms on the level site, volunteers used round river rock, pit-run gravel, and broken concrete from a residential renovation. The native forest flora can be invasive, so the base material was built up, then covered with landscape fabric. The groundcloth also prevents the gravel used as the next layer from washing into crevices and settling too much. After the gravel was spread, the boulders were arranged. The height of the berms brings the plants closer to eye level, and the designers kept the berms small enough that the plants are easily visible from the paths. A small crevice area and several scree slopes were incorporated into the plan. The rock placement and planting were inspired by the natural patterns of rock slides in nearby mountains. A couple of large trees at one end of the site were incorporated into a shaded raised-bed rock garden to ease the transition from perennial beds to alpine berms. The soil in this bed contains more peat and humus than that of the berms, allowing for a different range of plants, notably several species of *Cypripedium*. The garden, built and planted in just a few months by a dozen volunteers, is Alaska's largest public rock garden.

A small public rock garden at the Matanuska Agricultural Showcase Garden in Palmer, next to the Palmer Visitor Center, has two beds. The older, built in 1988, is a low berm measuring only about 12 inches (30 cm) tall, 8 feet (2.4 m), across and 30 feet (9 m) long. Adorned with too few wonderful rocks from a local fossil vein, it is composed of the native topsoil with a bit of gravel mixed in. The garden is very densely planted and mulched with pea gravel. The many treasures in this bed include an old white-flowered *Silene acaulis* almost 2 feet (0.6 m) in diameter and *Primula scotica*, which has naturalized here.

Next to the Visitor Center log cabin is an abandoned fountain that has been converted into a rock garden. The octagonal bed of beautiful stonework is about 12 feet (3.6 m) across, with walls about 2 feet (0.6 m) high. When the waterworks broke, the pool was filled with gravel and then ignored for years. In 1998 workers using a small front-end loader dumped in a scoop of pit-run gravel and several scoops of boulders, creating a berm about 4 feet (1.2 m) tall. The boulders were arranged by hand and then covered with topsoil and a pea-gravel mulch. The entire bed took less than a day to build and a day to plant. It features many Alaskan native alpine plants, including *Salix reticulata*, *Salix phlebophylla*, *Salix rotundifolia*, *Androsace chamaejasme*, and several saxifrages. One of its showiest plants is a fine *Saxifraga oppositifolia*.

PLATE 74. A display rock garden under construction at Recluse Gardens, the nursery of Jeff and Rhonda Williams in Wasilla, Alaska, near Anchorage. Photograph by Rhonda Williams

Several private gardens are worth mentioning for their contributions to the art of Alaskan rock gardening. Verna Pratt has a lovely rock garden around a small pond in her back yard. An addition, designed to eliminate some of the lawn mowing around an existing lilac, incorporates hypertufa troughs as edging.

Recluse Gardens is a small nursery owned by Rhonda and Jeff Williams. Rhonda created a niche for herself when her hobby of growing unusual perennials grew into a business. In 1997 Jeff bought her a number of car-sized boulders as an anniversary gift, promising to build her a rock garden where she could plant the rare treasures she was growing. This was rock garden construction on a grand scale, with the use of heavy machinery to lift and place the boulders. Jeff became skilled at making a pile of boulders appear to be bedrock rising out of a berm. Two years after building their first rock garden, they sold the property and moved their nursery to a better location. It wasn't long before Jeff began placing boulders for the new rock garden. His kind of grand design can take several years to complete. Rhonda and Jeff have rewritten the rules for rock garden construction in Alaska, to good effect. One old rule says that rocks should be angled and buried in a way so that the crevices between the stones catch rainwater. Instead, Rhonda has created small dry microclimates with tiny ledges or little caves that mimic natural formations. Another old rule suggests using a homogenous type of stone, but mountains often show layers of very different rocks, and glaciers mix and deposit many varieties of stone. Rhonda and Jeff incorporated this characteristic into their construction.

Doug and Florene Carney's spectacular garden is on a site featuring a short slope that faces east-southeast. From the back porch of the house, the rock garden is obscured from view. Not until one walks across the sweep of lawn is a majestic distant mountain view revealed, mirrored by a rock garden that rivals many botanical gardens. It is 30 feet (10 m) deep and 100 feet (30 m) long, with many large boulders placed by heavy equipment, and includes a stone stairway and scree leading to a major water feature at the southern end. The pond started out smaller, but the sandy gravel glacial deposit that lies beneath the property kept collapsing during excavation. This proved serendipitous: a larger water feature and falls were really necessary to balance the size of the rocks and the mountains in the distance. Providing an example of how plants can survive with proper drainage, one of the most beautiful plantings flows down the steps—a river of *Phlox subulata*, a plant that has been difficult elsewhere in south-central Alaska. Florene cleverly labels her plants by using a paint pen to write the names on small, flat, river-washed cobbles, sealing them with clear varnish. These little markers blend perfectly with the pea-gravel mulch.

These rock gardens and dozens of others are changing gardening in Alaska. The good drainage and lean soil allow plants to survive here that reference books claim are hardy only to USDA zone 6 or 7. (Many of the plants listed as hardy to zone 3 or 4 do not survive in Alaska because of the peculiarities of our seasons.) The rock gardening experiments being conducted all over the far north will rewrite the rules on hardiness, and the results promise to be stunning.

FURTHER READING

Verna Pratt, *Field Guide to Alaskan Wildflowers*

Rock Gardening in Mild-Climate California

SANDRA LADENDORF

It is difficult to generalize about gardening in California because the state has many microclimates. Often, these considerable climatic differences are found over very short distances. This climatic diversity is so marked, in fact, that the editors of the *Sunset Western Garden Book* (2001), the bible of California gardeners, ignore the USDA plant hardiness zone map and instead describe and map twenty-four different zones in the western United States and Canada.

On the Monterey Peninsula this pattern is clearly exemplified. We live only 9 miles (14.4 km) from the Pacific Ocean. The coast is frostfree and frequently foggy. Ancient bougainvilleas cover trellises there, and old geraniums (*Pelargonium* cultivars) act like the perennials they are in the wild, tumbling down banks in huge swathes. The Salinas Valley, where most of the nation's lettuce, broccoli, and other cole crops grow, is 9 miles farther inland from our home; it is also essentially frost-free, thanks to the mist and fog that roll in from the ocean in late afternoon and burn off by midmorning almost every day. Between the cities of Salinas and Monterey, however, there is a sun belt of hills and complex canyons, where we garden. This area experiences some frost in most winters and can reach as low as 16°F (–9°C) in extreme years. Because we are gardening on a gentle slope at the base of a canyon, the frost often rolls down the hill, leaving our garden frost-free but nipping the neighbor's tender plants. Microclimates and topography affect rainfall as well. At our house, there is 7–14 inches (18–35 cm) of rainfall per year, but in a canyon twenty-five minutes' drive away, near Watsonville, as much as 125 inches (313 cm) has fallen in the same period.

The climate of northern California (of which Monterey is near the southern limit) is relatively benign. Most days are sunny, dry, and warm. The hot days, cool nights, and low rainfall are reminiscent of conditions in Greece. Although daytime temperatures occasionally climb above 90°F (32°C), when the sun goes over the hill, the air begins to chill. We live like the people of the siesta countries around the Mediterranean, closing up the house in the early morning hours and late in the afternoon flinging open the windows to let the cool breezes blow through; we sleep under a blanket every night of the year.

In many ways, this is a gardener's paradise. If we water them, almost any plants will thrive. When we moved here from Connecticut in 1972, however, the year-round need to water, prune, and fertilize came as a shock. We were accustomed to a winter hiatus from gardening, a quiet time to read catalogs, order seeds, and dream of next year's garden. This leads to another specialty of the California rock garden: more than any

PLATE 75. The garden of the late Harland Hand in El Cerrito in the San Francisco Bay area is now maintained by Marjorie Harris. This view from above shows Hand's mastery of using boulders, small pools, and architectural plants. Photograph by Pamela Harper

other, it is a year-round garden, where Mediterranean bulbs and small plants from South America, Australia, or South Africa can be seen in bloom even on New Year's Day.

We have learned that if we want plants to survive in dry sites with no water from April to October or November, we must look to the Mediterranean. Greek *Cistus* species grow side by side with native California *Ceanothus* in roadside plantings. Olive trees thrive here in unwatered sites, along with native oaks (*Quercus* spp.), buckeyes (*Aesculus californica*), manzanitas (*Arctostaphylos* spp.), and toyon (*Heteromeles arbutifolia*). A host of Californian and Mediterranean natives serve us all well in this era of drought-tolerant gardening. When these dryland species are newly planted, we water them occasionally the first year, and then they are on their own.

The choices for rock garden design and construction in California are the same as in any other part of the country: troughs and other containers, raised beds, terraces, screes, berms, and crevice gardens, in

PLATE 76. The New World Desert area at the University of California Botanic Garden at Berkeley was designed and planted by Sean Hogan. The barrel cacti are examples of *Echinocactus grusonii*. Photograph by Sean Hogan

either sun or shade. In the many parts of the state that have little or no surface rock, there is no opportunity to purchase a lot with wonderful ledges to act as the bones of a rock garden. Here we have to bring in rock and construct those bones. The placement of large rocks is an art in itself—too often, they look as if they had just been dropped from a truck into someone's front yard. Whether you are trying to suggest a mountain boulder field or a rugged ledge, the rocks should look as natural as possible. Probably the best way to mimic nature in a rock garden is by burying the rocks so that only the top two-thirds or less shows above the ground.

Rock gardening is the most idiosyncratic form of gardening, so there are no rules, no absolutes—just a great many ideas, suggestions, and inspirations. My husband and I love to explore the rocky alpine regions of the world, from the Cascade Mountains and the Sierra Nevada to the Bighorns and abroad in the Alps and the mountains of Greece. We travel vicariously through lectures at NARGS study weekends and chapter meetings, where plant explorers take us to remote places such as eastern Turkey or the beautiful, rugged western mountains of China. Whenever possible, we visit created rock gardens, both private and public. We find inspiration everywhere.

Photography is a great tool for rock gardeners. You can record the image of any plant combination or rock placement that appeals to you and refer to the pictures when planning your own rock garden. For example, on Mount Evans in Colorado, I learned that one could grow a shade-loving plant in the hottest, sunniest area by placing it under an overhanging rock. It is a useful technique for any sunny rock garden.

Rock gardeners are collectors, wanting one of every dwarf plant, the more unusual the better. A few are purists, raising only the true alpine plants of the high mountains, but most grow anything that is compatible in size and scale—and scale is the important concept. What you choose to grow in a trough will be miniature indeed compared to plants, trees, and shrubs you choose for a rock garden that covers several acres. Whatever the site, there is an appropriate dwarf conifer to

PLATE 77. The careful rockwork of the University of California Botanic Garden's limestone-endemic bed can be seen here. Cacti and succulents thrive in such alkaline conditions. Photograph by Sean Hogan

suggest the scale of the planting (see "Dwarf Conifers and Woody Plants" for details.)

The trick of designing a pleasing rock garden is to develop a place for the successful growth of each plant, and yet make the garden an interesting place to visit. Repetition of form is one useful technique, and repetition of color is another tool. Sometimes we plan it and sometimes it happens serendipitously, as when we planted *Iris tectorum* in our North Carolina woods and its lovely blue-lavender echoed drifts of native blue phlox in bloom across the path. In our shady California rock garden, irrigated *Primula sieboldii* combines nicely with an unwatered white cistus in the sunniest back corner of this bed. Because this shade garden is of generous size, I use plants of a larger scale than in the sunny rock garden area.

We are now developing a terraced scree with a planted dry wall as support, followed by a low mound that includes a couple of modest crevice elements. We will use the crevices for saxifrages, ramondas, lewisias, and other plants that thrive in such sites (see "Crevice Gardens" for details). There is a small sand bed for the most challenging plants, such as *Dicentra peregrina*, found in gravel banks in its native Asian habitat.

In this dry, sloping site, we are digging down, in contrast to the raised scree we created in North Carolina. All the garden sections, including one for perennials and roses near the back, are excavated 24 inches (60 cm). Because gophers are major pests in much of California, the garden sections are lined with small-mesh chicken wire (also called aviary wire), followed by 6 inches (15 cm) of ¾-inch (19-mm) gravel and then a very lean mixture of ⅜-inch (9-mm) gravel, sand, and soil, top-dressed with pea gravel. The perennial bed has an appropriately richer soil. Our native soil is miserable alkaline hardpan clay, with decomposed granite on the hillsides, so any gardening area needs considerable amendment.

Drainage is the secret to successful rock gardening everywhere. When we see where our beloved mountain plants grow, mostly among rocks with very little soil or sustenance, we understand how little nourishment alpines need. Many grow in cracks and crevices, with their roots extending many feet into the mountain. They are fed only by the occasional decaying leaf or bits of manure left by some animal.

Many Mediterranean plants are indispensable and forgiving, flourishing in the heat and humidity of the East Coast as well as in California's dry, hot climate, but others have more specific needs for dry, baked ground. Acantholimons, for instance, are spiky, flower-covered cushions that often fail in the moist Midwest and East, so I am looking forward to their thriving here. Other Mediterranean plants I treasure are *Euphorbia myrsinites*, *Aubrieta deltoidea*, many dwarf campanulas, and a host of drabas, saxifrages, and sempervivums, all very satisfactory in the California rock garden.

I remember exploring the roadsides and slopes of Greece, being wafted along by the heady fragrance of the herbs I was brushing through. Most of those herbs, thymes (*Thymus*), oreganos (*Origanum*), savories (*Satureja*), and rosemaries (*Rosmarinus*), have small forms, either species or cultivars, that are ideal for a rock garden. Among their mats and cushions, many California gardeners enjoy planting small spring-flowering annuals. Avoid the invasive California poppy, however.

Succulents, large and small, are mainstays in California rock gardens. The large-scale gardens designed by Harland Hand (plate 76) make effective use of bold agaves and echeverias, but smaller settings can accommodate dwarf species of these, as well as little cacti and the tiny-leaved, brilliant-flowered South African *Delosperma* species.

A huge group of treasured plants are the bulbs. Many species of crocuses, tulips, irises, fritillarias, narcissus, and ornithogalums are native to Greece, Turkey, and other countries that border the Mediterranean Sea. Most of these bulbs are extremely adaptable. *Anemone blanda* grows as happily in shady North Carolina woods as it does in the sunny meadows of Greece, and *Cyclamen* species thrive on both coasts of North America. However, the Oncocyclus irises from hot, dry Near Eastern countries demand a summer baking that few gardeners can provide without special bulb frames to protect the dormant plants from summer rains. These irises should do very well in California. The dwarf *Iris attica* demands the same dry, sunny conditions. In dry areas with a little more shade, native Pacific Coast irises (section Californicae) happily tolerate six months of drought, flowering well even if totally neglected.

The Xeric Rock Garden:
An Intermountain Style

GWEN KELAIDIS

Rock gardening as a horticultural art arose in the moist coastal regions of the Northern Hemisphere, especially in England, and it developed in the United States earliest in the Northeast and Northwest, but many of the world's loveliest associations of compact, saxatile plants grow in the natural rock gardens of arid, sun-drenched climates. In regions where sunny days prevail and rain seldom lasts more than a few hours, rock gardens are a sensible kind of landscape.

Only quite recently have settlers in North America's arid inland turned from survival, usually by ranching, mining, or agriculture, to the more leisurely pursuit of gardening for pleasure. In the past fifty years, both disposable income and leisure time have increased. The stunning scenery and wide open spaces of the West have lured more and more people to the western plains and the intermountain region, while air conditioning has made living in the hot Southwest tolerable for more people.

Recent immigrants from moister climates, as well as some longtime residents, are often drawn to the lush beauty of maritime horticulture: enthusiastically blossoming annuals, traditional perennial borders, and the rich green of lawns. Yet all these are expensive, not only in terms of the very precious water it takes to maintain them, but also in terms of the emotional havoc that can result when they are destroyed by the natural forces of searing wind, hail, unexpected water scarcity, or an unplanned absence from home that leaves the garden subject to normal climatic conditions. It is much more practical to create gardens in harmony with the local climate and scenery, to strive to bring into our home gardens some of the Intermountain West's distance and drama, the effects of sun and drought impressed on the land. It is more in

harmony to plant a garden that reflects the beauty of the natural landscape by incorporating its colors, textures, and spare aesthetic quality.

Most early gardens of the inland West consisted of a few roses, irises
(my grandma watered them with the rinse water from the dishes), lilacs
in northern areas, or crepe myrtle to the south. These hardy plants and
the blossoms of fruit trees provided joy to those who came here a century
ago. The plants were reliable and, most important, they could be grown
with little or no irrigation. The first intentionally xeric gardens (unirrigated designs using drought-adapted plants) in the Intermountain West
were probably developed by native plant enthusiasts who wished to re-
create a portion of nature in their own yards and who were motivated by
the desire to conserve water. They used yuccas, agaves, and native grasses
such as little bluestem and buffalo grass, possibly adding penstemons,
rabbit brush (*Chrysothamnus nauseosus*), and an eriogonum or two.

In the early 1980s, the Denver Water Board trademarked a concept
of zoned irrigation, Xeriscaping®: the outlying areas of a residential lot
were to be planted with drought-tolerant, largely native plants, whereas
the inner areas close to the house would be more heavily watered. Since
the mid-1980s, a few daring gardeners have combined a passion for
dryland plants with a passion for gardens rich in botanical interest and
year-round beauty. We are still searching for a term for the result: dryland perennial gardening, xeric rock gardening, or perhaps naturalistic
dryland gardening. The term *rock gardening* works well, because it
implies using not only rocks but also a diverse range of wild plants that
have been little tamed by horticulture.

Whatever term we finally settle on, this kind of gardening is novel,
great fun, and even labor-saving. The soil need not be altered from its
natural state. Soils in the Intermountain West are typically clays, mineral soils with little organic matter, or sands. We might add humus—if
we can find it, for the climate causes the rapid decomposition of any
plant material. Leafmold can be obtained in urban areas where trees
have been grown in irrigated conditions; well-processed sewage sludge
is sometimes available. Beware of bark and woodchip products, how-

PLATE 78. A xeriscape crowned by *Eriogonum niveum* in the Kelaidis garden in Denver, Colorado. Photograph by Gwen Kelaidis

ever; their decomposition brings microorganisms to the soil that are not beneficial to dryland plants. Adding humus may make the soil easier to work, and it adds to aeration and to the soil's ability to retain nutrients. On modified soil, we may be able to grow a wider range of plants, but perhaps not, especially if we modify too much.

The xeric rock garden need have no particular shape. It may be on flat ground, along a ridge, or atop a rock outcrop. I prefer mounding up the soil into ridges or rolling mounds, because I enjoy the height and diverse topography this creates (for details, see "Berms"). Building a dryland garden in a very small area may be difficult from a design perspective. The garden should be in full sun; even the winter shadow of trees or buildings, lengthened by the lower angle of the sun, may cause survival problems for dryland plants.

No water systems need be installed for the xeric garden, but in the years when you are adding many new plants, it is convenient to have easy access to a hose. The ultimate goal is to do no watering—to create an independent landscape.

PLATE 79. This streetside berm planting by the author is a tapestry of low mat and cushion plants. Photograph by Gwen Kelaidis

Whether mulch is used on a xeric garden depends on the gardener's preference, situation, and needs. My border of dryland shrubs and small trees is mulched variously with pine needles, scooped up when maintenance crews are raking the parks, or with leaves, bagged generously by homeowners with large shade trees. Because we are surrounded by open fields with an abundant and constant supply of weed seeds, my steep ridges are mulched with pea gravel. You could even plant the shortest prairie grasses as a sort of mulch between larger plants, such as castillejas, composites, phloxes, and penstemons. The genus *Muhlenbergia* has contributions to make, as does grama grass (*Bouteloua*). These grasses live in a natural companionship with dryland plants and should be much easier to control than the moisture-hungry and aggressive bluegrasses and crabgrass. Never mulch small dryland plants with bark or wood chips. I have a strong preference for gravel mulch, which works best if no soil shows through. Don't worry that your garden will be lumped with the all-too-common rockscape expanses of barren gravel mulch; it will have abundant plants, with the gravel underneath providing only a backdrop.

Acquiring plants is the biggest challenge for the dryland gardener. Today a great many more native plants are available commercially than twenty years ago, but many others are not offered because they do not tolerate typical growing conditions in nurseries. Nevertheless, local retail or wholesale nurseries are the first source to check and fellow xeric gardeners the second. Finally and most dependably, propagate the plants yourself. In general, digging up xeric plants from the wild is not only environmentally objectionable (except where habitat is being bulldozed or otherwise destroyed) but also ineffective. The sunny, austere climate demands that plants evolve deep roots, often taproots, which will register their discomfort with transplantation by dying, now or in six months.

Two categories of plants are obvious candidates for the xeric rock garden. First come plants native to your region. Some gardeners limit themselves to plants that grow naturally within a thirty-mile radius of home. Others grow only North American plants. Some disdain hybridized plants and grow only naturally occurring species. The most voracious of us, however, grow or attempt to grow all appropriate plants from regions with similar ecological conditions around the world—whatever may thrive with us and delight our senses.

If you decide to limit your palette to North American plants, indulge in the several hundred penstemons available. My favorites include *Penstemon nitidus*, the earliest and most sky blue; *P. barbatus* and *P. eatonii*, for their durability and red flowers; and the low mats of *P. caespitosus* and the horticultural selection 'Claude Barr' (now referred to the species *P. procumbens*). *Penstemon pinifolius*, bearing red or yellow flowers on short stems tufted with narrow green leaves, is nice in some dry gardens but looks tortured in others. All the blues of the Glaber group (for instance, *P. glaber*, *P. strictus*, *P. subglaber*) delight with blossoms of azure to purple and have larger flowers than the other species mentioned. Some sun gardeners succeed with *P. fruticosus* or *P. davidsonii* var. *praeteritus*. The choicest species, such as *P. gairdneri*, *P. acaulis*, and *P. laricifolius*, have proven difficult for me except in troughs, which can be kept more evenly dry than the best xeric rock

PLATE 80. Dry gardens can
look full and floriferous.
Photograph by Gwen
Kelaidis

garden. *Penstemon ambiguus* has expressed a strong preference for sand, dying everywhere else I have planted it.

Grow as many eriogonums as you can accommodate. Depending on the size and scale of your garden, grow *Eriogonum umbellatum* varieties, *E. subalpinum*, *E. jamesii*, *E. douglasii*, *E. ericoides*, *E. wrightii*, *E. niveum*, which reach at least 1 foot (0.3 m) in height, and the lovely buff pink *E. corymbosum*. For smaller-scale areas, the most essential species are *E. ovalifolium* in its many forms, *E. caespitosum* for dense mounds of tiny foliage, and the more particular *E. douglasii* and *E. sphaerocephalum*.

For lovers of big, spiny rosettes, yuccas and agaves are a must. A number of species are available in warmer climates, but choices diminish as you go below zone 5. These plants are despised by some gardeners, and they do constitute a cliché of Southwest rockscape gardening. The sharp spikes at the ends of their leaves can be very useful in deterring trespassers in the garden, though. The related genus *Hesperaloe* is another possibility, adding color with red flowers.

There are many, many more natives. Don't forget zauschnerias (*Epilobium canum*), available in at least six forms; rabbit brush (*Chrysothamnus*), which is glorious in late summer; and the lovely, evergreen bearberries *Arctostaphylos nevadensis* and *Arctostaphylos patula*. In California, you can find many more species and selections at the better retail nurseries.

Remember that all these plants do best in undiluted sun, and with little or no water. Under shady or heavily watered conditions, they will grow lanky and languid. Not a few will die if overwatered, although they may tolerate more water when they are young.

As we move on to other continents, we find a vast array of plant wonders. More and more are being introduced, notably by adventurous seed collectors who market their collections through advertisements in rock garden journals. They come from central Asia, South Africa, and the dry regions of Chile and Argentina. Important genera for the xeric garden include *Acantholimon, Verbascum, Veronica,* many genera of the mint family (Lamiaceae), Juno and Oncocyclus irises, *Tulipa, Eremurus, Crocosmia, Delosperma, Othonna, Euphorbia,* and *Gazania.* Trials at the Denver Botanic Gardens and elsewhere are constantly introducing new material for gardens in the inland West.

The planting objective for sunny rock gardens is seldom to have complete ground cover like that seen in perennial borders or public bedding. Although this can be attempted with larger perennials, the austere aesthetic of the desert, dryland, and sunny mountains calls for a bit more space between plants. Designing the plantings offers many possibilities. In some part of the garden, I group ground-covering plants of approximately equal aggressiveness, such as *Veronica liwanensis* and the small *Eriogonum umbellatum* selections, where they can compete only with one another and where their winter color pleases the eye. Sometimes I place a tall plant, such as a penstemon or a dryland salvia, in the midst of a carpet of ground cover. Generally, many dryland plants tolerate neither the shade of other plants nor crown competition (another plant growing over them). As in typical perennial and annual borders, place the tall plants behind the shorter ones, as seen from the path. On a long xeric ridge I placed the tallest plants at the higher end and along its crest, tapering plant sizes downward both along the ridge as it loses elevation and along the sides as they drop to the path. This allows me to view the small plants close up and protects the smaller plants from the overzealous growth of larger neighbors.

I don't consider color combinations much—although I no longer plant autumn-blooming, orange to scarlet zauschnerias anywhere near autumn-blooming magenta liatris! Nor do I worry about early and late

PLATE 81. Spring color on an unirrigated slope in mile-high Denver. Photograph by Gwen Kelaidis

color, because there are many dryland plants that bloom in nature with the autumn or late-summer rains, and it is not difficult to have color from spring until snow. Early bloomers include many crucifers (*Physaria, Iberis, Alyssum*), townsendias, many veronicas, some penstemons, and the glorious array of tulips, both botanical and hybrid. I plant tulips where they are backlit by the early or late sun, and I would do the same with the desert irises. Midsummer bloomers include acantholimons, many penstemons, most eriogonums, *Asclepias, Salvia, Stachys, Satureja,* and *Castilleja.* Bringing glory to the late garden, when other rock gardens have faded into a vegetative state, are *Zauschneria, Eriogonum niveum* and *E. corymbosum, Chrysothamnus,* dryland asters, and *Salvia pachyphylla. Zauschneria* alone will take your breath away, and they bloom here until the first snows bear them to the ground.

Choice small plants for the dryland garden, echoing the cushions and buns of the traditional rock garden, include townsendias, small ball cacti, cushion *Hedyotis* (dryland relatives of *Asperula*), the tiny penstemons of the Caespitosi group (for instance, *Penstemon thompsoniae* and *P. desertipicti*) and penstemons of the Erianthes group, cushion *Astragalus* species, sand lily (*Leucocrinum montanum*), and fritillaries. There are many cushion erigerons, lomatiums, and lesquerellas.

Gardeners can reclaim the heritage of the Great Plains and intermountain valleys and grow more of these plants, build more xeric landscapes, and celebrate the austere beauty of the land we have settled.

FURTHER READING

Beth Chatto, *Beth Chatto's Gravel Garden*; Jim Knopf, *The Xeriscape Flower Gardener*; Lauren Springer, *The Undaunted Gardener*

The Northeastern United States
and Eastern Canada

TOM STUART

The yin and yang of gardening are the impulses of the designer and of the collector. The best of rock gardens meld these into a unified whole. In the northeastern United States, the garden of Nina and Jack Lambert in the Finger Lakes area near Ithaca, New York, exemplifies how a rock garden can develop. The stone is slate, abundant in the area and collected over many years, trunkful by trunkful. A slab of common slate in itself is unimpressive, but used sensibly—here, echoing local road cuts and rough farm walls—it makes a fine terracing material. The original fill was native clay amended with sand, gravel, and rotted stumps. Photographs taken in 1972 show classic rock garden plants dotting a gentle, terraced slope. In succeeding years, the collection grew in diversity, and the sharp edges were softened by mosses. The combination of native stone, artfully employed, and a wealth of interesting plants sets this sanctuary apart. The garden has seen many shrubs pass through maturity to senescence; it has undergone tree-destroying storms; and the gardeners have countered exuberance with pruning, transplanting, and replacement. Yet the essential character has not changed—it is merely richer today.

Right from the beginning, the team documented this undertaking. Jack, who understands his world by drawing it, sketched, while Nina took to mapping. In her words, "It never occurred to me not to. How else to keep track of what is where, particularly when dormant, and to keep up with the name changes over time? A map gives spatial constancy, a sense of place." One result of these documents is the elimination of all those labels, the aesthetically annoying "mouse tombstones" endemic to collectors' gardens. Another is the ability to keep track of what lies underground, dormant or late-emerging. Such knowledge is useful when you are trying to move a plant from mere subsistence to full, thriving potential. "Full potential" implies the right conditions. Like other successful gardens, the Lamberts' is designed with a multitude of needs in mind: those of sun- or shade-lovers, of xeric and moisture-requiring species.

Climatic Factors

The Northeast can be envied by gardeners elsewhere for its precipitation pattern. Despite the many feet of snow in upstate New York (mentioned by newspapers every Ground Hog Day), the mean annual precipitation in Rochester, New York (32 inches, 80 cm), and nearby Toronto (33 inches, 82 cm) are at the low end for the region. Most people in the Northeast can count on more than 40 inches (100 cm) annually, spaced almost evenly throughout the months, although January and February contribute less than others. What more could a gardener want?

PLATE 82. Millstream, the garden of the late Lincoln and Laura Louise Foster in Falls Village, Connecticut, created on natural rock formations around a rushing creek, epitomized rock gardening in the Northeast during the mid-twentieth century. Photograph by Pamela Harper

Nevertheless, *mean* precipitation does not tell the whole story. We can count on at least one spell per year of three to five weeks of drought. In the winter, drought matters less; in the summer, many plants well adapted to this climate suffer. A rainy summer can be equally devastating: ten days of downpour will try the soul of any bun plant. Here are some techniques for retaining and discarding moisture. None is useful in every situation, however. Learn the plant and its needs, then apply these methods sensibly and methodically until it thrives.

Evaporation and transpiration are directly proportional to the heat of the sun. Reduce light, and you increase moisture; increase light, and you reduce moisture. Many plants have a tolerance range that gives you some latitude in choosing sites, so try a difficult plant in multiple sites. If you have a high alpine that insists on a full dose of sun in your low-altitude garden, adjust other parameters, especially soil drainage. If you are stuck with full shade everywhere (many suburban ordinances prohibit cutting trees), the best advice is to move—or to learn the art of woodland gardening.

Grouping plants closely together results in less water per plant, an invisible siphon depleting soil moisture. All plants are not equal, however, even those with the same apparent mass. Maples and dogwoods have shallow roots, resulting in voracious competition with perennials; oaks and hickories draw from deeper sources. On lesser scales, the same principles apply: the typical lush perennial border is no less a thirsty sponge than an expanse of lawn.

Use the early season. Deciduous shade has little effect on sun-loving bulbs or perennials if they make most of their growth before the trees leaf out, particularly if they go dormant by early summer. (These plants are sometimes called "spring ephemerals.") You can plant these almost anywhere; soil moisture will be adequate during all the time they spend in the sun. If you have an area of thin soil, planting spring ephemerals is a fine way to make good use of it.

Ground covers are often recommended as companions for spring ephemerals, but most are more likely to transform their companions from ephemerality to death by draining off water and nutrients. The natural vigor of any plant suggested for rapid increase ought to be enough warning. There are a few exceptions: in shade, native *Maianthemum canadense* (false lily of the valley) is vigorous, only weakly thirsty or hungry, shallow-rooted, and easy to remove. *Androsace sarmentosa* has similar attributes in sunnier spots. The majority of ground covers are satisfactory where you want *only* a ground cover.

Mulch is a ground cover without needs. It cuts evaporation and reduces weeds and their water and nutrient consumption. Organic mulches deplete soil nitrogen as they decay, however, so it may be advisable to sprinkle a balanced fertilizer lightly on them each spring. A well-chosen mulch can improve the garden's appearance, contribute organic matter, and improve soil structure, whereas a poor choice may bring along weed seeds or unsightly breakdown. Cocoa hulls are an example of the last problem. Consider carefully; run a test site if you are unsure. Stone mulches are often recommended for rock plants susceptible to crown rot, such as lewisias.

You can increase soil's water-holding capacity by adding organic materials. Decrease water retention by adding sand, grit, or gravel, planting on a slope, or building a raised bed. For succulents and plants native to the Mediterranean region—plants with higher drainage needs in the climate of the Northeast—go all out with pure sand or gravel (see "Dry Sand Beds"). I grow a dozen succulents in only 1 inch (25 mm) of gravel on a roof with a 15° slope. For more technical details of achieving good soil drainage, see the chapter "Soils."

Higher pH, limestone-derived soils are relatively uncommon in the Northeast but are found sporadically in the Allegheny and Appalachian Mountains and in western Newfoundland. For most of us, acid rainfall in this heavily developed region increases the acidity (that is, lowers the pH) of already acid soils. Luckily, most plants are tolerant of lower pH than that of their native soils, and acid-loving ericaceous plants include many great species for rock gardens. However, if your priority list includes encrusted saxifrages or other alpines from the Dolomites, plan on amending soils to raise the pH. Use limestone or bring in a truck-load of tufa (see "Working with Tufa"). Dolomitic limestone for lawns is a slow-release medium to raise pH, but wash it first, or risk burning plants with all the surface dust. Better yet, purchase it in prilled, or encapsulated, form. Tufa is easiest to obtain by mortgaging the house or getting yourself named in the wills of local NARGS chapter members.

Don't be afraid of native plants. Nonnatives are a challenge, but natives can be a fabulous backbone for your garden. Native plants have been through the dry and wet spells, the summers and the winters, and they've made it just fine. They take much of the guesswork out of determining hardiness. Be selective, however; there are plenty of com-mon ones, but the Northeast has its share of the world's finest rock gar-den plants.

PLATE 83. A berm rock garden created by Catherine Hull in Massachusetts. The statue at the end of the vista ties the naturalistic feature to its more formal setting. Photograph by Pamela Harper

Creating habitats in a climate that is less than perfect for your plants is also achieved by working with topography. In the Northern Hemisphere, the northern side of a mountain has the richest flora. Because it does not receive the full intensity of the sun, a northern exposure has more moderate conditions and stays moist longer, particularly in summer. Make use of this by siting a rock garden on a northern slope. If you don't have one, build a raised bed or make a trough with a miniature mountain in it.

Freestanding raised beds are an effective way to provide good microclimates. A raised bed ensures good drainage, and a freestanding bed offers northern, eastern, southern, and western exposures. As an alternative—or in combination—build a dry stone wall (see the chapter "Planted Walls and Formal Raised Beds"). For materials, simply look around. Many areas of the Northeast provide relatively stable shale or slate, great for crevices or terraces. Softer, porous stones, such as sandstone, are sometimes available; such rock is a happier home for the roots of saxatile plants than harder materials. Boulders left by the last ice age, used to mark off fields in the eighteenth century, are often granite encrusted with lichens and moss. These add instant beauty to a dry stone wall.

Fill the bed (or backfill the wall) with slow-rotting organic material, plenty of sand and gravel, and whatever small rock serendipity provides. (I offer an exception, however: although limestone gravels are not often available in the Northeast, their use should be deliberately matched with compatible, lime-loving plants.) The individual components are less important than their proportions, which must allow free passage of air and water at the root level (see "Soils"). A disadvantage of a raised bed is the extra watering required. There is no free lunch, and rock gardening is not a low-maintenance activity.

Successful rock gardeners create a multiplicity of habitats: shade to sun, wet to mesic to dry, clay to sand to gravel, flat to steep, acid to alkaline. When a new acquisition arrives on the scene, find out what you can about its native habitat, factor in the Northeast's climate, and choose a

PLATE 84. The transition between terrace and woodland, frequent in Northeast gardens, is accomplished in the Hull garden by a planted stone wall and mulched path. Photograph by Pamela Harper

spot. If it doesn't work, choose again. Stop only when you are utterly convinced no one ever has grown it, or ever will.

Plant Choices

We rock gardeners want to grow the ungrowable, don't we? Yes, but pause along the way to challenges such as *Dionysia*, and explore plants from an environment similar to your own. The flora of northeastern Asia offers direct counterparts to many native plants of northeastern North America, and often the former are superior (if you have no prejudices). For example, Korean *Jeffersonia dubia* is much showier than American *Jeffersonia diphylla*. Whether botanically related or not, the plants of northeastern Asia evolved with similar temperature and rainfall patterns. Seek them out.

When we begin to grow true alpines, the manipulation of soil and topography comes to the fore. As a beginner, I took the mantra "alpines need perfect drainage" to imply that alpines can deal with drought. Although some can, many demand ideal moisture levels at different stages of their growth cycle. Except in bogs above tree line, most alpines have evolved with perfect drainage. Consider, however, that higher elevations are always accompanied by higher precipitation: in the Ruby Mountains in the middle of the Nevada desert, the mean annual precipitation at 10,000 feet (3000-m) elevation is 47 inches (118 cm), more than almost anywhere in the Northeast. If you look only at the geographical provenance of a plant and use that to decide to put it in the sand bed, pray for rain. Pray frequently.

Here is a conundrum. If we grow alpines on a flat area in the Northeast, many will surely succumb during wet periods. If we grow them on raised beds or hillsides and leave them untended, many will die from desiccation. Although there is no universal solution, a promising starting point is a raised bed with supplemental water provided by building an artificial moraine (see "Moraine and Scree Gardens"), which is a lot of work, or by occasional assistance from the hose. You

PLATE 85. A rocky, dry streambed offers access to the garden and extra drainage during downpours in the Connecticut garden created by the late Ted Childs. Photograph by Pamela Harper

can also try building a bed above a tank—at its simplest, a pit lined with a tarp—to ensure sufficient water via capillary action. In my garden such an arrangement has been successful with saxifrages, primulas, and gentians, and it even allows for vacations. The larger the capacity of the tank, the longer the time you can spend on the Continental Divide collecting seed.

Anne Spiegel, a New York collector especially of western North American plants, provides no supplemental water. Her favorites require different solutions. Some parts of the garden thrive on traditional soil mix, but a major section is a creviced outcrop deep in gravel (some of it limestone), supporting a fine array of *Eriogonum*, *Penstemon*, *Oxytropis*, and *Physaria*—plants strong on drought tolerance and impossible to grow without catering to their needs. This and other collectors' gardens in the Northeast (see also "The Cactus and Succulent Specialist's Rock Garden") prove that knowledge, creativity, and meticulous attention—along with plenty of hard work—can expand the regional plant palette in many directions.

FURTHER READING

William Cullina, *Growing and Propagating Wildflowers*; H. Lincoln Foster, *Rock Gardening*; Anne Halpin and Robert Bartolomei, *Rock Gardens*

The Southeast and Mid-Atlantic Region

MICHAEL CHELEDNIK

Nowhere is rock gardening a pursuit for the lazy or timid gardener. This is especially true in the Mid-Atlantic and Southeastern regions of the United States. Here, a climate characterized by long, wet, hot summers has forced enthusiasts to rethink what rock gardening really is and to alter both their plant palette and the manner in which the plants are grown.

The Mid-Atlantic and Southeast, for our purposes here, includes the area from New York City and Philadelphia south and southwest through Maryland, Delaware, and the District of Columbia, much of Virginia, and the coastal states south of Virginia. Near the Atlantic shore, particularly in the northern portion of this region, the ocean acts as a moderating influence that results in cooler daytime and evening temperatures. In the Appalachian Highlands, which border much of the region to the west, higher elevation provides similar cooling. Even in these areas, however, the climate can be problematic for most alpine plants.

PLATE 86. A raised bed at Tony Avent's nursery near Raleigh, North Carolina. Photograph by Bobby Ward

The Mid-Atlantic and Southeast experience summers of almost tropical heat and humidity. Starting in mid to late May and lasting into September, daytime highs are generally in the range of 85 to 100°F (29 to 38°C). In and of itself, the heat is not necessarily bad for all rock plants; those native to the American Southwest and parts of Turkey endure temperatures in this range without complaint. However, when we factor in humidity levels of 60 to 80 percent or more, nighttime temperatures that rarely drop below 70°F (21°C), and generally high summer rainfall, the combination spells death for the vast majority of alpine and dryland plants under normal outdoor growing conditions.

The reasons for this are twofold. First, plants respire at a higher rate at elevated temperatures, burning large amounts of the sugars they have produced during the day, rather than using the sugars for growth, as they would in areas with cooler nighttime temperatures. As a result, the plants eventually (and often fairly rapidly) die of the botanical equivalent of fatigue: they wear themselves out in an effort to keep their cells supplied with oxygen. The other major problem is soil-borne and air-borne pathogens, which thrive in the warm, damp air of a Southeastern summer. Those who have never gardened in a humid climate would be shocked at the rapidity with which dense-growing, compact, or tomentose (hairy-leaved) plants can succumb. Seemingly healthy plants can turn into an unrecognizable mass of slime literally overnight, especially following an afternoon thunderstorm, the most common form of summer precipitation in the region.

In contrast, the winter climate in the Mid-Atlantic and Southeast is friendly to most garden plants. Wet winters can cause problems, as they do anywhere—for instance, limiting the use of South African succulents. As in the Pacific Northwest, markedly colder winters come along once every five or ten years, culling the more tender subjects in the rock garden.

In spite of these obstacles, rock gardening has a long history in the Southeast and Mid-Atlantic. In the early twentieth century, there were celebrated rock gardens in much of the area, even as far south as Louisiana and Alabama. These gardeners realized (probably the hard

PLATE 87. Norman Beal's garden, Raleigh, North Carolina. Photograph by Bobby Ward

way) that if they were to have successful rock gardens, the range of plants recommended by the dominant British and European authors of the time would not do. Silvery saxifrages, mats of Asiatic gentians, and sheets of raoulias simply were not an option. Like gardeners everywhere, they learned to adapt the style of gardening to suit their climate, in terms of both plant selection and cultural techniques.

The types of rock available for construction vary around the region. In the coastal plain of eastern North Carolina where I garden, there are no native rocks. Other areas of Piedmont (foothills) North Carolina feature mostly sedimentary rocks, often limestones, with extrusions of granite and slate. Although soils, too, vary widely, they are generally acidic. Heavy clay can be a problem for rock gardeners, especially in the Piedmont, because it impedes drainage during summer rainfall.

One style of rock gardening common to the region is the semi-shaded rock garden. Typically, this is a woodland garden featuring low-growing plants. Plants such as ferns, heucheras, small hostas, violas, and numerous small native spring ephemerals (*Hepatica*, *Jeffersonia*, and *Sanguinaria*, for example) populate such gardens.

PLATE 88. A shaded rock garden scene in Asheville, North Carolina, showing
Hakonechloa macra 'Aureola', *Amsonia montana*, and a selection of *Spiraea japonica*.
Photograph by Pamela Harper

Purists may cringe to hear such a planting called a "rock garden," but
few of those purists live where the temperature routinely climbs past
90°F (32°C) each summer day.

More traditional rock gardens are certainly possible in the region,
but care must be taken with plant selection. Many of the more pedes-
trian rock plants do wonderfully; for example, most *Phlox*, *Iberis*,
Origanum, and *Sedum* species and cultivars can be grown as well here
as anywhere. Other popular subjects, such as thymes and even sempervivums, can be tricky, rotting off in wet periods. An especially wide
variety of bulbs can be grown: everything from the Mediterranean and
southwest Asian species, which appreciate the hot summer dormancy,
to many South American and South African bulbs that are too tender
for areas with colder winters. Indeed, a rock garden could be comprised
solely of bulbous material and provide bloom nearly every day of the
year, at least in the southerly portion of the region. Another characteristic of rock gardens of the Mid-Atlantic and Southeast is a reliance on

native plant material such as *Viola pedata*, *Iris cristata*, *Iris verna*, and *Phlox subulata*.

Gardeners in this region also manipulate sites and cultural techniques, especially to grow moisture-sensitive dryland plants by building sand beds, raised berms, and troughs (see chapters in part 2 for details). By providing sufficient moisture combined with perfect drainage, southeastern gardeners have been able to grow plants such as eriogonums and western *Penstemon* species, which are extremely difficult to grow here in traditional rock garden settings.

Rock gardening in the Mid-Atlantic and Southeast can be difficult, but it is far from impossible. I garden in eastern North Carolina (USDA zone 8), a climate far removed from that of the Dolomite Alps or the Tien Shan mountains of China, yet I manage to have a respectable rock garden. It is a continuing challenge to experiment with new plants and learn how to grow familiar ones better.

PART 5

Visiting Public Rock Gardens

Botanic gardens, with their mandate to display as wide a variety of species as possible, often construct significant rock gardens to provide proper conditions for alpines and other rock plants. The rock garden may be a central attraction, as at the Edinburgh (Scotland), Wisley (England), and Denver (Colorado) institutions, or it may be a small feature, perhaps recently added as a public park or garden gains horticultural sophistication. Because small rock features are often the work of area chapters of NARGS or other rock garden societies, they are likely to offer many hints about appropriate construction that has been found to work at each locality. In addition, curators and committees usually stock public rock gardens with vigorous, relatively easy-to-grow plants that have a long season of interest and that can stand up to varying levels of care and mishandling by visitors.

When you visit these gardens, be sure to take a camera and notebook to record what you see and ideas for your own garden design. Visit during various seasons to observe which plants are particularly appealing then. If you live nearby, you may wish to volunteer at the garden—a good way to learn and, often, to obtain surplus plants or seeds. Most botanical gardens offer classes, including seminars on trough-making, and most have plant sales, where species not available commercially can be purchased.

Beyond public gardens, many members of NARGS regularly open their gardens to visitors. The society's directory, available to members, gives information on these for all of North America and also for the group's many members abroad. Always telephone or e-mail the gardener in advance to arrange your visit.

The sketches of public rock gardens in this section, each contributed by a curator or volunteer associated with the garden, are only a sample of what you can find for inspiration. The following also hold collections of alpine or other rock plants in specially constructed settings: Devonian Botanic Garden, Edmonton, Alberta; Rhododendron Species Foundation, Federal Way, Washington, rhododendrons and other ericaceous genera; University of California Botanic Garden, Berkeley, California; Huntington Botanical Garden, Los Angeles, California; Mount Goliath Bristlecone Pine Forest, Clear Creek County, Colorado, a crevice garden at the visitor parking lot, the highest public garden in North America at 11,600 feet (3480 m); Hudson Gardens, Littleton, Colorado, extensive alpine and dwarf conifer plantings; Betty Ford Alpine Garden, Vail, Colorado, native and exotic alpines growing above 8000 feet (2400 m); Allen Centennial Garden, University of Wisconsin, Madison; Olbrich Botanical Garden, Madison, Wisconsin; Rotary Gardens, Janesville, Wisconsin; Lake Harriet Park, Minneapolis, Minnesota; Dyck Arboretum, Hesston, Kansas; Royal Botanic Gardens, Hamilton, Ontario, with rock garden in a deep quarry pit; Berkshire Botanic Garden, West Stockbridge, Massachusetts; Stonecrop, Cold Spring on Hudson, New York, open by appointment and includes a retail nursery; Wave Hill, Bronx, New York.

St. John's, Newfoundland:
Memorial University Botanical Garden

TODD BOLAND

Located on Mount Scio Road in St. John's, Newfoundland, the Memorial University Botanical Garden was begun in 1971 and opened in 1977. About 750 feet (225 m) above sea level and within 2.5 miles (4 km) of the open Atlantic Ocean, the site is regarded as USDA zone 5b, with a mean maximum summer temperature of 68°F (20°C), mean winter temperature of 27°F (–3°C), and about 60 inches (150 cm) of annual precipitation. More than half of the cultivated area is occupied by the extensive rock gardens, woodland garden, and peatland beds. The latter two features and the ericaceous border host more than two hundred rhododendron hybrids and species (mostly dwarf); ninety cultivars of heaths, heather, and related genera; thirty varieties of *Primula*; and many other acid-loving plants. The site also encompasses a 111-acre (44.5-ha) nature reserve with trails traversing a spruce-fir forest, bog, fen, marsh, regenerating burn-over, and pond. No trip to

PLATE 89. The rock garden at Memorial University Botanical Garden, St. John's, Newfoundland. Photograph by Todd Boland

269

Newfoundland would be complete without a visit to this wonderful botanical garden, whose rockery is claimed to be the best in eastern Canada. The garden is open May through November.

The first rockery was built on a south-facing slope, using relatively small rocks and terraces to represent a mountainside. The soil is composed of equal parts of screened topsoil, leafmold, and coarse sand, and the area is mulched with a 2-inch (5-cm) layer of granite chips. The southern end has a scree slope. The newer rock garden, completed in 1989, contains a limestone garden and a mountain gully complete with stream. The former houses many of Newfoundland's native arctic-alpine species. In the gully, very large rocks were placed by heavy machinery; more than 200 tons (180 metric tons) of rock and 80 tons (72 metric tons) of mixed soil were used in this feature alone. The alpine house, constructed in 1991, has two display benches as well as a small rockery. Alpines are planted in clay pots and plunged in a sand bed; these are replaced throughout the growing season to present a maximal floral display at all times.

Montreal, Québec: The Alpine Garden at the Montreal Botanical Garden

RENÉ GIGUÈRE

Montreal's reasonably reliable snow cover (USDA zone 4; winter minima around $-30°F$, $-34°C$) allows growing a wide spectrum of plants. Good drainage must be provided for alpines because of long-lasting autumn wetness before solid frosts occur. Spring growth begins by April, and May is an explosion of color featuring typical alpine gems.

The alpine garden at the Montreal Botanical Garden was planned by the garden's first curator, Henry Teuscher, who in 1940 proposed a vast rock garden of 15 acres (6 ha). He believed that alpine, arctic, and subarctic plants should be grouped by geographical distribution in an alpinum, whereas other small ornamental plants should occupy a

PLATE 90. Cliff at the Montreal Botanical Garden. Photograph by René Giguère

separate rock garden. A small formal rock garden, built in 1949–1950 and still present, consists mainly of raised beds contained by dry stone walls laid out along formal lines and edged with paths. Today, however, rock garden plants and alpines are concentrated in the alpinum. The alpine flora of eight major mountainous regions of the world are placed on distinct hillocks, and cultivars are planted apart from natural species and grouped according to their geographical relationships with Europe, Asia, or North America. The alpinum was completed in 1961, when water finally poured over the magnificent artificial cascade. The mountains comprise more than 2500 rocks weighing as much as several tons apiece; the rock is weathered limestone obtained from surface deposits, effective for imitating exposed cliffs. The alpinum today holds more than three thousand taxa in a 10-acre (4-ha) area. Species never seen before in this region are continually tried, despite uncertainty about their hardiness.

Niagara Falls, Ontario:
Niagara Parks Botanical Gardens

ANNA LEGGATT

Students of the Niagara Parks Commission School of Horticulture, established in 1936, have created more than 100 acres (40 ha) of gardens at the southern end of the Niagara Peninsula. Nearby Lake Ontario and Lake Erie moderate the climate most years to USDA zone 7 (minimum temperature 0 to 10°F, –18 to –12°C); however, extremes of –13°F (–25°C) can occur in January and February. Snow cover is usually incomplete for most of the winter. The highest recorded temperature was 100°F (38°C), in August. Average rainfall is 32 inches (79 cm), mostly in September and June.

The rock garden, begun in 1956, is built of local limestone laid over a soil mound. In the 1990s, the rocks were repositioned to create a more natural background for the plants, and the native heavy clay soil was replaced by more hospitable mixtures. Scree areas, an alpine meadow, an ericaceous bed, and an artificial moraine were created. In 1998 the

PLATE 91. Water-worn rocks are used effectively at the Niagara Parks Rock Garden in Ontario. Photograph by Anna Leggatt

renovations were completed by a graduate student funded by a NARGS internship grant. The present rock garden is about 69 × 52 feet (21 × 16 m), rising to a height of 6.5 feet (2 m). There were approximately 240 different taxa in the garden in early 2001.

This good example of a relatively simple rock garden will give visitors ideas for their own gardens, and because it is a teaching garden, there is always something new to see. The garden is situated beside the Niagara Parkway, 5.6 miles (9 km) north (downstream) from the Canadian Horseshoe Falls. Follow signs to the Butterfly Conservatory. The garden is open every day from dawn to dusk, year round.

New York City: The New York Botanical Garden
STEVE WHITESELL

This garden is located on a 2.5-acre (1-ha) walled and fenced site in a small valley in the New York Botanical Garden. It was constructed, beginning in 1932, in a naturalistic style with rock gathered on the grounds. The large rocks used on the waterfall slope and streambed were maneuvered into place with teams of horses and manpower. Although intended to give the impression of natural rock formations, all the rockwork except for a large outcrop at the crest of the waterfall slope is constructed.

By the late 1980s, the rock garden appeared to be transitioning into a woodland garden. Thus began a twelve-year program of restoration undertaken by director Bob Bartolomei to reset fallen rockwork and reopen obscured vistas and sight lines. Existing scree beds, alpine meadow, and ericaceous beds were cleared, and new sand and peat beds constructed. Species diversity was increased to more than 2500 taxa. The base of the waterfall is now planted with sun-loving woody and herbaceous rock garden genera; the facing alpine meadow holds dwarf bulbs emerging from carpets of *Thymus* and *Dianthus*. The sand bed beyond, obscured by a low ridge surmounted by contorted *Pinus mugo*,

PLATE 92. A view of the rock garden at the New York Botanical Garden. Photograph by
Steve Whitesell

shelters *Cyclamen* species and other choice plants. Beyond, a path loops
around the ericaceous bed, interplanted with subjects suited to a peat
habitat. The path continues to a new crevice garden with an elaborate
three-tiered moraine beyond. Gravel spills across the path to a lawn,
which slopes to the streambed that bisects the garden. The stream is
bordered by water-loving *Primula* species, large *Rhododendron keiskei*
specimens, and ornamental trees that frame views to the waterfall
slope, the pond near the entrance, and the distant Native Plant Garden.
The garden is a laboratory of sensation in all seasons—particularly in
early to midspring, when bloom is heaviest.

Kansas City, Missouri:
The Limestone Rock Wall at Powell Gardens

ALAN BRANHAGEN

Powell Gardens, a municipal public botanical garden, is situated 35 miles (56 km) southeast of Kansas City, Missouri, in the center of the continental United States. The garden's soil is Missouri gumbo clay, limiting the palette of plants grown. A dry-stacked limestone wall provides a place for rock garden plants that can survive in the region's erratic climate. Summers are hot and humid; winters are wet, with bitter cold snaps and inconsistent snow cover (USDA hardiness zone 5b). The frost-free growing season extends from mid-April to late October.

The rock wall is just under 600 feet (180 m) long and averages 4 feet (1.2 m) in height. Light brown limestone with highlights of buff, gray, and rust was selected because it is warm in winter and nonglaring in summer. The wall lines a main access route, bringing its plants within easy access, and serves as a retaining wall into a sloping island. The wall rests on a concrete footing that was cast in place along with the adjacent concrete path. An extensive drainage-tile system gathers excess water from above the wall and carries it beneath the walk into a lake. The soil mix between and behind the stones is composed of 1 part each crushed limestone, compost, and local topsoil (a mixture too rich for many western North American plants).

More than 250 species and cultivars from around the world were selected, first for their adaptability to the site's soil, exposure, and climatic conditions, and then for their beauty. There are eight indentations along the wall to accommodate seating, one with a shade arbor. The wall's curving face and indentations provide eastern, southern, and western exposures, but little northern exposure. Plants colonize all the crevices; they creep, mound, and cascade to create a changing tapestry that forms a living wall. Plants native to Ozark glades have performed best, but the hot summers with either excessive or scant rainfall, high humidity, and high nighttime temperatures take their toll on most montane or alpine species.

Denver, Colorado: The Rock Alpine Garden at the Denver Botanic Gardens

SANDY SNYDER AND RICH BISHOP

It was not until the 1970s that Denver was ready to accept the idea of building a rock alpine garden in the southwestern corner of the Denver Botanic Gardens, situated just east of downtown Denver at 1005 York Street. The flat site was sculpted and shaped by Herb Schaal of the landscape design firm EDAW, Inc., and the new feature was dedicated in June 1981. The garden receives an average of 14 inches (35 cm) of rainfall annually. There is little shade, and the alpine species must survive occasional daytime temperatures above 90°F (32°C) in most summers.

PLATE 93. The Rock Alpine Garden at the Denver Botanic Gardens. Photograph by Panayoti Kelaidis

There is rarely enough snow cover in winter for reliable protection from the desiccating winter sun, and winter lows can reach −20°F (−29°C).

This rock alpine garden is testimony to the principle that a great range of plants can be grown if gardeners work with nature. Microclimates abound in the varied grades. Irrigation selectively furnishes moisture as needed by plants in specific areas. The garden, therefore, is planted according to the plants' cultural needs, not their geographical origin. In two areas—the hot, dry steppe and the upper meadow—the clay and bentonite soil has not been amended. The soil grows native xeric plants beautifully, and plants from climates like Denver's are real stars.

A large island has been constructed of immense limestone chunks, in-filled with a decomposed limestone soil ideal for Mediterranean plants. Some plants from South Africa do surprisingly well here, too. Salvias from Turkey, the Balkans, and the mountains of the Caucasus have made the moraine mound and the scree mound their homes. The lower meadow, a flat area in the middle of the garden, has soil with a high organic content, enjoyed by species from high mountain meadows.

PLATE 94. The Rock Alpine Garden at the Denver Botanic Gardens. Photograph by Panayoti Kelaidis

Bulbs put on an intense show from February through May here. The montane slope duplicates woodsy soils and is top-dressed annually with leafmold. A path winds through the fell field, an area of broken rock, and climbs to the garden's summit, from which the visitor can see 14,000-foot (4200-m) Mount Evans in the distance.

A rock garden planted with four thousand different plants from all over the world is truly a delight for the senses. The Rock Alpine Garden gives hikers a preview of the plants they will see on their Rocky Mountain wanderings and introduces the seasoned rock gardener to new plants from Africa, New Zealand, China, and South America. The garden also showcases design: it contains granite boulders through which a stream cascades and mists crevice plantings; limestone chunks and porous tufa, where plants have seeded themselves into tiny cracks; and red and white sandstone used in retaining walls. There are also innovative designs for larger-scale planting in semi-arid western landscapes.

Homer, Alaska:
The Pratt Museum Botanical Garden
VERNA PRATT

This small garden filled with Alaskan native plants is situated in front of the Pratt Museum in Homer, Alaska, a small community on Kachemak Bay backed by hills up to 1500 feet (450 m) in elevation. The maritime climate is equivalent to USDA zones 5–6 (winter minimum temperatures between –20 and –10°F, –29 and –23°C). The garden was renovated in 1989, and it now offers an effective array of habitats. Species are placed in appropriate plant communities, including beach, meadow, peat bog, bog-to-forest transitional zone, and alpine. Native shrubs form a barrier between the garden and the street and nearby buildings. A rail fence topped with cattle wire keeps the local moose at bay in winter. A small peat-bog garden contains wetland shrubs and many volun-

PLATE 95. Alpine plants of the subarctic at the Pratt Museum rock garden, Homer, Alaska. Courtesy of the Pratt Museum Photo Archives. Photograph by Nancy Levinson

teer moss species. The latest addition is the alpine rock garden, surrounded by handicapped-accessible trails. Obtaining plants from the wild for the rock garden required volunteers to travel by air to the mountains across Kachemak Bay. A slightly domed area mimics the alpine settings where the rocks and plants were gathered. Crushed rock has been used as scree material.

Varied leaf textures and foliage colors make this a delightful garden from early spring through autumn. Visitors who cannot reach the rocky peaks in the distance have the opportunity to view some of their natural beauties here. The fascinating plant material of this arctic-alpine garden lacks the waves of color often seen in rock gardens of warmer climates, but it has no need for them, for it has a charm all its own.

Vancouver, British Columbia:
E. H. Lohbrunner Alpine Garden

BRENT A. HINE

This feature of the expansive botanical garden is named in honor of a pioneering local alpine plant nurseryman, Edward H. Lohbrunner, who donated some of this garden's first plants. Part of the University of British Columbia Botanical Garden, the alpine garden was built in 1975, completed in time for an international rock gardening conference in Vancouver the following year. Under the direction of James MacPhail, the first curator, 2200 tons (1980 metric tons) of pyroxene andesite (a type of volcanic rock) were sited.

PLATE 96. The European section of the E. H. Lohbrunner Alpine Garden, Vancouver, British Columbia. Photograph by Judy Newton

The garden's design is based on broad geographical units, each representing a continent. In the African section, the focus is on Mediterranean and South African plants. In the Australasian section a wide array of exotic plants thrive. Trials of subalpine *Eucalyptus* species have led to permanent additions. The European section has many specialized niches: under a mature contorted hazel (*Corylus avellana* 'Contorta') grow self-sown *Cyclamen coum*, *Galanthus* species, and *Eranthis hyemalis*, an early spring show in January. Prominent outcrops built of tufa satisfy many *Dianthus* and *Saxifraga*. There is also ample space for classic crevice plants, scree-lovers, and cliffhangers. In the North American section grow some of the most intriguing plants. The warmest possible aspect and a very well drained, gravelly soil allow some southerly species to flourish well north of their ranges. Under the shade of a western maple is a hybrid swarm of trilliums. The large Asian section features a pond 20 feet (6 m) in diameter. Just south of it is a small woodland area; a bark-chip path winds through it, bisected by a dry streambed.

PLATE 97. The African section of the E. H. Lohbrunner Alpine Garden. Photograph by June C. West

In the nearby trough courtyard, most of the many troughs are made from hypertufa, but a few are hewn from solid stone. The hypertufa troughs have a life span of twenty to thirty years in this climate. These containers, in a range of sizes, contain some true alpine plants that are more comfortable where exceptionally free-draining soil mixes can be formulated and artificial irrigation closely monitored. Some of the plantings are thematic, from a particular geographical region or a sample of a genus, such as *Lewisia*.

The garden is only 100 feet (30 m) above sea level and very close to the bay, so trying to grow alpines is a challenge. Southwestern British Columbia winters are mostly snowless and wet. It is not sheer cold that causes problems for alpine plants, but the combination of cold and wet: the region's average annual rainfall is 50 inches (125 cm). To achieve the needed drainage, the garden was designed on a roughly 35° west-facing slope (opposite to the direction of wind-driven precipitation). The typical soil mixture used throughout the garden contains 1 part loam, 1 part coarse sand or fine (less than ⅜ inches [9 mm] diameter) gravel, and 1 part leafmold. Much of the garden is regularly replenished with additional soil. Vancouver has a cool Mediterranean climate, and supplementary irrigation is essential during July and August. When the boulders were placed, innumerable microenvironments were created for hundreds of alpine and rock plants from throughout the temperate world. Yet the wonder of this garden lies in its simplicity: it combines earth, air, water, and sunshine (and a little love) in such a fundamental way as to give enduring pleasure to all who visit. It reminds us that the earth is a garden, after all.

Bellevue, Washington: The Alpine Rock Garden at Bellevue Botanical Garden

MICHEAL MOSHIER

Bellevue, adjacent to Seattle, is Washington's second largest city and the home of the young but popular Bellevue Botanical Garden, begun in the early 1990s. Among its many features is the 6000-square-foot (540-square-meter) Alpine Rock Garden, constructed in 1996. The garden is situated on a north-facing, bowl-shaped slope adjacent to the main entry. The botanical garden is jointly managed by the City of Bellevue Parks and Community Services Department and the Bellevue Botanical Garden Society, with assistance from many volunteers, including members of the Northwestern Chapter of NARGS.

Although small in size, the garden was a monumental undertaking. Detailed construction drawings were prepared, along with specifications including more than 300 cubic yards (230 cubic meters) of custom-mixed rock garden soil: 150 tons (135 metric tons) of crushed and washed ⅜-inch gravel, 60 cubic yards (46 cubic meters) of ground

PLATE 98. The newly laid granite and paths of the Bellevue rock garden before planting. Photograph by Micheal Moshier

PLATE 99. The same garden one year after planting. Photograph by Micheal Moshier

pumice, and 90 cubic yards (69 cubic meters) of a commercial organic soil mix. This soil was spread over the site to a depth of 14–18 inches (35–45 cm). Into it, more than 300 tons (270 metric tons) of granite rock were carefully placed according to the plan, some of the stones weighing as much as 10 tons (9 metric tons).

Reminiscent of a natural alpine cirque, the rock garden's curving contours offer a variety of exposures from full sun to cool afternoon shade, providing ideal conditions for a wide variety of alpine plants. More than five hundred species and five thousand individual plants were placed in the garden in its first two years, with an emphasis on alpine genera native to the northwestern United States, complemented by compatible species from alpine regions around the world. The peak floral display begins in early spring with a wide array of miniature bulbs; as the seasons progress, a generous selection of conifers adds rich bronzy and plum-colored hues.

The rock garden has an intimate scale that home gardeners can easily relate to, and it provides many ideas to adapt to particular sites and circumstances. As well, it offers educational points about alpine habitats. In 2000 an interpretive plan was developed for the rock garden, resulting in reconfiguration of the pathways to accommodate increased access for disabled visitors and to encourage greater traffic flow. It was divided into zones for plants associated with specific alpine habitats, such as scree, subalpine, and moraine environments. Many plants were moved accordingly to new positions in the garden, and many other plants were added. This feature has become one of the most popular parts of the Bellevue Botanical Garden.

Portland, Oregon: The Berry Botanic Garden and Leach Botanical Garden

BONNIE BRUNKOW OLSON AND NEAL MAILLET

Portland has a relatively mild climate, with the Mediterranean rainfall pattern typical of the Pacific Coast. Approximately 36 inches (90 cm) of precipitation falls yearly, mainly between October and April. Average annual low temperatures are 15°F (–9°C) near the urban area. Both of these public gardens were carved from the native, dense Douglas fir forest by keen gardeners.

The Berry Garden is in a secluded residential neighborhood near Lewis and Clark College, about 4 miles (6.4 km) south of downtown Portland. Rae Selling Berry, the founder, raised many of her plants from seed acquired through subscriptions to early-twentieth-century botanical expeditions by explorers such as Frank Ludlow and George Sherriff, Joseph Rock, and E. K. Balls. In the 1930s, she began her forty years of rare-plant gardening in Lake Oswego. After Mrs. Berry died in 1976, a group formed to purchase the garden and save the extensive plant collections, to be administered as the Berry Botanic Garden.

The rock garden lies in a bowl-shaped, sunny slope with good drainage—crucial in a wet, western Oregon bottomland, where frost melts off foliage before the sun hits it. Drainage pits with tiles were laid beneath the site. The raised beds were initially bordered with Douglas fir logs chinked with moss. The planting medium, spread about 3 inches (75 mm) deep, consisted of 4 parts coarse washed river sand,

PLATE 100. The rock garden at the Berry Botanic Garden consists of low screes supported by lava rock, with wide paths for public access. Photograph by Bonnie Brunkow Olson

2 parts pea gravel, 1 part peat, and 1 part screened leafmold. The surface was mulched with stone chips. Mrs. Berry chose this style with an eye to enjoying it in her old age, saying the "agony of hopping over stones and bending down to see the plants . . . sometimes slipping off and doing untold damage takes away from enjoyment."

Eventually, the log edges broke down and water no longer penetrated the beds evenly; drainage systems failed in some beds; and overgrown dwarf conifers and surrounding trees cast too much shade. Gardener Jack Poff began to rebuild the beds in 1968 and also made the first of the many troughs, which are grouped in a separate display area today. He reconfigured the beds and paths to soften the old grid system and added much more rock, in a style featuring tiered serpentine rows of rockwork with planting pockets. In the 1990s, a new rockery was built in the front of the house, remodeled as an office and visitor center. Two small beds hold a Siskiyou Mountains–themed ecological planting, incorporating serpentine rock outcrops. An 8-foot (2.4-m) tall rock retaining wall at the eastern edge of the scree beds is now incorporated into the rock garden display.

PLATE 101. Construction of the rock garden at the Leach Botanical Garden: a crevice garden on a precipitous south-facing slope, where creating public access was a challenge. Photograph by Bonnie Brunkow Olson

Today the rock garden collection consists of approximately thirty individual beds and forty-nine troughs covering 0.25 acre (0.1 ha). The plants come from around the world, with perhaps half native to western North America. Except for an ericaceous bed, the Siskiyou bed, and a rare and endangered plant area, most plants are placed not thematically but by microhabitat preference; some succeed only after numerous moves into new sites. The garden is now being refocused toward Northwest native plants and ecological displays. It is open to the public by appointment.

The rock garden at Leach Botanical Garden is a work in progress that began small and failed in its first attempts. John and Lilla Leach, botanical explorers of the Siskiyou Mountains, purchased 4 acres (1.6 ha) of forested land in suburban Southeast Portland in 1931. The land is steep, straddling an east–west ravine with an elevation gain of nearly 50 feet (15 m) from Johnson Creek to the upper boundaries. The first rock garden was built on a precipitous slope behind the house, above a 4-foot (1.2-m) brick retaining wall. It was not a very successful planting site, possibly because of the challenges presented by the steep, south-facing clay slope. In 1967, Jack Poff worked on the existing outcrop to make it more habitable, digging soil out from behind the rocks and replacing it with sand and scoria debris.

After the Leaches died, the garden and house were given to the City of Portland to use as a park and museum. A volunteer foundation, the Leach Garden Friends, organized in 1982 to raise money for programs, capital improvements, and staff. To showcase Northwest native plants from rocky habitats and alpine zones, the foundation decided to build a rock garden on the site of the old outcrop, one of the few places in the garden with a sunny exposure. After removing shrubs and old rocks, volunteers dug a drainage trench at the bottom of the site and filled it with perforated plastic drainpipe and round rock. Mixed sand, peat, and compost amended the soil. The Oregon Cactus and Succulent Society and gardener Scotty Fairchild installed a rock garden display of hardy cacti and succulents from the Northwest and Great Basin on the hottest part of the hillside slope, where they are covered in winter against rain.

In the early 1990s, Fairchild constructed a Columbia River Gorge plant display area, connected the cactus and succulent segment to the initial rock garden, and continued expansion uphill with a scree zone, a strata and cliff area, and a deep planting pocket—adding 1700 square feet (153 square meters) to the rock garden. To mitigate the hot exposure, one portion of the path is sunken between sunny and shady walls. The steep slope, averaging between 30 and 50 percent grade, limited the construction style to a hybrid between a sloped retaining wall and a crevice garden with a few small planting ledges. The rock used is dark, blocky central Oregon lava, which can be set tightly to discourage soil erosion. Part of the garden's main circulation trail bisects the upper part of the rock garden, allowing visitors to wander through the collection. Today the rock garden covers approximately 2445 square feet (220 square meters). There is still room to expand, and a water feature is planned. There are also problems of age, clay percolation, and shade to correct.

The Leach Botanical Garden is just east of Interstate 205 on 122nd Avenue south of Foster Road. It is open from dawn to dusk throughout the year but may be closed on summer weekends, when the garden is often rented out for wedding parties. Plants are sold at the garden, as well.

Eugene, Oregon:
The Sebring Rock Garden, Alton Baker Park
LOUISE PARSONS

Diverse talents within the Emerald Chapter of NARGS combined to build and maintain the Sebring Rock Garden in Alton Baker Park, just across the Willamette River from downtown Eugene in Oregon's southern Willamette Valley. This unusual project was sponsored by a NARGS grant in 1996 that enabled the society's local chapter to combine more than 100 tons (90 metric tons) of boulders and countless loads of soil and amendments into an artistic landscape covering more than 6000 square feet (540 square meters).

PLATE 102. The Sebring Rock Garden under construction, with grit mulch ready to be spread. Photograph by Louise Parsons

PLATE 103. Plants suited to a sunny public site soon created a brilliant floral display at the Sebring Rock Garden. Photograph by Louise Parsons

Metabasalt boulders form the structural backbone of the garden. It is surrounded by pavement, offering good overall visibility and vantage points, and wide gravel paths make it entirely wheelchair-accessible. The paths, with curves and visual breaks with varying orientations, allow a good representation of exposures and planting areas. The native soil used as a foundation is a rich silty loam, to which was added plenty of scoria (dark, nutrient-rich lava) grit, very sandy loam, and composted forest products. Contoured mounds of foundation soil secure the large boulders, in keeping with the scale of the project.

There is bloom and foliar interest in the garden year round: cyclamen, heathers, ferns, and berries in winter; bulbs and saxifrages in earliest spring; the native *Dasanthera* penstemons in late spring; rhododendrons in April; Mediterranean plants in summer. Penstemon cultivars can bloom until hard frost, as do many hardy rock garden geraniums. Autumn brings a display of *Helichrysum*, heathers, hebes, and *Pimelea*, and the renewed growth of rock ferns.

APPENDIX
Ingredients for Rock Garden Soils

Basic ingredients derived from rock and soil

Ingredient	Characteristics	Sources
sandy loam	predominantly sand with a variable quantity and quality of loam; a good basic ingredient	active and ancient river channels, outwash areas; purchase from landscape and construction suppliers
sand	varies by locality; upland river deposits preferred for sharp, salt-free sand; builder's sand has even particle size distribution; masonry sand is very fine textured	ancient dune deposits, river deposits lake and sea shores; purchase from sand and gravel quarries or dig by permit
aeolian soil, loess	fine grained but gritty; lacks cohesion and water retention; good rock garden soil, good substitute for sandy loam	wind deposits from the end of the Pleistocene, especially in western North America; purchase from landscape and aggregate suppliers or dig by permit
pumice	lightweight volcanic rock	volcanic deposits; purchase from quarries, masonry block plants, or in bags from landscape suppliers
scoria	heavier volcanic rock, usually dark	volcanic deposits; purchase from landscape suppliers (as "lava rock") or dig by permit
perlite	industrially hydrated pumice, white, very lightweight; unsuitable for outdoor use but employed in potting soils	purchase in bulk or bagged from garden centers or agricultural suppliers
rock chips	broken or crushed rock; angular; diameter may be specified	sand and gravel quarries, aggregate suppliers
pea gravel	rounded rock particles, diameter usually specified	quarries, aggregate suppliers
river gravel, river rock	water-rounded rock particles, usually larger than pea gravel	quarries, aggregate suppliers
grit	rock particles of small diameter (less than ¼ inch [6 mm]); various sizes available	landscape suppliers, feed stores (as poultry grit), aquarium suppliers (as aquarium gravel or sand)

Basic ingredients derived from rock and soil, continued

Ingredient	Characteristics	Sources
recycled aggregate	usually crushed concrete intended for roadbeds; if used as garden filler, be sure it does not contain asphalt or oiled bed material	construction companies, aggregate suppliers
expanded clay or shale	clays and shales calcined or otherwise industrially treated; trade names include Turface® and Axis®	landscape suppliers, garden centers
vermiculite	hydrated magnesium, aluminum, and iron silicates processed into evenly sized flakes; holds water well; often used in potting soils	garden centers, agricultural suppliers

Mineral soil amendments

Ingredient	Effects	Supplier
rock phosphate	provides calcium phosphate and limited elemental calcium with slow release	gardening suppliers, especially organic gardening specialists
glacial rock flour	may provide nutrients especially good for alpines, but very fine textured and can impede drainage	suppliers catering to organic gardeners; collect in nature by permit
greensand	provides potassium and trace minerals such as magnesium and iron; mined from prehistoric marine-organism deposits	organic gardening suppliers; cost varies depending on local availability
lime	provides calcium	available powdered, granulated, or in slow-release prilled form from agricultural and garden suppliers
dolomite lime	calcium-magnesium carbonate; has less effect on soil pH than lime and provides magnesium	agricultural and garden suppliers
other limestone products	granulated and hydrated forms, processed to minimize dust in handling; provides more rapid release of lime	agricultural and garden suppliers
gypsum	calcium sulfate; changes texture of certain soils and can enhance drainage; may aid nutrient	availability and release calcium and sulfur agricultural and garden suppliers; rock products companies

Mineral soil amendments, continued

Ingredient	Effects	Supplier
rock sulfur	sometimes used to modify pH	agricultural and garden suppliers
superphosphate	supplies phosphate; use with caution after soil testing	agricultural and garden suppliers; agricultural product must be carefully diluted with masonry sand for garden use
balanced fertilizers	provide equal ratio of nitrogen, phosphate, and potassium (N, P, and K); use weak applications on rock garden by lowering spreading rate and purchasing slow-release forms	agricultural and garden suppliers
potash	provides potassium; use only if soil test indicates deficiency	agricultural suppliers
water-retention polymers or gels	expand after moistening to globs that retain water; often used in hanging containers; *not recommended* for rock garden plants	garden suppliers
oyster shell	when finely crushed, provides soluble and absorbable minerals, especially calcium; wash well to remove salt	feed stores

Organic materials

Ingredient	Characteristics	Sources
peat, peat moss	retains water well, but difficult to remoisten if it dries	deposits in old bogs; sold in bags or bales by garden and agricultural suppliers
coir, coconut fiber	aerates soil and holds water; adds fiber to clay; can hold too much moisture; turns slimy in warm conditions	industrial by-product; sold in bales at garden centers
cocoa bean, buckwheat, and other nut and bean hulls	long-lasting; variable effects on soil chemistry; untested in rock gardens; cocoa may repel cats and rodents	agricultural by-products; sold in bags at garden centers and, locally, at agricultural processing plants
leafmold	retains water and rewets readily; few weed seeds; decomposes rapidly (oak leafmold is longer lasting)	sold in bags or in bulk by garden centers and, in some areas, by municipal composting facilities

Organic materials, continued

Ingredient	Characteristics	Sources
compost	highly variable; be sure it does not contain unacceptable levels of herbicide or pesticide; may contain weed seeds; homemade is safest	sold in bulk at garden centers, landscape suppliers, and some municipal waste and composting facilities; agricultural by-products such as mint compost are locally available
mushroom compost	contains spent manure and well-rotted straw; decomposes rapidly and provides rapid nutrient supply; contains lime and may have harmful levels of salts	by-product of mushroom growing; sold by growers; sold bagged or in bulk by garden and landscape suppliers
sawdust	quality varies; must be rotted before use in soil	quality varies; must be rotted before use in soil
bark fines, bark dust	texture often uneven; must be rotted before use in soil; bulk product often contains weed seeds	by-product of lumber industry; sold in bulk by landscape suppliers and mills, in bags at garden centers
bone meal	provides many minerals, primarily calcium phosphate; tolerance by alpine plants varies; may attract pest animals	by-product of meat industry; sold bagged by agricultural and garden suppliers
blood meal	provides nitrogen and trace elements; may attract pests	by-product of meat industry; sold bagged by garden suppliers
bat guano	releases nitrogen quickly; but too hot for alpines and expensive	mined in caves, sometimes to detriment of bat populations; sold by organic garden suppliers
fish meal, fish fertilizer	weak source of various minerals; attracts pest animals, snails, and slugs	sold as powder or liquid by garden suppliers

Glossary

aeolian soil: wind-deposited soil

aggregate: the mixture of sand and small stones used in concrete

alpine house: a specialized greenhouse with extra ventilation

backfill: soil placed behind a retaining wall or other rock feature

berm: a mound of soil, usually elongated, raised above the general grade of the garden

bun: a plant that grows in a dense, compact, more or less spherical shape; also called "cushion"

chasmophyte: a plant that grows naturally on vertical cliff walls, especially in canyons or gorges

cobbles: somewhat square or spherical rocks, ranging in diameter from about 4 to 8 inches (10 to 20 cm)

compost: in American usage, rotted leaves and other vegetable material; in British usage, any soil mixture, such as potting soil

crushed rock: sharp gravel produced in various sizes by quarry operations; often used for paving

cushion: *see* bun

dry wall: a wall constructed of stone or concrete blocks without mortar

duff: the upper layer of soil in a forest, consisting of almost pure organic matter from fallen leaves, conifer needles, and twigs

dwarf: a vague term applied to a plant that is smaller than most of its relatives or a clone that is smaller than the typical form in its species; herbaceous plants shorter than 1 foot (0.3 m) are considered dwarf, and dwarf shrubs are a bit larger

ericaceous: belonging to the family Ericaceae

fieldstone: rocks of various sizes mixed in the soil; they tend to rise to the surface through frost action

fines: particles of very small size

grit: fine, sharp, crushed rock of any type, usually with a diameter less than ¼ inch (6 mm)

hardscaping: landscape elements other than plant material

humus: highly organic soil

leafmold: well-rotted leaves and other vegetable material

lights: the glazed panels of a cold frame or greenhouse

loam: soil consisting of an easily crumbled mixture of clay, silt, and sand

loess: wind-deposited soil

moraine: an accumulation of earth and stones carried and finally deposited by a glacier; see "Moraine and Scree Gardens"

naturalistic: resembling forms or scenes found in nature, unmodified by human activity

outcrop, outcropping: a natural feature occurring where underlying rock rises above a generally soil-covered area

pea gravel: somewhat rounded stones with a diameter of about ¼ inch (6 mm), obtained by grading material from sand and gravel quarries; often used as a mulch

peat: organic material quarried from ancient bogs, primarily derived from sedges and sphagnum mosses; in North America, usually sold milled and baled as a soil amendment

peat bed: in North America, any planting area heavily amended with peat; in Britain, a bed constructed of block peat

perlite: a lightweight mineral product often used in potting soils

pore space: air space between the particles of a soil mixture

pumice: a volcanic rock that is light and fragile due to many tiny air spaces; horticultural pumice is ground into angular particles with a diameter of about ¼ inch (3 mm)

raised bed: a planting area, often rather formal in design, raised above the general grade of the garden

retaining wall: stone, concrete blocks, railroad ties, or other material set against a steep soil slope

river rocks: rocks worn round and smooth by the tumbling action of
rivers

root run: the area in the soil available to a plant for root growth

scoria: a volcanic rock, usually dark in color, with tiny air spaces;
heavier and harder than pumice

scree: a substrate composed almost entirely of decomposing rock,
usually without much organic matter or fines; mobile scree is found
on steep slopes in the mountains

sharp sand: quarried sand that has not been rounded by water action;
usually obtained at higher elevations on rivers

soil mix, soil mixture: any combination of soil materials, mixed in
proportions suitable for growing a specific range of plants

stratified rock: rock formed by being laid down in level layers, such
as water-deposited sediment, and that fractures into more or less
flat slabs

talus: a natural feature consisting of stone rubble of larger diameter
than scree

tufa: a soft, water-deposited calcium carbonate rock, usually gray and
highly textured; the word *tufa* is often misapplied to volcanic tuff, a
type of pumice

xeriscaping: a style of planting using species that do not require supplemental irrigation

Annotated Bibliography

Periodicals and Societies

The Alpine Garden (formerly *Bulletin of the Alpine Garden Society*). 1932–. This journal of the Alpine Garden Society, included in membership, is illustrated in color throughout. Articles cover specialist gardening, features on genera, and extensive reports on prize winners at AGS shows and new introductions. The Alpine Garden Society, AGS Centre, Avon Bank, Pershore, Worcestershire WR10 3JP, England, United Kingdom. www.alpinegardensociety.org

The Rock Garden. 1975–. This journal of the Scottish Rock Garden Club, included in membership, is illustrated in color. The content is similar to that of *The Alpine Garden* but focuses on the colder climate of Scotland. Scottish Rock Garden Club Membership Secretary, P.O. Box 14063, Edinburgh EH10 4YE, Scotland, United Kingdom. www.srgc.org

Rock Garden Quarterly (formerly *Bulletin of the American Rock Garden Society*), 1940–. The journal of the North American Rock Garden Society; subscription included in membership. Each issue contains eighty pages, sixteen in full color; articles cover gardening, features on genera and individual species, travels to wild plant sites, and book reviews. Executive Secretary, North American Rock Garden Society, P.O. Box 67, Millwood, NY 10546. www.nargs.org

Rock Gardening in North America and Its Antecedents
compiled by Marnie Flook

Bissland, James. 1938. *Common Sense in the Rock Garden*. New York: De La Mare. Identifies two types of rock gardens: the architectural (or structural) rock garden, containing pavement plantings and planted walls, and the naturalistic rock garden, developed to duplicate a piece of nature.

Cabot, Francis H. 1984. "As It Was in the Beginning: The Origin and Roots of Rock Gardening in North America." *Bulletin of the American Rock Garden Society* 42.5: 22–48. A history of practice, primarily in the Northeast, and early activities of the (North) American Rock Garden Society.

Canning, Edward J. 1900. "Rock Gardens." In *Cyclopedia of American Horticulture*, ed. by Liberty Hyde Bailey. New York: Macmillan. By the head gardener at the Smith College Botanical Garden's rock garden, completed in 1897 and still in existence.

Correvon, Henri, and Philippe Robert. 1911. *The Alpine Flora*. Trans. and rev. by E. W. Clayforth. London: Methuen. English edition of Correvon's *Les Plantes des Alpes*, first published in French in 1884.

Davidsonia. 1978. Special issue: Dedication of the E. H. Lohbrunner Alpine Garden. Journal of the Botanical Garden, University of British Columbia, Vancouver. A landmark in a prime center of North American rock gardening.

Farrer, Reginald. 1908. *My Rock Garden*. London: Edward Arnold. Farrer's books had the greatest influence on the rock and alpine gardeners of the early twentieth century.

Farrer, Reginald. 1919. *The English Rock Garden*. London: T. & E. Jack. 2d ed., 1925. For many years the bible of rock gardening.

Flook, Marnie. 1997. *A History of the American Rock Garden Society, 1934–1995*. Manhattan, Kans.: North American Rock Garden Society. Primarily organizational history, but mentions some noted gardens.

Foster, H. Lincoln. 1968. *Rock Gardening: A Guide to Growing Alpines and Other Wildflowers in the American Garden*. New York: Bonanza. Reprint. Portland, Ore.: Timber Press, 1982. Often called the "American Bible of rock gardening," this books describes 1900 plants in 400 genera and contains advice on how to build a classic East Coast rock garden, as well as other ways to grow the plants.

Kolaga, Walter A. 1966. *All About Rock Gardens and Plants*. New York: Doubleday. Primarily a plant list, but construction of gardens is also discussed.

Robinson, William. 1870. *Alpine Flowers for the English Garden*. The early advocate of naturalistic gardens ventures into the mountains.

Schenk, George. 1964. *How to Plan, Establish and Maintain Rock Gardens*. Menlo Park, Calif.: Lane. 2d ed., Palo Alto, Calif.: Sunset Books, 1972. An early work by a writer known for his strict approach to principled design. Includes detailed instructions, with illustrations, on how to build a natural-looking rock garden.

Schnare, Susan. 1991. "Some Massachusetts Gardens." *Journal of the New England Garden History Society* 1 (Fall). Describes some nineteenth-century New England rock gardens.

Symons-Jeune, B. H. B. 1932. *Natural Rock Gardening*. London: Country Life.
Although published in England, this book also exerted influence in
North America with its advice to lay rocks according to nature's rules.

Thomas, Graham Stuart. 1989. *The Rock Garden and Its Plants*. Portland,
Ore.: Sagapress and Timber Press. A history of rock gardening, mainly in
the United Kingdom and Europe.

Recent Books on Rock and Alpine Gardening

Carl, Joachim. 1990. *Miniature Gardens*. Trans. from the 2d ed. by Martin
Kral. Portland, Ore.: Timber Press.

Chatto, Beth. 2000. *Beth Chatto's Gravel Garden*. New York: Viking
Studio/Penguin. Many ideas for the xeric garden, although focused on
larger plants.

Fingerut, Joyce, and Rex Murfitt. 1999. *Creating and Planting Garden Troughs*.
Wayne, Pa.: B. B. Mackey. A more extensive version of the material found
in the present volume, illustrated throughout.

Foerster, Karl. 1987. *Rock Gardens through the Year*. Rev. by Bernard Rollich.
London: Macdonald. Foerster's northern European perspective is useful,
especially to Midwestern gardeners.

Good, John, ed. 1988. *Handbook of Rock Gardening*. 2d ed. Birmingham,
U.K.: Alpine Garden Society. Articles by leading British gardeners on
various aspects of the craft, for the novice; although many of the
materials mentioned are not available in North America, this is a useful
and inexpensive paperback, available from the AGS book service.

Halpin, Anne, and Robert Bartolomei. 1997. *Rock Gardens*. New York:
Clarkson Potter. A fine account, but difficult to find.

Hills, Lawrence D. 1959. *The Propagation of Alpines*. 2d rev. ed. London: Faber
& Faber. Reprint. Sakonnet, R.I.: Theophrastus, 1976. Although many of
the materials mentioned have been superseded by advancing technology,
serious growers still turn to this manual for help in propagating choice
plants.

Rolfe, Robert. 1990. *The Alpine House: Its Plants and Purposes*. London:
Christopher Helm; Portland, Ore.: Timber Press. An information-packed
little book on the British style of growing difficult plants in pots under glass.

Regional and Specialized Works

Allison, James. 1991. *Water in the Garden*. London: Salamander Books.

Burrell, C. Colston, ed. 1995. *Woodland Gardens*. Brooklyn Botanic Garden, Handbook 145. New York.

Burrell, C. Colston, ed. 1998. *The Shady Border*. Brooklyn Botanic Garden, Handbook 155. New York.

Case, Frederick W., Jr. 1962. "Growing Native Orchids of the Great Lakes Region." *American Orchid Society Bulletin* 31: 437–445.

Case, Frederick W., Jr. 1992a. "Bog Gardens and Bog Plants." *Bulletin of the American Rock Garden Society* 50: 45–46.

Case, Frederick W., Jr. 1992b. "Plants for the Bog Garden." *Bulletin of the American Rock Garden Society* 50: 129–144.

Case, Frederick W., Jr. 1992c. "Carnivorous Plants for the Bog Garden." *Bulletin of the American Rock Garden Society* 50: 205–210. (Includes "A Siphon System for the Bog Garden," by Roberta B. Case.)

Case, Roberta B. 1992. "A Sphagnum Bog Garden." *Bulletin of the American Rock Garden Society* 50: 11–12.

Elliot, Jack. 1998. *The Woodland Garden*. Pershore, U.K.: Alpine Garden Society..

Elliott, Joe. 1981. *Alpines in Sinks and Troughs*. Pershore, U.K.: Alpine Garden Society. Elliott was one of the earliest rock gardeners to perfect the use of troughs.

Fingerut, Joyce, and Rex Murfitt. 1999. *Creating and Planting Garden Troughs*. Wayne, Pa.: B. B. Mackey Books.

Glattstein, Judy. 1998. *Made for the Shade*. Hauppage, N.Y.: Barrons.

Hawthorne, Linden. 1999. *Gardening in Shade*. American Horticultural Society Practical Guides. New York: DK Publishing.

Jans, Harry. 1993. "A Freestanding Tufa Wall." *Bulletin of the Alpine Garden Society* 61.2: 196–199. Jans is a brilliant innovator in techniques for the small rock garden.

Kelaidis, Gwen. 1999. "A Glossary of Gravel." *Rock Garden Quarterly* 57 (winter): 62. Sorts out local terminology for rock products.

Knopf, Jim. 1991. *The Xeriscape Flower Gardener*. Boulder, Colo.: Johnson Books.

Lawrence, Elizabeth. 1986. *The Little Bulbs*. Durham, N.C.: Duke University Press. Bulbs for the Southeast.

Lawrence, Elizabeth. 1990. *A Rock Garden in the South*. Ed by Nancy Goodwin and Allen Lacy. Durham, N.C.: Duke University Press.

Lawrence, Elizabeth. 1997. *A Garden of One's Own*. Ed. by Barbara Scott and Bobby J. Ward. Chapel Hill: University of North Carolina Press.

Lowry, Betty J. 1986. "In the Northwest." In *Rocky Mountain Alpines*, ed. by Jean Williams, pp. 275–281. Portland, Ore.: Timber Press.

Mathew, Brian. 1997. *Growing Bulbs: The Complete Practical Guide*. London: Batsford.

Mellichamp, T. L. 1992. "Hybrid Pitcher Plants." *Bulletin of the American Rock Garden Society* 50: 3–10.

Nash, Helen, and Eamonn Hughes. 1997. *Waterfalls, Fountains, Pools and Streams: Designing and Building Water Features in Your Garden*. New York: Sterling.

Pratt, Verna. 1990. *Field Guide to Alaskan Wildflowers*. Edited by Frank Pratt. Anchorage, Ala.: AlaskaKrafts.

Pratt, Verna. 1991. *Wildflowers along the Alaska Highway*. Edited by Frank Pratt. Anchorage, Ala.: AlaskaKrafts.

Pratt, Verna, and Frank Pratt. 1993. *Wildflowers of Denali National Park*. Anchorage, Ala.: AlaskaKrafts.

Rix, Martyn. 1986. *Growing Bulbs*. Rev. ed. Bromley, U.K.: Christopher Helm; Portland, Ore.: Timber Press. Especially valuable for its description of worldwide climates and how they affect plant communities and gardening.

Schenk, George. 1997. *Moss Gardening: Including Lichens, Liverworts, and Other Miniatures*. Portland, Ore.: Timber Press.

Slocum, Perry D., and Peter Robinson. 1996. *Water Gardening, Water Lilies and Lotuses*. Portland, Ore.: Timber Press.

Spain, John. 1997. *Growing Winter Hardy Cacti in Cold/Wet Climate Conditions*. Middlebury, Conn.: Privately printed.

Springer, Lauren. 1994. *The Undaunted Gardener*. Golden, Colo.: Fulcrum. Strategies, including rock gardens, for the dry-climate Intermountain West.

Sunset Books. 2001. *Sunset Western Garden Book*. K. Norris, ed. Menlo Park, Calif.: Sunset Books.

Plants for the Rock Garden

NOTE. Some of the works listed in the historical section contain extensive
plant lists, especially those by Farrer, Foster, and Kolaga. The works in this
section describe individual plants and their cultivation; even the older
ones listed are useful reference books for the modern rock gardener.

American Rock Garden Society and Denver Botanic Gardens. 1986. *Rocky
Mountain Alpines*. Portland, Ore.: Timber Press. A collective volume
prepared for an international conference on alpine plants, with sections
on plant geography, seeing plants in the wild, and growing species from
this region.

Anderson, Edward F. 2000. *The Cactus Family*. Portland, Ore.: Timber Press.
A beautifully produced compendium, the best work presently available
on cacti.

Barr, Claude. 1983. *Jewels of the Plains: Wild Flowers of the Great Plains
Grasslands and Hills*. Minneapolis: University of Minnesota Press.
Worthwhile plants of the prairies and plains, by a founder of American
rock gardening.

Beckett, Kenneth, ed. 1993. *Alpine Garden Society Encyclopaedia of Alpines*. 2
vols. Pershore, U.K.: AGS Publications. Certainly the most complete and
up-to-date reference in the field, and the only widely available source on
South American alpines in particular; although very expensive, it is
indispensable to the committed grower of alpine plants and hardy bulbs.

Benson, Lyman. 1982. *The Cacti of the United States and Canada*. Stanford:
Stanford University Press.

Clausen, Robert. 1975. *Sedum of North America North of the Mexican Plateau*.
Ithaca, N.Y.: Cornell University Press.

Cullina, William. 2000. *Growing and Propagating Wildflowers*. New York:
Houghton Mifflin. Focuses on the Northeast but extends beyond it, by
the propagator for the New England Wild Flower Society.

Elliott, Jack. 1991. *Alpines in the Open Garden*. London: Christopher Helm;
Portland, Ore.: Timber Press. A great grower discusses plants suitable for
unprotected conditions in England; the plants are arranged by type of
habitat.

Fincham, Robert L. 1983–1984. "Little-known Miniature Conifers." *Bulletin of
the American Rock Garden Society* 41: 189–192, 42: 31–35, 73–75.

Grey-Wilson, Christopher, ed. 1989. *A Manual of Alpine and Rock Garden Plants*. London: Christopher Helm; Portland, Ore.: Timber Press. The most up-to-date of the English manuals listed here, but coverage is very selective and limited to the more commonly available species.

Griffith, Anna N. 1973. *Collins Guide to Alpines and Rock Garden Plants*. Reprint. London: Collins, 1983. Many growers use this older English manual for its clarity, but it is now outdated in terms of plant names and coverage.

Heath, Royton E. 1983. *Collectors' Alpines: Their Cultivation in Frames and Alpine Houses*. Portland, Ore.: Timber Press. First published in the United Kingdom and written from a British perspective; the long plant list is especially good on European species.

Ingwersen, Will. 1991. *Alpines*. Portland, Ore.: Sagapress and Timber Press. In a sense, a supplement to Ingwersen's *Manual* (below), written in a pleasant conversational style and issued in an attractive large, color-illustrated format.

Ingwersen, Will. 1991. *Manual of Alpine Plants*. 2d ed. London: Cassell. This (or the first edition of 1978) are particularly accessible to the novice grower, written with clarity and enthusiasm; no illustrations, however.

Irish, Mary, and Gary Irish. 2000. *Agaves, Yuccas and Related Plants*. Portland, Ore.: Timber Press.

Koerner, Christian. 1999. *Alpine Plant Life*. Berlin: Springer. A technical work on plant ecology, useful for understanding the needs of alpine plants.

Krussmann, Gerd. 1985. *Manual of Cultivated Conifers*. Portland, Ore.: Timber Press.

Kummert, Fritz. 1989. *Pflanzen für das Alpinenhaus*. Stuttgart: Ulmer. In German; the introduction and plant list contain tips for growing many very unusual species in a cold climate, so this is valuable for North American gardeners who find the English books unsuited to their conditions.

Lowe, Duncan. 1991. *Growing Alpines in Raised Beds, Trough, and Tufa*. London: Batsford.

Lowe, Duncan. 1995. *Cushion Plants for the Rock Garden*. London: Batsford.

Mathew, Brian. 1989. *The Genus Lewisia*. Bromley, U.K.: Christopher Helm; Portland, Ore.: Timber Press.

Mineo, Baldassare. 1999. *Rock Garden Plants: A Color Encyclopedia*. Portland, Ore.: Timber Press. Features 1350 color photos and is written from an

American perspective, unlike most of the "plant-list" works cited here; by the proprietor of the famous Siskiyou Rare Plant Nursery.

North American Rock Garden Society. 1996. *Rock Garden Plants of North America: An Anthology from the Bulletin of the North American Rock Garden Society*. Ed. by Jane McGary. Portland, Ore.: Timber Press. Articles, many with authors' revisions, selected from fifty years of the Society's journal, covering plants native to North America, where to see them in the wild, and how to grow them.

North American Rock Garden Society. 2001. *Bulbs of North America*. Edited by Jane McGary. Portland, Ore.: Timber Press.

Paterson, Allen. 1987. *Plants for Shade and Woodland*. Markham, Ont.: Fitzhenry and Whiteside.

Phillips, Roger, and Martyn Rix. 1989. *The Random House Book of Bulbs*. Ed. by Brian Mathew. New York: Random House. The most useful illustrated manual of hardy bulbs.

van Gelderen, D. M., and J. R. P. van Hoey Smith. 1996. *Conifers: The Illustrated Encyclopedia*. 2 vols. Portland, Ore.: Timber Press.

Contributors

Rich Bishop was horticulturist for the Rock Alpine Garden at the Denver Botanic Gardens for seven years. He holds a degree in environmental planning and management.

Todd Boland is a college instructor in general horticulture in St. John's, Newfoundland. He is a dedicated birder and, in his garden, focuses on conifers and ericaceous plants.

Alan Branhagen is director of horticulture at Powell Gardens in Kingsville, near Kansas City, Missouri. He holds a degree in landscape architecture and is the author of *The Gardener's Butterfly Book* (2001).

Bonnie Brunkow Olson, a botanist, was formerly director of the Leach Botanical Garden and worked at the Berry Botanic Garden, both in Portland, Oregon.

Michael Chelednik has a degree in biology and lives and gardens in Greenville, North Carolina, specializing in bulbs. In 1999 he explored the native plants of northern and eastern Mexico.

Robert Fincham is a science teacher and conifer enthusiast whose collection became a mail-order nursery, Coenosium Gardens. He has written for *American Nurseryman*, *Rock Garden Quarterly*, *Fine Gardening*, and the *American Conifer Society Bulletin* and has produced three videos on conifers and propagation methods. He was a founder of the American Conifer Society and served as its president for eight years.

Joyce Fingerut has a background in psychology and data analysis as well as training in horticulture and landscape design. She designed and built award-winning exhibits for the Philadelphia Flower Show and gives lectures and workshops on trough-making and rock gardening. She served as president of NARGS during 2001–2002.

René Giguère is curator of the alpine garden at the Montreal Botanical Garden and founder of the Québec Chapter of NARGS. He holds a degree in biology and has been teaching and learning about landscaping, nurseries, and horticulture for more than twenty years.

Phyllis Gustafson is a nursery propagator and operates a seed company, Rogue House Seeds, from her home in Medford, Oregon. An avid hiker and skilled gardener, she specializes in plants of her native Siskiyou Mountains and similar climates and is very active in NARGS.

Brent A. Hine is a curator at the E. H. Lohbrunner Alpine Garden at the University of British Columbia. His other interests include Japanese culture, language, and plants.

Eamonn Hughes is the proprietor of Hughes Water Gardens near Portland, Oregon. He has designed and built pools, waterfalls, and artificial streams in scores of private gardens, as well as water features in major public spaces such as the Oregon Garden (Silverton) and Crystal Springs Rhododendron Test Garden (Portland). He is the coauthor (with Helen Nash) of *Waterfalls, Fountains, Pools and Streams*.

Rob and Sharon Illingworth of northwestern Ontario, Canada, are self-taught gardeners interested in "pushing the limit." In addition to their rock garden, they have a woodland garden and perennial borders. They also enjoy propagating plants and photography.

Gwen Kelaidis, a botanist and garden designer, was editor of the *Rock Garden Quarterly* from 1990 to 2000. She frequently lectures to rock garden and other horticultural groups, especially about xeric plants. She and her husband, Panayoti, live in Denver and have two children.

Panayoti Kelaidis is director of the Denver Botanic Gardens, where he developed the world-famous Rock Alpine Garden. He has traveled around the world pursuing his botanical interests and has introduced numerous choice plants to North American horticulture. He is a popular lecturer to garden groups at home and abroad.

Nicholas Klise is now retired from a career as a landscape architect, during which he designed some notable rock gardens. He and his partner, Morris West, have created a beautiful, remarkably varied, and innovative garden around their home in Pennsylvania.

Sandra Ladendorf recently built a new rock garden at her home in the hills outside Monterey, California. A longtime NARGS member and former president of the society, she has also gardened in North Carolina.

Anna Leggatt, a botanist, is active in plant conservation efforts in Ontario, Canada. She conducts educational workshops on native plants, maintains her own extensive rock garden, and travels frequently to view plants in the wild in other parts of the continent.

Rick Lupp is the proprietor of Mt. Tahoma Nursery at the foot of Mount Rainier near Seattle, Washington, where he propagates and distributes a wide range of rare and choice true alpines. A dedicated hiker and climber, he has discovered several new introductions in the wild and continues to explore the mountains of the West.

Neal Maillet is executive editor at Timber Press and grows rock garden plants at his home in Portland, Oregon.

Jane McGary, a freelance editor specializing in scholarly reference books, has edited the *Rock Garden Quarterly* since November 2000. She edited two previous NARGS/Timber Press publications, *Rock Garden Plants of North America* and *Bulbs of North America*. She has a large garden east of Portland, Oregon, and specializes in hardy bulbs.

Baldassare Mineo studied architecture before becoming the proprietor of the well-known Siskiyou Rare Plant Nursery in Medford, Oregon, in 1978. He has introduced hundreds of new subjects for horticulture and is the author of *Rock Garden Plants: A Color Encyclopedia*. The display gardens at his nursery and adjacent home exemplify the potential of rock gardening, an art he brings to audiences through his popular lectures.

Micheal Moshier, now living in Port Angeles, Washington, is a landscape designer and graphic artist. His paintings illustrate *Lewisias* by B. LeRoy Davidson.

Rex Murfitt was born in England, trained at the famous Ingwersen alpine nursery Birch Farm, and traveled widely with Will Ingwersen to build rock gardens. He was later head gardener to Constance Spry, the flower-arranging doyenne, and worked with Graham Stuart Thomas. After moving to North America, he helped Frank Cabot develop Stonecrop Nursery and its noted alpine display beds and designed exhibits at the New York and Philadelphia Flower Shows. Now retired, Mr. Murfitt lives in Victoria, British Columbia.

Louise Parsons, a geologist and cartographer, operates a surveying company with her husband from their home in Corvallis, Oregon. She is also an avid rock gardener, hiker, and small-plane pilot.

Sheila Paulson of Calgary, Alberta, founded the Calgary Rock and Alpine Garden Society and organized the 1999 NARGS annual meeting in Banff. She enthusiastically promotes alpine plants and tufa rock gardens for Calgary's cold-winter climate.

Verna Pratt and her husband, Frank, operate AlaskaKrafts in Anchorage, Alaska. She is the author of *Field Guide to Alaskan Wildflowers*, *Wildflowers along the Alaska Highway*, and *Wildflowers of Denali National Park*, all illustrated with the Pratts' beautiful nature photographs. She is a founder of the NARGS Alaska Chapter.

Ray Radebaugh, an engineer, maintains a rock garden with many choice specimens in the mountains of Colorado.

Lee Raden has built his garden, Alpenflora, in central Pennsylvania over the past thirty years. He founded the Delaware Valley Chapter of NARGS in 1965 and was president of NARGS from 1986 to 1989. He has exhibited plants at the Philadelphia Flower Show since 1966 and received the Distinguished Achievement Medal of the Pennsylvania Horticultural Society in 1998.

Jaime Rodriguez switched careers from health care to horticulture and now works at a nursery near Anchorage, Alaska. He is an active founding member of the Alaska Chapter of NARGS and organized the hiking tours for the 2002 NARGS national meeting there.

Loren Russell, an entomologist who turned his interest to botany, lives and gardens in Corvallis, Oregon. He is an active member of NARGS and other horticultural and conservation groups; he lectures across the United States on Pacific Northwest plants and his other plant-related travels. He is also renowned for his generous donations of wild-collected seed to society exchanges.

Michael Slater and his wife, Jan, garden in western Pennsylvania. He frequently shows plants at the Philadelphia Flower Show and has a special interest in woodland and western American species.

Sandy Snyder worked for sixteen years at the Denver Botanic Gardens. Now retired, she lives and gardens in Littleton, Colorado.

John Spain, a retired corporate trainer, has had rock gardens in Grosse Pointe, Michigan; Wayne, New Jersey; and Middlebury, Connecticut. He is the author of *Growing Winter Hardy Cacti in Cold/Wet Climate Conditions* and articles for several gardening periodicals.

Tom Stuart, a database consultant, tames the woods in his large New York State garden. A very active member of NARGS, he has held several offices and is presently manager of the society's seed exchange.

Lawrence Thomas, a retired magazine editor, gardens in the alpine zone of New York City on an eleventh-floor balcony. Founding chairman of the Manhattan Chapter of NARGS, he has written and lectured extensively on container gardening.

Steve Whitesell, a graduate of the Rhode Island School of Design, is a landscape architect in New York City. He gardens in Kew Garden Hills, New York.

Harvey Wrightman is the proprietor of Wrightman Alpines, a nursery in Kerwood, Ontario, where he offers a wide range of plants, many rare, as well as materials for rock gardening. His workshops on crevice garden construction are popular with horticultural groups.

Index